The State of Palestine

The Palestinian national movement reached a dead end and came close to disintegration at the beginning of the present century. This critical analysis of internal Palestinian politics in the West Bank traces the re-emergence of the Palestinian Authority's established elite in the aftermath of the failed unity government and examines the main security and economic agendas pursued by them during that period.

Based on extensive field research interviews and participant observation undertaken across several sites in Nablus and the surrounding area, it provides a bottom-up interpretation of the Palestinian Authority's agenda and challenges the popular interpretation that its governance represents the only realistic path to Palestinian independence. As the first major account of the Palestinian Authority's political agenda since the collapse of the unity government, this book offers a unique explanation for the failure to bring a Palestinian state into being and challenges assumptions within the existing literature by addressing the apparent incoherence between mainstream debates on Palestine and the reality of conditions there.

This book is a key addition to students and scholars interested in Politics, Middle-Eastern Studies and International Relations.

Philip Leech is Senior Fellow at the Institute for Government at the University of Ottawa, Canada, and a Visiting Fellow at the Kenyon Institute in Jerusalem. He has a PhD from Exeter University's Institute for Arab and Islamic Studies and is the co-editor of *Political Identities and Popular Uprisings in the Middle East* (2016).

The State of Palestine provides a comprehensive critique of the false messiah of state-building as a strategy for Palestinian emancipation. Based on extensive research in the occupied Palestinian territory, particularly in the city of Nablus, Leech critically assesses 20 years of the Palestinian Authority, but with a focus on the post-2006 era. This book is essential reading for those who wish to understand Palestinian politics today and for why the so-called 'two-state solution' was – and remains – so fundamentally flawed.
Dr Mandy Turner, Director of the Kenyon Institute in Jerusalem
(Council for British Research in the Levant)

The first thorough and scholarly examination of the post-Oslo reality in the West Bank. This careful and forensic study exposes the fallacies surrounding the reality on the ground in the areas under the Palestinian Authority control. A highly important source of information and deconstruction for anyone who wishes genuinely to understand, and change, the dismal reality on the ground in the West Bank and beyond.
Ilan Pappe, Professor of History at the Institute for Arab
and Islamic Studies, Exeter University

Drawing upon original fieldwork in the north of the West Bank, Phil Leech provides a meticulous and much-needed critique of the Palestinian Authority's 'state building' project. This is a fascinating and timely account of Palestinian politics that deserves to be widely read.
Adam Hanieh, Senior Lecturer in Development Studies, the School of
Oriental and African Studies, University of London

Leech makes a compelling case that the Palestinian Authority's and the international community's statebuilding project in the Occupied Territories never stood a real chance. Extensive engagement with the lived experience of those in cities, villages and refugee camps is married to a grasp of the higher politics and economic models at play. Although accessibly written, this is not a comfortable read, challenging many of the hopeful scenarios politicians and activists have held on to. Laying bare the real dynamics at work, Leech's analysis is a prerequisite for moving beyond the pious hopes and assertions of the past.
Gerd Nonneman, Professor of International Relations,
School of Foreign Service, Georgetown University

In this excellent account, Philip Leech goes beyond the rhetoric of countless policymakers and journalists to deliver a meticulous critique of the Palestinian Authority's doomed statebuilding project. He convincingly demonstrates how a security agenda and a neoliberal economic strategy took precedence over democracy and the path to Palestinian independence.
Rory McCarthy, *The Guardian*'s Jerusalem correspondent, 2006–10

The State of Palestine
A critical analysis

Philip Leech

LONDON AND NEW YORK

First published 2017
by Routledge
2 Park Square, Milton Park, Abingdon, Oxon OX14 4RN

and by Routledge
711 Third Avenue, New York, NY 10017

Routledge is an imprint of the Taylor & Francis Group, an informa business

© 2017 Philip Leech

The right of Philip Leech to be identified as author of this work has been asserted by him in accordance with sections 77 and 78 of the Copyright, Designs and Patents Act 1988.

All rights reserved. No part of this book may be reprinted or reproduced or utilised in any form or by any electronic, mechanical, or other means, now known or hereafter invented, including photocopying and recording, or in any information storage or retrieval system, without permission in writing from the publishers.

Trademark notice: Product or corporate names may be trademarks or registered trademarks, and are used only for identification and explanation without intent to infringe.

British Library Cataloguing in Publication Data
A catalogue record for this book is available from the British Library

Library of Congress Cataloguing in Publication Data
Names: Leech, Philip, 1984– author.
Title: The state of Palestine : a critical analysis / Philip Leech.
Description: New York, NY : Routledge, [2016] | Includes index.
Identifiers: LCCN 2016006439 | ISBN 9781472447760 (hardback) |
ISBN 9781315573649 (ebook)
Subjects: LCSH: Palestinian National Authority–History–
21st century. | West Bank–History–21st century. |
West Bank–Politics and government–21st century.
Classification: LCC DS119.76.L435 2016 | DDC 956.95/3044–dc23
LC record available at http://lccn.loc.gov/2016006439

ISBN: 978-1-472-44776-0 (hbk)
ISBN: 978-1-315-57364-9 (ebk)

Typeset in Times New Roman
by Out of House Publishing

To
Khai-Trí,
Freya,
Arthur, Albert and Audrey,
and
Xeius, Lana, Lilly, Lois and Lucy

Contents

List of illustrations viii
Preface ix
Acknowledgements xi

1 Introduction 1

2 The 'state' and Palestine 13

3 The fragmentation of Palestine 35

4 Making plans 62

5 Palestinian authoritarianism 88

6 The 'State of Palestine' 108

7 'Economic peace' 129

8 Disaster, capitalism and Palestine 147

9 Conclusions 171

Bibliography 182
Index 202

List of illustrations

Figures

1.1	Total Israeli settlement population	5
6.1	Legitimacy of governments	111
6.2	West Bank: public perceptions of safety and security compared to approval ratings for the Fayyad government	112
6.3	President Abbas' approval rating (West Bank and Gaza)	124
7.1	Breakdown of West Bank GDP by sector (economic activity), 2013	138
7.2	Unemployment as a percentage of labour force, Palestine vs. average of developing states in the region	141
7.3	Average daily wage in the West Bank by sector (real terms)	142
8.1	Percentage change in GDP growth rates 2000–12, West Bank and Gaza Strip vs. regional average (developing countries)	148
8.2	Perceptions of corruption in the PA among West Bank Palestinians	151
8.3	Unemployment rates among refugees vs. non-refugees and according to location of residence, West Bank, 2014	157
8.4	PA current account 2000–12	163

Tables

5.1	Structure of Palestinian security services c. 2005	93
6.1	West Bankers: what should be the PA's top priority?	110
6.2	Structure of Palestinian security services c. 2009	120
8.1	Percentage of the Palestinian workforce employed in Israel and the settlements 2007–13	161
8.2	Data from June 2010 opinion poll on public attitudes to PA boycott policies	161

Preface

Research for this book began in 2008. Since then, the project has developed, grown and – I hope – improved a great deal. There are two main reasons for this trajectory. The first is a natural product of learning more and more through my own research and writing. This is partly a result of the welcome advice from more senior colleagues, partly a product of undertaking further research and also partly resulting from simply sitting with the subject and thinking about it for longer, allowing sometimes disparate thoughts to coalesce into more solid ideas.

The second major reason was my strong desire to make this book accessible to a general audience as well as to academics. Obviously this volume remains a fairly focused account of a topic that might, at first, seem quite obscure to most readers. But I hope that this apparent opacity does not cause the reader to underestimate the topic's significance. My desire to make this account more accessible was – to some extent – born out of a sense of urgency of which I became conscious during my first experiences of teaching undergraduate and graduate courses at universities in the UK.

None of the main texts available at the time were capable of conveying the complexity and nuance of the Israel–Palestine conflict that truly spoke to what I had learned from my own research. The seriousness of this problem was intensified because of the fact that, for many students, much of the information on this issue that they absorbed was from the general media, which emphasised the most sensational events, often with little regard for the subtler or more complex detail.

The third reason for the changes was in acknowledgement of – and in response to – the reality of the so-called 'Arab Spring'. While I have suggested in this volume that the protests in Palestine in 2011–12 are better seen as the consequences of distinctly domestic dynamics (and therefore I downplay the idea of a 'contagion' or anything similar with respect to Palestine and protests elsewhere), the uprisings of 2011 and their respective aftermaths certainly shook my understanding of how to approach the topic of contemporary Palestine. In particular I have become aware that media accounts – particularly in the UK and North America – apparently suffer from an acute form of

Eurocentrism in relation to the Middle East. It sometimes appears as if most English-language accounts of politics in the Middle East are only capable of interpreting events in the region through a lens defined by European regional concerns.

For example, human catastrophes in North Africa and the Levant in recent years have been transmuted into issues of European security and immigration; the resurgence of authoritarian rule in some countries is applauded as a necessary bulwark against 'terrorism'; and, perhaps most arrogantly, the complex political, economic and social causes of strife – no matter where in the region it takes place – are grouped together and discussed under the blanket heading of a 'reformation' in Islam – or similar – as if the agency of nearly 400 million people across 18 countries can be simply explained away with the analogy of Europe's own bellicose and combustible past!

A similar perspective continues to frame the discussion of Israel and Palestine in the West. Though a new discipline of Palestine Studies has emerged recently – involving some of the best academic expertise available – popular discourse remains dominated by Eurocentricism and exhibits signs of a seriously blinkered logic. As Rashid Khalidi (2009, 70) has put it:

> The Middle East attracts, and for a very long time has attracted, an inordinate share of people who are obsessed. This is true whether they are obsessed with God, with themselves and their own narratives, or with something else. Those obsessed with one area or aspect of the Middle East often lose sight of larger patterns that may in fact determine or explain outcomes throughout this region and beyond.

As an observer who is at least conscious of this context, I have no desire for this book to add more of the same. I am neither a Palestinian nor an Israeli and I cannot speak for anyone other than myself. However, what I intend for this book is that it puts forward a clear and coherent argument that is supported by evidence and – hopefully – makes a contribution to broader debates.

With this in mind, this book is directed primarily at a Western audience. In particular, it is intended to appeal to those readers who are willing to challenge conventional approaches to the Israel–Palestine conflict and keep their minds open to alternative perspectives and new ideas.

Acknowledgements

I owe my greatest debt of gratitude to all the people in Nablus, and elsewhere in the West Bank, who have helped me complete this research through agreeing to be interviewed, having informal conversations with me and often simply by extending their warm hospitality and allowing me some insights into life in the occupied West Bank. Especially to Anan, Ismat, Kifah, Bessan, Taleb, Mustafa, Ahmed, Ibrahim, Omar and Ez, I am extremely grateful.

I am also tremendously thankful for the help and support of my parents, Oliver and Lyn Leech. They have given up an enormous amount of time and effort proofreading myriad drafts of this work. I am truly grateful for their encouragement in this project and for so much more.

I am also very appreciative for the support, both moral and material, given by my family, particularly my grandmother, Jean, my sister and brother, Kate and Mark, my cousin Liz and their respective families. Right from the start, they have all helped me focus when necessary and distracted me when I needed that too. I also thank my wonderful partner Mai Ngo and her parents for their kind support and encouragement. I could not have finished this project without my family around me.

I am also greatly appreciative of the assistance and backing of the faculty members at Exeter University's Institute of Arab and Islamic Studies. I have been very fortunate to work closely with Dr Sophie Richter-Devroe, Professor Ilan Pappé, Professor Christine Alison and Dr Ruba Salih. I also wish to extend my sincere thanks to Professor Gerd Nonneman, who gave me the opportunity to learn an enormous amount by working with him as a teaching assistant on his excellent courses.

My gratitude is also extended to colleagues at the Council for British Research in the Levant, particularly Dr Mandy Turner, Dr Carol Palmer, Dr Bill Finlayson and Dr Jamie Lovell. And also to others who have helped me from other institutions, especially the staff of Birzeit University's Right to Education Campaign and Faculty members at An-Najah National University. Also to staff at (or formerly at) the Palestine Economic Policy Research Institute (MAS), the Bisan Center for Research & Development, the

Alternative Information Center, Human Rights Watch, International Crisis Group and Christian Aid.

I was also strongly encouraged by friends and colleagues where I have worked, particularly Dr Jamie Gaskarth, Dr Shabnam Holliday, Dr Patrick Holden and Dr Ian Murphy during my time at Plymouth, and, while I was at Liverpool University, I valued and appreciated the guidance of Professor Erika Harris in particular. I also thank Professor Caroline Andrew for kindly facilitating my fellowship at the University of Ottawa and to the anonymous reviewers for their extremely helpful feedback.

Finally, thanks also to my friends and colleagues who I have not mentioned by name – I am grateful for the innumerable demonstrations of kindness and encouragement you have shown me. Of course, any errors in the pages that follow are my own.

1 Introduction

In 2010, As'ad Ghanem described the apparent demise of the Palestinian national movement:

> The Palestinian national movement reached a dead end and came close to disintegration at the beginning of the present century. In the Post-Arafat period, in particular in 2006, internal and external processes ripened in the Palestinian national movement, which provided clear evidence of its failure and made it a 'failed national movement'.
>
> (2010, 18)

This book offers a critical analysis of internal Palestinian politics in the West Bank during the period 2007–12, when the Palestinian Authority (PA) appeared to be searching for an escape route out of Ghanem's 'dead end'. It tracks the re-emergence of the PA as a significant institutional force in the context of Palestinian politics in the aftermath of the Second Intifada – a major uprising by Palestinians against Israeli rule between 2000 and 2007 – and the main security and economic agenda pursued by the PA during that period. Its primary concern is to challenge the popular interpretation of the PA's governance, that is, to challenge the idea that the PA's statebuilding project represented a realistic path to achieving Palestinian independence.

Instead, the argument of this book paints a very different picture: that Palestinian statebuilding never stood any real chance of success. This is for two main reasons. First was simply that any and all efforts that would be undertaken by the PA – regardless of what underlay the motivation for them – could never be capable of challenging the strategic envelope imposed on the Palestinians by Israel. The second reason was that, despite a great deal of rhetoric emanating from international actors – including foreign states, donor organisations or multinational groups – that pledged commitment to the creation of a Palestinian State, there would be no real help forthcoming. A strong case can be made that international interference in the conflict was never intended to rein in Israel's occupation, but, instead, was largely self-serving. Moreover, the impact of international actors actually bolstered Israeli supremacy over the Palestinians and, when it counted, they even abandoned their rhetorical support for the PA by rolling back on their own promises of seeking a two-state solution through peaceful means (for instance, when the US threatened its veto-power to scupper Palestinian hopes of a United Nations (UN) Security Council Resolution recognising its independence in 2015). In short, any effort to challenge the status quo during this period – including the PA's statebuilding project – was doomed even before it had begun. This was because, from below, Palestinian agency alone had insufficient force and, from above, the international actors that did have the power to change the situation were deficient in their commitment to the cause. Thus, there was never a real hope of challenging Israel's debilitating occupation of Palestinian lands and Palestinian lives during this period.

More generally, this book's three main original contributions to contemporary Palestine Studies are as follows: first, it is based on extensive field research undertaken across several sites in Nablus – a place with a unique heritage of resistance and a historic centre of Palestinian intellectual and political life (Moors 1994; Doumani 1995) – and the surrounding region. This distinguishes it from the majority of academic research in this field to date, which tends to be based on fieldwork conducted primarily in Ramallah (the PA's *de facto* capital) or East Jerusalem (the *de jure* capital of Palestine, which exists under direct Israeli occupation). Second, it serves as the first book-length account of the PA's statebuilding agenda – which has been discussed at length in academic and journalistic circles – as an apparently distinct and previously untested path to independence. Third, this book's argument does not take for granted an analytical framework that is predicated on either the 'one-state' or 'two-state solutions', which have become near-ubiquitous as the sole points of reference in most contemporary academic literature on the subject. (The 'two-state solution' refers a possible partition of the land between the River Jordan and the Mediterranean Sea, while a 'one-state solution' describes the possibility of Israelis and Palestinians sharing it, perhaps in a bi-national state.) Rather, drawing on Antonio Gramsci's 'War of Position', this book presents a broader standard that rests on a more comprehensive analysis of the deeper power dynamics in this context.

This book presents a detailed critique of the PA's statebuilding project. While it argues that the statebuilding agenda never really offered a serious challenge to the status quo, it suggests that a better way to understand the project was as a programme of internal reforms that were designed to make the PA more efficient in terms of executing the priorities of interested external parties. These priorities were (a) reform and development of the Palestinian security forces in order to make them more capable of combating Hamas – an Islamist movement that rejects negotiations with Israel – and (b) the implementation of a range of austerity-focused reforms of the Palestinian public sector. The first of these priorities was driven by the Israeli desire to stave off a potential third popular uprising and it also aligned with broader Western concerns regarding Islamist political movements in the context of the 'Global War on Terror'. The second priority was also a product of multiple drivers.

In the short term, the major priority of the international community was to curtail the serious issue of corruption within the PA that had syphoned off an indeterminate (though reportedly significant) quantity of foreign aid donations. At the same time, this statebuilding project appeared to offer international actors a renewed opportunity to implement an economic agenda that combined the concept of 'functionalism' – a sub-school of liberal peace theory emphasising the idea that though working together in the day-to-day mechanics of governance, broader peace becomes more likely – with a long-standing commitment to neoliberalism as a development strategy.

However, neither of these agendas would play out that way. The improvement of the Palestinian security forces effectively served to strengthen the hand of some of the PA's most anti-democratic forces. Moreover, the neoliberal economic agenda suffered from the fact that the basic framework underlying Israel's domination of the West Bank was never challenged. This included the basic legal norms that were in use, as well as the structures – both legal and material – that constrained Palestinian agency and frustrated Palestinian political coherence. Rather, in a continuation of the same philosophy that underlay Israel's 'disengagement' from the Gaza Strip – a strategic withdrawal to militarised borders in 2005 – the material structure of the occupation in the West Bank was further entrenched during this period of time.

There was another factor, however. This was a surge of popular outrage that coincided with the uprisings across the region known as the 'Arab Spring'. There were several factors that produced these events in Palestine. First was the resumption of so-called peace negotiations between the PA's leadership and Israel despite the fact that Israel continued to construct illegal settlements in the West Bank, effectively undermining its rhetorical commitment to peace and continuing the expropriation of Palestinian lands and resources in the process. Second was a failure on the part of international donors to maintain the level of financial support to the PA necessary for it to meet its outgoings. This resulted in a severe fiscal crisis for the PA that was so bad that public sector salaries went unpaid. All of this added to already significant levels of popular discontent. In the end, this series of events brought about the demise of the statebuilding project as it had originally been formulated. It also allowed the President of the PA, Mahmoud Abbas, to take advantage of the situation to remove his perceived rival, the then Prime Minister Salam Fayyad, and opportunistically hijack the notion of statebuilding by taking the issue to the UN General Assembly in pursuit of high-profile, but largely meaningless, symbolic recognition.

These events also exposed the fact that the roles undertaken by Western donors in terms of the statebuilding project were apparently often incoherent. For example, where on the one hand there is strong evidence to support an argument that the Western governments – particular the UK and the US governments – played an instrumental role in inculcating authoritarianism in Palestine for the sake of preventing unrest, the fact that donors failed in the relatively simple task of ensuring that the PA did not run out of money – and thereby indirectly inculcating popular strife – demonstrates that their approach to the project was inconsistent to say the least. In addition, while it was clear that some of the institutions working on the ground (for instance, the policy team from the UK government's Department for International Development (DFID)) seemed to be seriously committed to Palestinian 'statehood' in some form or other, achieving parity between the two sides was never a serious prospect. Rather, the 'state' that they had in mind would have been little more than a façade designed to mask continued Israeli dominance.

Background to this discussion

At a donors' conference in Paris in 2007, the PA launched the precursor to its statebuilding agenda, the Palestinian Reform and Development Plan (PRDP), which was met with an enthusiastic reception from representatives of various Western governments, all of which had – until only a few months before – supported a crippling boycott on all aid to the occupied Palestinian territories (oPts). However, having purged any Hamas influence from its ranks (effectively overturning the results of the 2006 legislative elections) in a brutal crackdown – with the support of Western intelligence agencies (see Rose 2008; Black and Milne 2011) – in the eyes of its donor audience, the PA was reborn as the presentable face of Palestinian governance.

Through both in the development of the PRDP itself and in its willingness to work with Western backers – in coordination with Israel – against Hamas, the PA appeared to be embarking on a previously untested strategy. This was to accede to the key demands of Israel and the international community with the aim of achieving economic development and, ultimately, ensuring Palestinian independence from Israel's occupation. This would be through statebuilding rather than through direct resistance or confrontation as had been tried in the past. According to this strategy – which was formalised in subsequent documents: *Palestine: Ending the Occupation, Establishing the State* (2009) and *Homestretch to Freedom* (2010)[1] – the PA would embrace the role that had been demanded of it by foreign governments ever since its inception as a product of the so-called Oslo 'peace process' (1993–2000). In practical terms, this meant that the PA would build on two major policies that were of central importance to Israel, the US and its allies. First, it would continue to comply with Israeli security demands, in particular disrupting and degrading Hamas and its support network in the West Bank. Second, it would confront issues of corruption, which had plagued its recent history and had become a serious concern for donor countries (some of which had invested and lost millions of dollars).

The international community was extremely receptive and, at the meeting in Paris's Hôtel Park Hyatt; donors pledged $7.7 billion (some $2.2 billion more than had been requested) in support of the PA. Tony Blair, the recently appointed representative of the International Quartet, adopted the role of an advocate to the Israeli government on behalf of the PA, lobbying

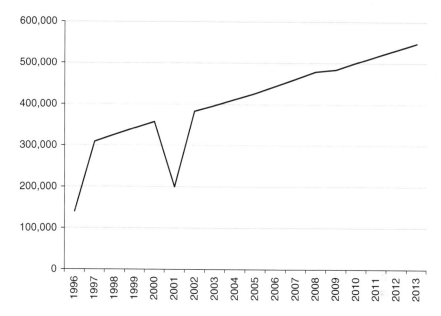

Figure 1.1 Total Israeli settlement population[5]

for greater cooperation between the two sides and the facilitation of the PA's agenda through, for example, the easing of some restrictions on movement. However, some five years on from these events, and despite winning overwhelming support from members of the UN General Assembly in 2012, the Palestinian national project stalled once again and the new 'State of Palestine' that emerged lacked independence, territorial integrity and sovereignty. Though various moves towards achieving more substantive progress had been attempted, Israel countered by accelerating the construction of illegal settlements in the West Bank and threatened expansion into the highly contentious 'E1' area, a move that would effectively and decisively cut off East Jerusalem from the rest of the West Bank, thereby terminating any prospect of a two-state solution to the conflict.

****

This book addresses the reasons behind how and why these events came to pass and offers an explanation from within the sphere of Palestinian political dynamics for the PA's failure to bring a meaningful Palestinian state into being. In addressing this question, the book presents a bottom-up analysis of the political and economic impact of the PA's statebuilding agenda. Thus, it offers a very different approach from the majority of commentaries and analyses that have become prevalent and have tended to adopt an external and often top-down perspective (for an example, see Bröning 2011). Towards this end, this book performs two important tasks. First, it serves as a diagnostic of the impact of the PA's agenda on the general Palestinian population in four sites in the Nablus region: (1) a major urban centre – Nablus city, (2) Balata Camp, the largest refugee camp in the West Bank, and two villages, (3) Qaryut and (4) Yanoun. Second, it interprets that data in the context of the broader conflict and its impact on the power relationships between Palestinian, Israelis and other relevant actors.

Data collection[2]

As mentioned above, one product of Israel's occupation has been to fragment and divide Palestinian society based on geography. In this context, it made sense to focus on geography as the main variable. This was in order to analyse the consequences of that statebuilding agenda on a cross-section of Palestinian society living under these fragmented conditions. The following sections provide background information on all four of the main sites that formed the basis for this research.

The city of Nablus

Nablus' rich and intricate history as a cultural and economic hub and as the political power base for a number of Palestine's oldest and most powerful families is an intriguing topic of study in its own right. There is not sufficient room here to outline a historical narrative of Nablus in any great depth. However, given the relevance of Nablus' role in Palestinian history to its current political status, for the purposes of this account, it is appropriate to outline a few of the reasons for Nablus' reputation. According to Beshara Doumani, the appellative 'Jabal an-Nar' (The Mountains of Fire) illustrates the city's reputation for fierce resistance to foreign conquest as the name originates from the turn of the nineteenth century when, in order to repel the invasion of Napoleon Bonaparte's army, the population of the city (colloquially known as Nabulsis) 'set forests and olive groves ablaze, burning the French soldiers' (Doumani 2004, 37). Further, in 1834, the city led a revolt against the Egyptian invasion under Ali Pasha, and 102 years later, it was an important nucleus of resistance in the Arab Uprising (1936) against the British mandate. Further, in 1963, four years before the beginning of the Israeli occupation, Nablus declared its autonomy from Jordanian rule. The city was also famously a focal point of resistance movements in both the First and the Second Intifadas and became known as the centre of terrorism in the Israeli media (Doumani 1995; 2004).

Nablus' Old City was symbolically important because of its historic role as the hub of soap and olive oil production, a vibrant commercial exchange and as the seat of power for the city's dynastic ruling class. It was also the nucleus for wider networks of social and economic relationships. Evidence of this was visible in the variety of churches, mosques and other sites of historical significance dotted in and around the Old City, including one of the highest concentrations of Turkish Baths outside Istanbul and Damascus. Such is the significance of the Old City to the character of Nablus that it is perhaps best considered as the heart of a wider, more recent, yet complementary, urban milieu.

However, because of its position as both the iconic and physical centre of Nablus, and because its architectural environment reveals some glimpses of Nablus' previous lives as an economic, political and social hub, contemporary shifts in the nature and distribution of power during the period of the PA's statebuilding agenda are shown in sharper contrast. For example, the destruction of Nablus' soap factories and the consequences of the city's detachment from both its traditionally productive hinterland and export routes are clear demonstrations of how Israel's occupation has plagued Palestinian economic and political life in the Old City and beyond. Moreover, the PA's efforts to breathe new life into the city through various projects – such as the building of a taxi station, a large shopping centre including a cinema and a series of 'shopping festivals' – as well as the overwhelming influx of foreign-made textiles (previously one of Nablus' key industrial outputs) are indicative of a the city's embrace of neoliberal economic and social norms.

Villages in Area 'C'

In 2007, the village of Qaryut has a population of 2,321 (Palestinian Central Bureau of Statistics (PCBS) 2008). It was located 20 km south-west of Nablus, on the edge of the governorate. Its main access to transport is via Route 60, a shared highway where both Palestinians and Israelis are permitted to drive (which is not the case on many 'Jewish-only roads' between settlements). Qaryut lies between the large Israeli settlements Eli and Shilo, though, throughout the research period, there was little interaction with the settlers, save for a few attempts by settlers to close off a dirt access road. The village remained largely unaffected by the direct violence during the Second Intifada.[3] However, the impact of Israel's closure policy was detrimental to the village's economy.

Yanoun on the other hand is significantly smaller than Qaryut. At the time, its population was 15 families, or approximately 102 people (PCBS 2008), though by December 2011, one family had moved away. The village was also split across two sites – Upper Yanoun, which is fully in area 'C', and Lower Yanoun, which is in area 'B.' There was a single-track road that connected the two parts of the village which are approximately three-quarters of a kilometre apart. The village had been entirely cleared of its inhabitants by Israeli settlers in 2002 (the first instance of this happening to a whole village since 1948). Because of this, since 2003, an Ecumenical Accompaniment Programme in Palestine and Israel (EAPPI) team has provided a constant international presence in the village. This team operated on two-and-a-half-month rotations (including responsibility for visiting other villages), which included filing regular reports on incidents that involved settlers from nearby Itamar and several small outposts that encircle the Upper Yanoun.

Balata Camp

Balata Camp is largest of the three refugee camps in Nablus. The camp measures a quarter of a kilometre squared and is home to 23,000 registered refugees (United Nations Relief Works Agency (UNRWA) 2008). Historically, it has been known as a strong centre for civil society and armed resistance. The UNRWA provides the following description of the society within Balata Camp:

> The refugees came from 60 villages and the cities of Lydd, Jaffa and Ramleh. Many are of Bedouin origin. Civil society and political actors in Balata are especially strong. The first West Bank group to defend refugee rights, the Refugee Committee to Defend Refugee Rights, was established in Balata in early 1994. The camp committee is one of the most active committees in the area. Three of its members serve on the Palestinian Legislative Council. The youth activities centre and the women's programme centre organise many activities as well. The camp fell under serious pressure from the Israeli army during the intifada.
>
> (UNRWA 2015)

Indeed, throughout the Second Intifada, Balata Camp was subject to some of the bloodiest fighting and numerous incursions by the Israeli military. At the time that this research was undertaken, scars of these conflict remained omnipresent in various forms, such as damaged – or destroyed – property, martyrs' posters and in the crowded graveyard adjacent to the camp.

Findings

There is an important distinction between the material changes undertaken as part of the PA's post-2007 agenda and the promises of statehood that accompanied it. In reality, the PA's material agenda comprised two main elements. The first was a security agenda that focused on (a) subduing the threat from Hamas and (b) collaborating with foreign governments at the expense of Palestine's democratic character and the basic rights of those under its rule. The second was an economic agenda that prioritised neoliberalism rather than challenging the real constraints on Palestinian development.

Of course, Palestinians in the West Bank experienced the impact of the PA's 2007–11 agenda differently according to a range of variables. However, the key conclusions of this research were relatively constant. These were that the underlying power imbalance between Palestinians and Israel in the West Bank did not narrow. Rather, it was evident from the outset that since its return to power, the PA's elites never intended to challenge the prevailing hierarchy of power. Instead, the PA pursued a very limited range of goals, defined by the restrictions imposed on it by Israel and the West, its own interests in terms of survival and the relative prosperity of its elite supporters, through complying with Israel's major demands and the requirements of international donors.

In practical terms, this meant that the apparatus of Israel's occupation was allowed to grow more entrenched in the West Bank, while the PA, in some respects, actively encouraged the growing influence of other foreign powers in Palestinian politics, while dramatically diminishing the ability of the general public to hold any sway over its own destiny.[4] Thus, the PA's programme effectively meant that the power exercised over Palestinian lives was taken even further out of the hands of those living on the lands that were – ostensibly – intended to become a Palestinian state. In more specific terms, the real impact of the PA's statebuilding agenda can be summarised in the following three points:

1. The statebuilding agenda was – in reality – not a serious attempt to challenge Israel's military, political and economic dominance over Palestinian lives and Palestinian lands in the occupied West Bank.
2. Though important divisions did exist within the PA leadership, the factions that dominated adopted a conciliatory approach towards the occupation and pursued a security agenda designed to integrate further entrenchment of the occupation. As a result, all aspects of democratic governance were prorogued and the PA essentially acceded to a role as an integrated part of the overarching power structure that did not offer any meaningful challenge the status quo.
3. The PA also embraced neoliberalism as at economic strategy, an approach that weakened what remained of Palestinian autonomy in its economic decision making, worsened the conditions of already vulnerable communities in the West Bank and helped undermine the basis for the productive sectors in Palestine's economy.

Other analyses have also outlined the deficiencies of the PA's agenda. According to Adam Hanieh, for instance, the reform programme had a severely deleterious effect on Palestinian society and Palestinian national claims (Hanieh 2008a, 2008b, 2011, 2013). Instead of furthering an agenda of Palestinian national liberation, in practice it allowed the occupation to become further entrenched (sometimes doing so with the PA's assistance), and the PA has abandoned most - if not all - of Palestinian political capital in pursuit of a 'state' that, given the limitations that Palestinians would have to accept, could only ever be symbolic (Hanieh 2008a). As Raja Khalidi - a prominent Palestinian economist - suggested in an interview, the statebuilding project seemed to be detached from reality:

> What's going to make this virtual state turn into a real state? Nobody seems to be addressing that. All the talk is about polishing this virtual state, reforming and fixing it, adding services here, privatizing there, saving money here and cutting budgets there. It's like the manner in which donors and international institutions approach the performance of a normal middle-income country. The PA seems to assume that by the will of the people, the citizens who proved themselves [of] being capable of respecting traffic signals, paying electricity bills and not carrying guns in public, statehood will 'impose itself'. Somehow statehood 'just arrives' in September because technically everything is ready.
>
> (Quoted in Smith 2011)

Thus, though similarities between the Arafat era (1994-2004) and the Fayyad era should not be overstated, at a deeper level, the PA remains constrained by many of the same basic determinant factors as was the PA during the 1990s. Further, the way in which the PA operated internally was also similar in some significant respects. To return to Ghanem's metaphor at the beginning of this chapter, even though the PA survived both Oslo and the Second Intifada intact, the Palestinian national movement did not. Though it was perhaps not clear until later, Palestine's national movement was indeed caught in a 'dead end' by the end of the 1990s and its link to the political activity of the PA had entirely disintegrated in the early 2000s. However, once this link between the PA and the goal of genuine national independence was finally severed, foreign actors breathed new life into the PA's institutional carcass and – with the help of some Palestinian elites – repurposed it to serve different ends.

Overview of the chapters

This book comprises nine chapters including this introduction. The following eight are as follows. Chapter 2, 'The "state" and Palestine', situates this book within the existing literature on the subject of Palestinian politics and statebuilding. It outlines the theoretical toolset that this account uses in order to answer the critical questions raised above, drawing from the fields of politics, economics and international relations. It defines critical terms that are relevant to this discussion and also provides definitions of vocabulary that is specific to the mechanisms involved in Israel's occupation.

Chapter 3, 'The fragmentation of Palestine', addresses the questions of (a) how the Oslo process emerged and (b) how the failure of the Oslo process combined with the period of intense destruction during the Second Intifada to lay the groundwork for what followed. Chapter 4, 'Making plans', focuses on what apparently makes the era of statebuilding different from what went before. It looks at Israeli policy, foreign intentions and the way in which the PA sought to present statebuilding as an achievable alternative. Chapter 5, 'Palestinian authoritarianism', focuses on the role of security at the heart of the PA's post-2007 agenda. It tracks the role of foreign agencies in the background of the reform of Palestine's security forces. Most troublingly, it also identifies how these reforms gave way to authoritarianism. Chapter 6, 'The "State of Palestine"', looks at the internal dynamics within the top tier of Palestinian politics and the relationship between the PA leadership and the population of the West Bank. It discusses how the relationship between Salam Fayyad – then Prime Minister – and President Mahmoud Abbas declined and the political outcomes of that. Chapter 7, '"Economic peace"', discusses the background to the PA's economic programme. It focuses primarily on identifying the main restrictions on Palestinian economic agency and goes into some detail as to the basic causes for the moribund state of Palestine's private sector and the PA's serious problem of fiscal leakage. Chapter 8, 'Disaster, capitalism and Palestine', looks at the PA's efforts to reform the economy. It notes how donor-led neoliberal policies failed the Palestinian population because they were essentially misdirected. In the end, it shows how there can be no serious progress in terms of Palestinian economic development unless and until the basic restrictions on economic agency are challenged. Chapter 9, 'Conclusions', brings the book to a close by reflecting on its major discussions and the contribution of its main arguments to the broader field of Palestine Studies.

A note on methodology

The main research methods utilised here for this project were participant observation and interviews. I conducted interviews with 82 different interviewees, some of whom I met multiple times, including four focus groups with three or more interviewees. I also interviewed four interviewees in Amman – specifically to discuss the topic of Qualified Industrial Zones and the background to Jordan's relationship with Israel and the PA – and several Israeli interviewees who provided details on specific areas of interest. I also solicited additional information from various institutions in writing, including from researchers at Israeli universities, Palestinian institutions and the DFID, a branch of the British government. The majority of my interviews were undertaken in English, though as my Arabic language skills developed, I became capable of engaging in longer conversations with Palestinian interviewees and understanding more of my environment directly.

I also maintained and developed much closer relationships with a core group of interviewees. In general, these were the people with whom I had both frequent contact and a good relationship. Many of these interviewees became friends during my time in Palestine and I grew to trust their interpretation of events. Often I found that discussing the political environment or recent events with these individuals was an extremely helpful practice that allowed me to clarify my own thoughts. This is not to say that I necessarily always (or even mostly) agreed with those who were part of this core group – or that they always agreed with each other – but, rather, they often directed me to other sources, opened up new ways of conceptualising an issue or a problem, or suggested new avenues of inquiry. However, most importantly, by observing and engaging with this close group as they navigated the political and economic milieu of contemporary Palestine, I learned a great deal about the practical nature of the day-to-day challenges that life under Israel's occupation and the PA's rule entails. These experiences challenged my own way of thinking and ensured that, at the very least, my interpretation was to some extent grounded in the everyday realities of a Palestine under occupation.

Notes

1 The full texts of all of these documents are available online via the Palestinian Authority's Ministry of Planning website: www.mopad.pna.ps/en.
2 Parts of this section draw on a previous account by this author, entitled 'Why Jabal an-Nar? Researching Nablus'.
3 Settlers killed one villager during an altercation and on two previous occasions, the first in the late 1990s and second during the Second Intifada, a villager had killed himself in a suicide attack in Israel. As a result of the first incident, the home of the bomber's family was demolished by the Israeli military (the second attack drew no similar retribution as the bomber had not been a resident in the village for some time).
4 The latter occurred as the PA embraced donors' requirements for a raft of neoliberal economic policies, which undermined the possibility of genuine development for the Palestinian economy.
5 All data from B'Tselem. Figures for 2012–13 are estimates.

2 The 'state' and Palestine

When the Oslo 'peace process' was made public in 1994, it was presented to the world as a series of negotiations that would work towards bringing an end to Israel's occupation of the West Bank and Gaza Strip that had begun some 27 years before. Yet, at the time of writing – 22 years later – this 'peace process' has been an evident failure (Massad 2014). Yet this lack of progress cannot be understood as a product of international neglect of the issue. Rather, the promise of creating a Palestinian state – as a means to end the conflict – has been one of the most often iterated goals of numerous political leaders. Moreover, the Palestinian case has also become something of a model for 'statebuilding' exercises elsewhere, as discussed in a wide range of literature produced by international organisations. So why, then, did it fail?

The primary goal of this chapter is to present a discussion of the relevant theoretical and empirical context in order to help answer this question. This chapter discusses both the key issue of Palestine in the context of general, mainstream statebuilding literature and also a range of critical approaches to the topic. Finally, it presents its own distinctive contribution to the discussion by engaging with the work of Antonio Gramsci in order to provide an enriched overall debate. The second, related, goal is to introduce detailed definitions of the key empirical concerns that are at issue here in order to outline the basic framework for this book's discussion. Overall this chapter seeks to deconstruct the broad, commonly understood, normative frameworks that are often applied in the Israel-Palestine case study. The chapter challenges these structures and, as an alternative, presents an analytical framework which stems from a more comprehensive understanding of applicable power dynamics. The first task, however, is to clarify the difference between concepts of 'statebuilding' and 'stateformation' in order to introduce some of the key critical ideas in this chapter.

Statebuilding, not stateformation

The question of how states are formed was explored, most famously, in the work of Charles Tilly. Tilly's focus was on how and why 'the state' became the most common form of polity since its emergence in the European Middle

Ages. Through tracing the processes of state formation in Europe, Tilly theorised that 'the state' became the dominant form of polity because of its efficiency in enforcing the will of the governing group on its own population and fighting its opponents. Or, as he memorably argued: 'War made the state, and the state made war' (Tilly 1975, 42). It might seem curious then that the creation of a 'Palestinian state' should be so often invoked as a mechanism to achieve peace.

The difference between what Tilly was describing and the kind of 'state' that Palestine might hope to become is also quite pronounced in other ways. Importantly, for Tilly, the state rested its claim to legitimacy on a long experience of refining its relationship to the populous through processes of negotiation, compromise and conciliation, as well as the ability to act as 'a needed shield' against threats (Tilly 1985, 1). Yet it is clear from even a cursory understanding of the relationship between Israel and the Palestinians that it would be unlikely that any future 'State of Palestine' would be capable of fulfilling these criteria, because of the likelihood of continued Israeli interference.

In the case of Palestine, then, 'statebuilding' – designed as a mechanism for making peace – is evidently quite different from the 'statemaking' or 'stateformation' that Tilly described in the European context. This difference hints at an important element at the heart of the critical analysis of the statebuilding project that this book seeks to present, namely, that the statebuilding agenda in Palestine – no matter how often ownership of this project may have been claimed by the PA leadership – was evidently largely brought in from outside, as opposed to emerging from Palestinian society itself. Of course, this factor alone is not enough to make the Palestinian case unique. Many states have come into being through the process of decolonisation and have therefore created, or adopted, state structures under the shadow of powerful foreign agents 'without the same internal forging of mutual constraints between rulers and ruled' (Tilly 1985, 21). As a result, in Tilly's view, the ruling classes in newly decolonised states were more likely to be dependent on external actors for their own security and also more likely to see the population as a potential threat to that security.

There is an important difference, then, between states that were products of the kind of formation process described by Tilly and those that have come to be through other means. Another way of describing this difference would be through the lens of Gramsci's terminology of an 'integral state'. For Gramsci, the 'integral state' describes an established and comprehensive structure of government wherein the ruling class' domination is well integrated with the entire machinery of rule – including political and civil society – and widely accepted as legitimate by the general population. The integral state 'has the functions *both* of coercion and consent. It contains *both* the apparatuses of government and the judiciary and the various voluntary and private associations and para-political institutions which make up civil society' (Gramsci and Forgacs 1988, 429). Decolonised states in the Middle East (and elsewhere) were much less likely to achieve this kind of 'integral' status because they had come into being not as a product of long periods of conflict, compromise and negotiation between the population and the ruling class, but as a result of the actions of foreign powers.

Evidence of this kind of statebuilding process in the aftermath of decolonisation is plentiful from across the Middle East (see, *inter alia*, Anderson 1987; Khoury and Kostiner 1990; Massad 2001) and elsewhere. Nazih Ayubi (1996, 12) explains:

> Part of the problem [of the post-colonial state] may be due to its 'lopsided' nature: to the fact that it is underdeveloped in certain respects but overdeveloped in others ... The state in the ex-colonial societies was not created by a national bourgeoisie but by a foreign colonial one which over-inflated the size of the bureaucratic machine, especially its military wing, to serve its own purposes in the colonies.

Though Ayubi does not ascribe this analysis to all states in the Middle East uncritically (making a particularly important distinction between states that were decolonised prior to the Second World War, and also drawing on other significant factors that have influenced the distinctions between Middle Eastern states and those in Europe), he goes on to make this case more specifically. The European-style state – which describes 'the daily "reality" of the state' for most Middle Eastern countries – 'has in the main come to the Middle East as an "imported commodity", partly under colonial pressure and partly under the influence of imitation and mimicry' (Ayubi 1996, 21).

While the first round of statebuilding in Palestine only began in the mid-1990s as a product of the Oslo peace process, there are numerous similarities between it and other states in the broader post-colonial Middle East of the early to mid-twentieth century. As Nathan Brown (2003, 9) argues:

> The parallels with the broader Arab experience were often far deeper than many Palestinians realized ... The PNA [Palestinian National Authority] – which found itself working around, confronting, avoiding, and outmaneuvering Israel and some Oslo provisions – was building a state in a way that Syrians looking to the 1940s or Egyptians looking to the 1920s and 1930s might find quite familiar.

As this book argues, there are also many important commonalities between the statebuilding programme beginning in 2007 and that of the initial formation of the PA in the 1990s, and in some respects this can be seen as a more intense phase in a continued process. In particular, the fact that the 2007 project would be paid for and directed by international actors would suggest that this process was never likely to bolster the PA's legitimacy any more than in the 1990s. In fact, the PA had never managed to achieve robust legitimacy within its polity – what Gramsci would have called 'hegemony' – throughout its existence and therefore had never come close to functioning like an 'integral state'. Moreover, it was the absence of that hegemony – and the problems that came along with it – that were important drivers behind launching the post-2007 statebuilding project. As this chapter will show, the PA's limitations as a governing body form a common theme that underlies all of the main events of this period.

Thus, we can see that the phenomena of 'statebuilding' – particularly in its post-colonial context – and 'stateformation' are very different. Moreover, on the basis of the differences between these two processes, we can theorise a basic categorical distinction between two different types of states: (a) those that have been 'formed' through vigorous evolutionary process over a long period of time and because of that fact are deeply rooted in their own domestic constituency – these are more likely to be 'integral states' (and less likely to be post-colonial states); and (b) those that have often been built in the aftermath of decolonisation and significant connectedness to a constituency outside their borders (usually the former colonial power) – these are less likely to be 'integral states'. Clearly these two different types of state are not likely to be equivalent in terms of their ability to secure hegemony among their domestic populations. In addition, the non-integral states are more likely to be subject to interference from outside forces. In other words, non-integral post-colonial states are likely to be weaker than integral ones.

Moreover, there are clearly parallels between the contemporary experience of statebuilding in Palestine and those that took place in the immediate aftermath of decolonisation. Both phases of statebuilding in Palestine (the 1990s – during the Oslo period – and after 2007) are interesting because they are often tied to the goal of achieving 'peace' or 'peacebuilding'. But both processes ultimately ended in failure because of an inherent contradiction between the following two goals: (a) no state strong enough to enforce peace effectively would be permitted to come into being (by Israel due to its fears of losing military and political advantage); yet (b) any state so weak that it remained obviously dependent on Israeli and external support would remain forever tainted by it; therefore (c) there was no realistic way in which the PA would ever emerge from the process position strong enough to sell (and enforce) the kind of measures necessary to secure peace. To put it bluntly, 'statebuilding' as 'peacebuilding' in Palestine was clearly bogus. In order to understand this contradiction further, it is necessary to explore the historical and political relationship between the concepts of peacebuilding and statebuilding.

Peacebuilding and liberalism

The predominant approach to both 'peacebuilding' and 'statebuilding' in contemporary International Relations is rooted in the philosophy of liberalism. This approach originates with Immanuel Kant's famous essay *Perpetual Peace: A Philosophical Essay* (1795). Kant outlines a programme for international peace between states. He suggested a series of reforms for governments to take internally as well as system of binding treaties between them. Key among these ideas were republicanism – which, though for Kant was not quite the same as democracy, represented a form of government that made the executive functions of government accountable to the people – and disarmament. Combined, Kant believed that these states would progressively form a 'pacific union' among themselves. This approach as a whole has been adapted and embraced as the foundational text for what is now called 'democratic peace theory', the notion that democratic governments are less likely to engage in conflict with each other than are other forms of government.

While the pros and cons of democratic peace theory have been widely discussed in academic journals (see Babst 1964; Rosato 2003; Doyle 2005), it has been effectively accepted wholesale as a core principle of International Relations by most major governments and supranational institutions. Indeed, the concept of democratic peace is deeply rooted in the founding principles of three international bodies that played a significant role in supporting the Palestinian statebuilding programme: the UN, the International Monetary Fund (IMF) and the World Bank.

The victors of the Second World War formed all three of these bodies with the intention of preventing major conflicts in the future, though their ideas rested on the principles outlined by US President Woodrow Wilson in the aftermath of the First World War. Wilson had argued against reverting to the kind of world order that was dominated by European states prior to the war, based on a 'Balance of Power' strategy between Europe's great powers and rapacious colonialism outside that continent. Wilson's vision was not quite the same as Kant's. Wilson intended a pacific union through the institutionalisation of international governance and the promotion of self-determination for colonised peoples, that is, 'not organized rivalries, but an organized common peace' (Wilson 1917).

The impact of 'Wilsonianism', as it has been called (see Paris 2004), had little impact on the nature of European colonialism in the immediate aftermath of the First World War. Rather, particularly in the Levant, the practical implications of 'Wilsonianism' did little more than to provide a veneer of international legitimacy for the division of lands taken from the defunct Ottoman Empire between Britain and France. Britain took control of Palestine under a mandate of the 'League of Nations' – the Wilsonian forerunner to the UN – yet in a series of duplicitous agreements, it continued to act as a colonial power. Famously, the British promised the creation of a Jewish State in Palestine, yet fiercely suppressed movements towards national self-determination by both Jews and Arabs (see Schneer 2011).

This system lasted until 1947, when, after being greatly weakened by the Second World War and in the context of growing insurrections against its rule, the British passed its mandate for Palestine to the newly formed UN for resolution. Again, the Wilsonian institutions were not strong enough to manage this conflict effectively. Instead, the UN Security Council proposed a partition of the land, only to have this immediately rejected by the various Arab governments as well as the Palestinian population. Hostilities continued to escalate into the 1948 war, which saw the new State of Israel proclaimed on 14 May 1948 and more than 700,000 Palestinians being forced to flee as refugees. While UN agencies were swift to respond to the crisis – including through establishing the UN Relief Works Agency (UNRWA), which remains the primary service provider to Palestinian refugees even today – the Wilsonian institutions remained essentially ineffective in the context of the Israel–Palestine conflict throughout the Cold War. Moreover, the notion of the application of democratic peace to solve international disputes became subsumed by the more immediate concerns of global bi-polarity and the potential of nuclear war between the US and the Soviet Union.

After the Cold War

It was after the Cold War ended that a new era of Wilsonianism was born. This signalled not only the end of a historical rivalry between two superpowers but also an apparent opportunity for human progress. As Robert Dahl, put it at the time, it appeared that there was 'an unprecedented global expansion in the acceptability of democratic ideas' (1991, 2). One view on how a more prescribed agenda to promote liberal democracy should be formulated was presented in detail by the then UN Secretary General, Boutros Boutros-Ghali, in a report entitled 'An Agenda for Peace' (1992). Boutros-Ghali suggested a programme of 'peacemaking' that 'may take the form of concrete cooperative projects which link two or more countries in a mutually beneficial undertaking that can not only contribute to economic and social development but also enhance the confidence that is so fundamental to peace' (1992, vol. 11, para. 55). Moreover, on the basis of this agenda, the Secretary General also explained that UN agencies would provide the technical assistance necessary to give 'support for the transformation of deficient national structures and capabilities, and for the strengthening of new democratic institutions' (Boutros-Ghali 1992, vol. 11, para. 59).

While Boutros-Ghali's report formalised the terms of this discussion, in reality the principles that he outlined had already become mainstream in much of the work around post-Cold War peacebuilding. In addition to these ideas about democratisation and institutionalisation, there was also the fact that the collapse of the Soviet Union – and the discrediting of Soviet-style communism – had also left neoliberal capitalism apparently unchallenged as the dominant political-economic ideology. As Francis Fukuyama (1989, 3) famously put it: 'The triumph of the West, of the Western *idea*, is evident first of all in the total exhaustion of viable systematic alternatives to Western liberalism' demonstrated by the 'ineluctable spread of consumerist Western culture' across a diverse array of contexts in the developing world.

Despite Fukuyama's exuberance as to the inherent superiority of Western civilisation, what he was witnessing can probably be traced to a collection of deliberate policies promoted by several global institutions throughout the late 1980s and 1990s. Collectively these policies became known as the 'Washington

Consensus' and comprised goals such as trade liberalisation, weakening the role of the state in some areas (e.g. reducing state spending and the privatisation of state industries) and strengthening it in others (e.g. greater state power over enforcing property rights) (Williamson 1990, 1993). As Roland Paris (2004, 5) explains, the impact on the concept of peacebuilding was profound:

> Peacebuilding missions in the 1990s were guided by a generally unstated but widely accepted theory of conflict management: the notion that promoting 'liberalization' in countries that had recently experienced civil war would help to create the conditions for a stable and lasting peace ... Although the fourteen peacebuilding operations launched between 1989 and 1999 varied in many respects, their most striking similarity is that they all sought to transform war-shattered states into 'liberal market democracies' as quickly as possible. Underlying the design and practice of these operations was the hope and expectation that democratization would shift societal conflicts away from the battlefield and into the peaceful arena of electoral politics, thereby replacing the breaking of heads with the counting of heads; and that marketization would promote sustainable economic growth, which would also help to reduce tensions.

This meant, then, that after the end of the Cold War, peacebuilding – an upgraded form of Wilsonianism – had become 'a specific kind of social engineering, based on a particular set of assumptions about how best to establish durable domestic peace' (Paris 2004, 5).

Good governance and security

Unsurprisingly, the term 'social engineering' did not make it into many official policy documents. Instead, the vocabulary of 'good governance' became more prevalent. Both the World Bank and the IMF began to embrace this concept as a key goal in their policy documents in the 1990s. The World Bank explained what this meant in a policy document in 1995:

> The most important attributes of good governance are accountability, transparency and participation ... Governments can contribute to economic and social progress by focusing on the things that they do best. At one extreme are public goods – law and order, national security, and an environment conducive to business – which only a government can provide. At the other extreme are sectors in which private producers are active and efficient.
>
> (World Bank 1995)

Again, it would be less economically developed countries or those involved in conflict that would be the primary targets of this agenda, especially as there was a clear increase in deployment of peacekeepers to conflicts around the world after the end of the Cold War. These included peacekeeping missions to Angola, Cambodia, El Salvador, Mozambique and Namibia, but there was also an effort to implement a range of less overt measures to encourage good governance in numerous other contexts around the world.

From the outset, then, good governance represented the conceptual tie that linked economic liberalism, security and the role of shoring up weak states (particularly those in parts of the world that had been colonised a few decades before). But the branding of 'good governance' as a policy framework also served as the means by which international institutions could conceptually break with the past. Where older policies such as 'structural adjustment programmes' – mechanisms used by international institutions to force developing countries to embrace economic liberalisation throughout the 1980s – had been discredited by popular resistance and the perception that they served thinly veiled neocolonialism (see, *inter alia*, Wallerstein 2004), good governance could been branded as something different.

The security aspect of this confluence of issues grew more prominent in the 1990s, especially as violence in civil conflicts in Africa and Eastern Europe escalated to the level of ethnic cleansing. In such cases – particularly with regard to Rwanda, Somalia and the former Yugoslavia – the situation was even described in terms of 'state failure' by commentators. Yet it was only after the dramatic terrorist attacks on the New York and Washington DC by Al-Qaida in September 2001 that the issue of 'state failure' and concerns over its potential impact on Western liberal democracies were really brought into sync. This was because, prior to 2001, Al-Qaida had been incubated in the 'failed state' of Afghanistan and was supported by the *de facto* Afghan government, the Taliban. In his response to those attacks, the US President George W. Bush made it very clear that the 9/11 attacks had precipitated a change in American foreign policy towards a doctrine of pre-emptive action and the exportation of values abroad, especially against regimes that 'harbor or support terrorism' (Bush 2001). If this policy programme appeared to be reminiscent of the imperialism of old, that was not without justification, as Michael Ignatieff (2002) explained:

> Imperialism used to be the white man's burden. This gave it a bad reputation. But imperialism doesn't stop being necessary just because it becomes politically incorrect ... Nation-building is the kind of imperialism you get in a human rights era.

As this policy platform developed and the US government turned its sights towards an invasion of Iraq, the language grew to mirror some of the criteria for 'good governance'. In particular, this included an emphasis on democracy and human rights. As Bush explained in November 2003, less than a year after the US led-invasion, his vision of democracy in the Middle East was much broader and 'must be a focus of American policy for decades to come' (Bush 2003).

Importantly, the President also made the democratisation in Palestine one of his issues of concern. However, the link between the Bush doctrine, exporting good governance and the question of Palestine was explained in more explicit terms by the then British Prime Minister, Tony Blair (2003):

> I do not believe there is any other issue with the same power to re-unite the world community than progress on the issues of Israel and Palestine ... All of us are now signed up to its vision: a state of Israel, recognised and accepted by all the world, and a viable Palestinian state. And that should be part of a larger global agenda. On poverty and sustainable development. On democracy and human rights. On the good governance of nations.

Thus, statebuilding in Palestine and the desire to build a more secure world for citizens within Western nations would now be seen as deeply interlinked. This conclusion helped precipitate a much more substantial involvement of British and American security forces in Palestine (discussed in later chapters) and a more sympathetic view towards maintaining the stability of the PA, after power had passed from Yasser Arafat to the more acceptable Mahmoud Abbas, at the expense of democracy.

The Palestinian context

In Palestine, the principal concepts of 'statebuilding' as 'peacebuilding' evidently demarcate the entire period since the end of the First Intifada (1987–93) to now. In Gramscian terms, this period can be seen as a distinct 'historic bloc', that is to say, it comprises a period throughout which there is general alignment among the relevant political and economic forces. This section discusses what this 'historic bloc' meant in terms of the experience of ordinary Palestinians.

The First Intifada coincided with the return of international interest in peacebuilding at the end of the Cold War. Moreover, the fact that the Palestinians represented a stateless people, most of whom were enduring the Israeli occupation, meant that this conflict could be seen as an ideal opportunity to implement the good governance agenda. Indeed, in 1994, less than a year after the 'Declaration of Principles' between Israel and the Palestine Liberation Organization (PLO) was announced, the World Bank launched a three-year programme designed to support the Palestinians in building the basic structures of the prospective state. According to the 'Emergency Assistance Program for the Occupied Territories' (World Bank 1994), $1.2 billion would be spent on public investment (housing, transport, sanitation, etc.); start-up costs for central government and other state-like institutions to take over from the Israeli Civil Administration; private investment (local credit institutions, telecoms, industry, etc.); and technical advice. This investment programme was designed to follow up on and implement the recommendations of a previous World Bank study, 'Overview: Developing the Occupied Territories' (1993), which – despite finding serious societal and economic problems as well as issues in terms of the collection of data – outlined how a 'good governance' agenda might be applied to that context:

> 'Good policy' would include, *inter alia*, a peace agreement that resolves strategic uncertainty sufficiently to provide the basis for private capital inflows and investment in productive activities; a relaxation of supply-side constraints, including deregulation and improvements in the supply of economic infrastructure and industrial land; trade arrangements that allow substantial trade expansion (in the region and elsewhere); a strong public finance framework with substantially expanded revenues (including taxes now accruing to the Israeli treasury); a major strengthening of the administrative and policy-formulating capability of the emerging, interim self-governing authority; and a strengthening of the human resource base both by stepped-up training programs and by access to entrepreneurial and professional skills of the Palestinians living abroad.
> (World Bank 1993, 15)

The Bank also predicted that if these policies were implemented, the Palestinian economy might achieve significant economic growth over the following decade. Unofficially, however, it seemed that the World Bank experts were also conscious that their proposed plan should be seen as a superior alternative to what the Palestinians themselves might implement if left to their own devices, as a contemporary *New York Times* article pointed out: 'World Bank experts hope that the Palestinians will avoid some of the mistakes that Arab governments have made in economic development … Economists say the Palestinians have one advantage of being economically underdeveloped: They can start from scratch in many areas' (Friedman 1994). Yet, evidently, even with the World Bank's involvement, there has been little progress in the 20 years since the launching of these plans. Indeed, as the World Bank's Economic Monitoring Report (2015b, 1) made clear:

> Palestinians are getting poorer on average for the third year in a row. As evidenced in previous World Bank reports, the competitiveness of the Palestinian economy has been progressively eroding since the signing of the Oslo accords, in particular its industry and agriculture. Even though donor aid had increased government-funded services and fuelled consumption-driven growth during 2007 to 2011, this growth model has proved unsustainable … In short, the status quo is not sustainable and downside risks of further conflict and social unrest are high.

So what explains this lack of progress? For the World Bank, there were a number of key issues, most notably the lack of a political agreement between Israel and the Palestinians, as well as inefficacies in governance, lack of private investment and failures by foreign donor organisations to keep to their commitments. However, while all of these elements certainly contributed to the creation and maintenance of a deeply miserable state of affairs for Palestinians, in order to understand the nature of this failure, it is necessary to view the entire process of statebuilding critically, in particular through examining the Palestinian history of its implementation.

The Oslo process in Palestine

Unsurprisingly, the implementation of this agenda in the oPts was perceived very differently by Palestinians from the way it was seen by outside organisations. In particular, quite apart from abstract goals such as 'good governance', the implementation of these 'statebuilding' processes during the mid-1990s in Palestine dramatically re-shaped the social and political reality for ordinary people. Indeed, the political and economic structure of life in Palestine today remains framed by the international agreements arrived at during the so-called 'Oslo process' in the mid-1990s. Therefore, this section provides a brief overview of these events in Palestine. It looks at three processes that were particularly significant from a domestic socio-political standpoint: (a) the impact on the class structure within Palestinian society; (b) the failure to create a governing body capable of achieving hegemony; and (c) the impact of the severe restrictions on the Palestinian economy that resulted from the Oslo process.

Class structure

The actions of elites and the changing nature of the Palestinian class structure overall played a significant role in the shaping of the events from the mid-1990s onwards. This development overlaid pre-existing class hierarchies within Palestinian society – where class status tended to be tied to land ownership (Doumani 1995; Dana 2014) – and can be traced to four main developments.

First was the means by which the PA was formed and how it sought to consolidate its rule. The new PA leadership – under Yasser Arafat, a charismatic leader, but with tendencies towards corruption and autocratic rule – sought to consolidate its power in the West Bank and the Gaza Strip having arrived from a long-term exile and owing its position to a compromise agreement with the occupying force. The method utilised by Arafat and his cronies entailed dominating and/or co-opting the social structures already in place in the oPts. This effectively turned the PA into a 'bully praetorian' government that relied on coercion and bribery in order to win the approval of its constituents (Henry and Springborg 2010, Chapter 5). Importantly, this method of rule was inherently weak and was not capable of reining in some important actors – for example, Islamist groups including Hamas and Islamic Jihad – or securing hegemony among the domestic population.

The second important process was produced by the return of elites from the Palestinian diaspora who had been influential in calling for negotiations. Many had seen the Oslo 'peace process' as an opportunity both to return to their homeland and as a chance to profit from normalising relations with the Israeli business community. After they returned to Palestine in the early 1990s, they continued to exert significant influence over Palestinian politics and they enjoyed preferential treatment by the PA. These factors encouraged further corruption and rent-seeking behaviour within Palestinian society and, as a result, weakened the PA's claim to legitimacy even further by making it obvious that power was concentrated within a small group of unaccountable elites.

The third process came about as a result of the return of lower- and middle-ranking cadres from the diaspora and their large-scale absorption into the apparatus of the PA. With a similar mentality as that which encouraged rent-seeking behaviour in the elites, the PA leadership sought to buy consent among these lower-ranked returnees by offering employment to large numbers of them upon their arrival in the oPts. This swelling of the public sector was particularly evident in the security forces, which comprised almost half of all public sector jobs.

The final process was brought about indirectly through the rise of a plethora of international non-governmental organisations (INGOs) in the oPts, which offered various means of accessing international funds for projects that they saw as worthy. As a consequence, a new industry was born and with it came new social networks, particularly in urban areas where well-connected individuals could capitalise on their education and demonstrate their worth to international donors.

What resulted from these processes was a transformed social structure. At the top was a ruling class that was highly concentrated and virtually impervious to penetration from below (though it remained subject to interference from foreign actors). Below that was an internationalised 'nouveau riche' – as Tariq Dana (2014) has called them – tied into the proliferating INGO sector and, below that, an enormous middle class supported, for the most part, by a bulging public sector. At the bottom were the rest of the Palestinian population – many deriving most of their income from either what remained of the Palestinian private sector or from working under harsh, albeit often relatively well-paid, jobs in Israel or the settlements (though even these were dramatically reduced in number as Israel imposed 'closure' on the oPts in the late 1990s).

The PA

Henry and Springborg's term 'bully praetorian republic' (2010) is a useful way of understanding how the PA's leadership ran the government. This term describes a particular type of government where power rests almost exclusively on the operations of the 'military/security/party apparatus' (Henry and Springborg 2010, 135). In 'bully praetorian republics', unlike in states with other regime types (for example, the 'bunker' states represented by Iraq under Saddam Hussein, Libya under Muammar Gaddafi or Yemen under Ali Abdullah Saleh) elites are not drawn from a clearly identifiable social group and as such 'they are at least not unrepresentative of their relatively homogeneous political communities' (Henry and Springborg 2010, 134). However, the most critical point about their nature is that the government tends to secure its dominance over the domestic hierarchy through the attribution of rents – payment of funds or awarding favourable contracts – rather than relying on direct coercion. As Henry and Springborg (2010, 134) explain:

> Since the state provides the primary underpinning for these [bully praetorian] regimes, they have relatively little incentive to build and maintain ruling coalitions based in their respective political societies. The rulers of each of them seem content to restrict their extra-state coalition building to the placation of rural and traditional elites. Rent seeking arrangements with crony capitalists are more for the purposes of serving state based patronage networks than for broadening ruling coalitions.

It is particularly significant that the crony capitalists that took advantage of this form of government and its distribution of rents during the 1990s continued to be extremely influential during the post-2007 period.

Economic torpor

The Oslo process also produced significant changes in terms of Palestinian economic governance. The most significant of these developments was the 'Gaza–Jericho Agreement Annex IV Protocol on Economic Relations between the Government of the State of Israel and the P.L.O., Representing the Palestinian People', otherwise known as the 'Paris Protocol', which was signed on 29 April 1994. It comprised 11 articles covering a broad range of areas. The Paris Protocol acknowledged a number of Palestinian economic rights, which had until that point been unrecognised, including the right to: (a) impose direct taxes; (b) renew direct Palestinian trade with Arab countries through imports on some goods (cement, iron and petroleum); and (c) establish an autonomous Palestinian Monetary Authority (PMA).

Yet the Paris Protocol also created the most significant impediment to Palestinian economic development (aside from the practical reality of the occupation itself). Indeed, even today the Protocol contributes to the three main categories of impediments to Palestinian development. These are: (a) fiscal instability – the inability of the PA to maintain a secure level of funding through taxation that meets its expenditure needs; (b) structural problems, in particular the overbearing nature of the Israeli economy; and (c) the loss of opportunities as a result of the restrictions imposed by Israel's occupation (each of these categories is discussed in depth in later chapters).

In addition to this, Israel increased the use of its system of 'closure' in the occupied Palestinian lands. First established in 1991 on the eve of the Gulf Crisis and enforced through a range of permits and other measures (Hass 2002), the policy as a whole manifested itself in two different ways: internal closure, which restricted movement within the West Bank; and general closure, which prevented movement between the oPts and Israel. The use of these methods was increased significantly throughout the 1990s and as Rex Brynen (2000, 65) explains:

> the costs of this were devastating. First and foremost, Palestinian labourers were cut off from work in Israel ... In September 1997 the wages lost during closure were estimated at $1.4 million per day, while local unemployment increased by approximately one-half.

The impact over the longer term was even starker, a clear and undeniable – if unsteady – decline in the utilisation of Palestinian labour throughout the 1990s and their replacement by foreign workers. Perry Anderson has pithily captured what the outcome of these processes meant at a socio-economic level: 'in villas around Ramallah a layer of bureaucrats and businessmen, enriched by theft or contraband ... prospers above a landscape of penniless labourers and unemployed, after Oslo shut them out of migrant jobs across the border' (2015, 5).

Overall, these three processes – the transformed class structure, the creation and operation of the PA as a 'bully praetorian republic', and the economic torpor produced by both the Paris Protocol and Israel's closure policy – reoriented the political and economic dynamics of Palestinian society, creating a kind of mass-scale dependency on the continuation of the Oslo process, even when it was not going well. Moreover, since the grossly one-sided nature of the relationship, in favour of Israel, was reinforced in the early 2000s, Palestine's ruling elite learned that, for the sake of its own critical interests, there could be no wiggle room when it came to adherence to a political framework that prioritised Israel's demands.

Influence from outside

Aside from supporting and sponsoring the Oslo process, foreign forces played a more direct and important role in influencing the political and economic framework of Palestinian society throughout the 1990s and into the 2000s. There are three particularly important aspects of this interference that we may consider: the first is the impact of foreign aid on Palestine; the second is the ideological influence of neoliberal statebuilding on Palestinian policy making; and third is the impact of foreign influence on the Palestinian security forces.

The impact of foreign aid

In keeping with the idea of building a state as a mechanism for producing a lasting peace agreement between Israel and the Palestinians, international donors also provided large-scale financial support. In particular, between 1994 and mid-2003, donor support totalled more than $6 billion, equating to approximately $670 million per year. This funding came from seven main sources: 'the Arab nations, the European Union, the United States, Japan, international institutions, European countries, and other nations' (Birzeit University 2005, 116). Combined, this funding made Palestinians, by some measures, the beneficiaries of the most foreign aid (per capita) in the world (Keating et al. 2005, 79). Yet at the same time, as we have seen, poverty grew and the economy contracted. Thus, it is worth examining briefly where this money went and why such an obvious contradiction between goals and outcomes should have occurred.

One factor that may help explain this is that each of the donor sources pursued somewhat different agendas from each other and also provided their funds according to slightly different conditions. Moreover, some donors pledged more than they would actually provide. All of this added to the murkiness of the issue and makes it harder to track precisely what the particular flaws in the process were. However, a more obviously problematic aspect can be understood by conceptualising the role of foreign aid as an intrinsic part of the broader political and economic context at the time. The Palestine Human Development Report 2004 (Birzeit University 2005) provides a helpful framework for understanding what this means. It suggests that the first ten years of international aid to the Palestinians can be divided into three distinct periods, each relating to a broader political-economic context in the oPts: these were the first state (1994–7), which was characterised by rising unemployment and poverty in spite of the influx of aid, largely as a result of Israel's closure policies; in stage two (1998–2000), however, there was 'tangible improvement in a number of economic and social indicators in the Palestinian territories, as seen in a rise in Palestinian GDP and declining rates of unemployment and poverty among Palestinians' (Birzeit University 2005, 115); and a third stage which was dominated by the violence of the Second Intifada and Israel's military response. During this final period, massive damage was wrought on Palestinian infrastructure and the focus of international aid efforts shifted away from development and towards providing basic humanitarian assistance and the preservation of some functioning order on the ground. The best two exemplars of these shifts are the funding provided by the Arab nations and that of the European Union (EU), as the Development Report states:

> A new factor came into play, which was the nature of assistance provided by the Arab nations and the allocation of the largest portion of that assistance to emergency relief programs and job creation programs,

> in addition to support for the PNA's current budget ... The amount of assistance provided by the European Union increased, especially that supporting the PNA's current budget and employee salaries.
>
> (Birzeit University 2005, 117–18)

If we view the report's analysis of three phases of international aid through the lens of the next ten years of developments in Palestine, it is clear that the third phase of emergency assistance and economic downturn did not actually end until 2007. At that point, international donors gathered once again in Paris and pledged support for the second attempt at Palestinian statebuilding. A fourth phase, then, is one that began in 2007, has excluded Gaza – which remains under Hamas rule – and has been one where aid has been devoted primarily to support the statebuilding project. However, this fourth period was also categorised by harsh instability in the actual levels of aid provided, which declined rapidly after a peak in 2009 (Wildeman and Tartir 2014).

Yet this fourth period was not just characterised by the, albeit inconsistent, return of aid flows to the West Bank, but also the strong emphasis on neoliberal economic policies. In Palestine this was particularly evident in the focus on restoring consumer demand, in particular in urban areas. This was a product of high levels of foreign aid, but was also funded by debt. As Wildeman and Tartir (2014, 434) explain:

> The neoliberal economic model enforced with vigour by a donor-backed Fayyad government from 2007 to 2013 was fuelled by aid, but also by personal and government debt, and drove up the cost of living for Palestinians in an economy that had already shrunk and de-developed during the peace process.

Given the importance of this neoliberal agenda, then, it is worth looking in more depth at the underlying philosophy and exploring the nature and meaning of its implementation in Palestine.

Neoliberalism in Palestine

The issue of a how and to what extent the impact of neoliberal ideology has shaped the current 'historic bloc' in Palestine is more complex. While the PA's approach to economics had always been rooted in a philosophy that ostensibly prioritised 'free markets', the way in which this was implemented developed over time. It is best to view this process as occurring in two phases. First was the initial formation of the PA on neoliberal foundations, but with some leeway for the leadership to utilise rent-attribution in order to curry favour. As Dana (2014) notes:

Early signs of capitalist influence on the nascent Palestinian Authority (PA) can be seen in Article 21 of the Palestinian basic law, which specifies that 'the economic system in Palestine shall be based on the principles of a free market economy'.

The second phase followed the end of the intifada and was based on a more direct adoption of a neoliberal, good governance framework. This was undertaken under the leadership of Salam Fayyad as was a core element of the statebuilding project.

As explained above, this first wave of neoliberalism was drawn out of the broader global dynamics that occurred at the end of the Cold War. This was the era of Francis Fukuyama's *End of History* (Fukuyama 1993) and the apparent triumph of liberal capitalism. In terms of the Israel–Palestine question, this philosophy was re-interpreted in terms known as 'functionalism'. 'Functionalism' refers to the belief that peace could be achieved through stressing the value of transitional relationships between states and sub-state institutions that develop through shared interests. In the context of the Oslo 'peace process', this was meant manifesting itself in the form of institutional collaboration between Israeli, Palestinian and other Arab institutions through which, it was hoped, there could develop enough common ground to form the basis of a successful resolution to the conflict.

However, this approach was flawed. The outbreak of popular discontent in the form of the Second Intifada demonstrated that popular support had not been forthcoming. Essentially, disillusionment was a product of the fact that although the participants in the functionalist 'peace process' were seen as legitimate representatives, the transformative narrative that was part of the process itself never became hegemonic. In other words, though the reasoning behind Palestinian participation in the Oslo process was widely disseminated within the population, the population was not able to take the critical step of consenting to the new paradigm that was being produced by the negotiations. Markus Bullion suggests this was because the 'peace process' had failed to bring about the basic improvements in life that had been promised in its legitimising narrative:

> Although support for the functionalist approach was reiterated as late as 1998 ... economic cooperation remained limited and overall economic development was not generated ... The autonomous Palestinian Territories experienced considerable setbacks even prior to the Intifada.
> (Bouillon 2004, 3)

Yet, despite the dramatic failure of the Oslo process, the second wave of statebuilding after 2007 did not pursue a fundamentally different strategy. Rather, it actually re-shaped the PA to fit the demands of external donors more closely. It is fair to say that post-2007, the PA was no longer engaged in a relationship with Israel that could seriously be described in terms of a 'functionalist' approach to peace. What replaced it was yet more neoliberalism, but with more up-to-date rhetoric. As Adam Hanieh (2013, 115–16) has put it:

> [The PRDP] was explicitly neoliberal, pledging the PA to undertake a series of economic reforms in order to reach a 'diversified and thriving free market economy led by a pioneering private sector that is in harmony with the Arab world, [and] is open to regional and global markets' ... In this vision, the unhindered operation of the market, coupled with the formal trappings of political democracy, would produce the best possible outcome. Rich and poor, Palestinians Israelis – would all benefit from the increasing spread of market relations.

Yet, as with examples of neoliberal agenda elsewhere, the scale of the state's role in the lives of ordinary people in fact grew. In particular, in Palestine this was driven by concerns over terrorism and/or other forms of political violence that might be directed against Israel or its ongoing occupation and manifested by a heavy emphasis on building up the capacity and loyalty of the security apparatus.

Impact on the security apparatus

As argued above, the building-up of the Palestinian security apparatus was a central aspect of foreign involvement in Palestinian statebuilding and should be understood in the context of the broader 'War on Terror'. Moreover, calls to 'end terrorism and incitement' (The Quartet 2007) – though seemingly a constant refrain throughout the conflict – were particularly emphasised when statebuilding was officially reborn at the Paris donors' conference in 2007, in the aftermath of the Second Intifada. Yet, behind the scenes international actors, led by the US and UK governments, had been secretly involved in re-structuring and supporting the PA security forces since the mid-2000s. (This ultimately culminated in the putsch against the Hamas-led government in 2006–7.)

The fact that such developments evidently run counter to the democratisation agenda that had been articulated by foreign leaders since the end of the Cold War (discussed above) demonstrates one of the key tensions at the core of statebuilding. Not surprisingly, after the removal or Hamas from the West Bank, the PA leadership was prepared to accept the suspension of its democratic structure in practice and instead 'fully embraced the logic of the security-development nexus ... according to which there can be no sustainable development without law and order – and conversely no sustainable security without development' (Samour and Khalidi 2014, 185). Of course, it is almost redundant to note that during this time of growing power for the non-democratic forces of the PA vis-à-vis the domestic population, there were no meaningful change in terms of Israel's strategic dominance. Indeed, Israel continued to enjoy the duel advantages of simultaneously being able to both dictate the standards by which 'security' was defined in this context and also – by various means, including derivatives of the closure policy of the 1990s and the legal and practical apparatus it gained through the Paris Protocol – to restrict Palestinian economic prosperity.

The outcome for the general population, then, was a profoundly unpleasant political-economic environment wherein the government of the West Bank grew ever more authoritarian, yet continued to offer no real protection from continued manipulation by Israel's occupation forces. Moreover, the wide-ranging influence of foreign donors seemed only to demonstrate just how far away power over Palestinian lands and Palestinian lives actually was from any of the domestic electorate. It was very clear then that 'statebuilding' in this form was an absurdity or worse. As Mandy Turner (2015) has argued, another take on these events is that foreign involvement in the 'development' of the PA may be better interpreted as a cover for something more insidious – that is, taken as a whole, foreign involvement in re-shaping Palestine's political economy fits more closely with a model of supporting Israel's counterinsurgency strategy than with anything that could reasonably be called 'statebuilding'. The changes that have taken place are subtle, but this makes them no less significant. Moreover, Turner's analysis explains that the underlying shift has been one that effectively made meaningless the difference between apparently independent Palestinian agency and the continuation of Israel's occupation:

> peacebuilding as counterinsurgency has complemented and meshed with the structures of domination and repression created by Israel in subtle but crucial ways that are not always visible, are often difficult to detect, and appear benign. And it is in this type of political economy that repression and choice are no longer polar opposites but merge.
> (Turner 2015, 25)

It should be noted, of course, that the somewhat erratic provision of aid by foreign donors – especially in the years prior to the outbreak of the Second Intifada and during the later 2000s – suggests that even if we accept Turner's argument (and it is compelling), we should do so in the sense that it represents the broad thrust of Western involvement in Palestine. In other words, it is reasonable to interpret the main objective of Western involvement in statebuilding as a form of counterinsurgency, but it is also reasonable to acknowledge that that objective was not always pursued consistently, nor was there complete coherence among all the parties promoting it.

The alignment of forces

The clear conclusion to be drawn from these arguments is that the alignment of forces at play in the current period – what Gramsci would call a 'historic bloc' – has thus operated like a centrifugal force; they have caused power in Palestinian politics to move away from the PA at the core. Yet this has not been in such a way as to empower the general population at the expense of elites, but rather to enable decision making to be monopolised by foreign forces and their proxies in the Palestinian elites. Far from anything like the kind of stateformation processes that might have created an 'integrated state' – the dynamic interactions of negotiation, compromise and conciliation – statebuilding in Palestine has been a series of short-term processes, mostly imposed from outside, that were designed to curtail dialogue between the ruling parties and the general population. In short, statebuilding in Palestine was always about assembling the structures of 'the state' as a top-down institution designed to impose order and suppress dissent. It was never a process capable of creating a state that was genuinely embedded in, or representative of, Palestinian society. The obvious question therefore arises: what can be done about this problem? If Palestinian 'statebuilding' as a means by which to achieve genuine independence from Israel is a misnomer, then by what framework may we analyse the utility of Palestinian political agency during this period? Helpfully, the work of Antonio Gramsci provides the outline of such a standard. This is the concept of a 'war of position'.

War of position

For Gramsci, a 'war of position' described the long and arduous battle through which the subjugated classes both grow to understand the nature of their domination by elites and resist and overcome it. This process takes place through challenging both the material structures of domination by the ruling classes and the intellectual, education and ideological framework through which their rule is justified. In other words, Gramsci sees a 'war of position' as something equivalent to attrition warfare taking place in the battlefield of civil society: 'The superstructures of civil society are like the trench-systems of modern warfare' (Gramsci and Forgacs 1988, 227).

The 'war of position' that Gramsci envisioned would have taken place in an integrated state (probably in Europe) where the ruling elite's position was secured not only through the coercive mechanisms they controlled – such as the police and the military – but also through their hegemonic narrative, that is, the widely held, or 'common sense', belief that such a government would be legitimate. In Palestine, however, as we have discussed above, no such hegemonic narrative has ever really been instantiated (at least not in such a way that embedded the PA or the version of 'statebuilding' associated with it into the popular consciousness). If that is the case, then it might appear that Gramsci's 'war of position' is unnecessary in the Palestinian context.

However, just because the PA has not successfully won over the majority of the population it rules with its legitimising narrative does not mean that people are willing to accept radical approaches to resistance easily, particularly if, along with it, comes the prospect of renewed chaos or an intense burst of violence. In other words, the fact that Israel has governed the oPts since 1967 via a menu of various repressive tactics – and that governance based primarily on the use of violence (both latent and manifest) – remains a daily reality in the oPts. The fact that it creates and normalises a worldview for those it subjugates cannot be overlooked (see Khalili 2007; Kelly 2008). This worldview too must be dismantled in order to allow for the emergence of an alternative 'historic bloc' (Hussein 2015).

What is critical about the 'war of position' concept, then, is that it not only makes resistance – and a different way of life – imaginable, but that it also begins the process of 'creating alternative institutions and alternative intellectual resources within existing society' (Cox 1983, 165). A genuine 'war of position', in other words, must not be focused merely on resolving superficial flaws in the appearance of this phenomenon – for example, by the anointing of a rump 'state' in Palestine – but rather the re-alignment of the relevant underlying forces in their entirety. It is, of course, not our task here to presume to lay out a plan for achieving such a transformation (if such a plan is possible to lay out). But this is not to say that such an ambitious conclusion cannot be relevant in a different way. By the simple act of acknowledging that real change in Palestine is a project that is both broader and deeper than that of merely achieving statehood, it is possible to draw out criteria that can act as a fairer and more reliable basis for framing this analysis.

Put simply, if the current 'historic bloc' is characterised by the disempowerment of most Palestinians, genuine change can only be judged to occur when most Palestinians are becoming more empowered by the forces at play. Therefore, it is possible to suggest some criteria against which change may be measured. These are:

- a reduction in Israeli control over Palestinian political and economic activity;
- an increase in the capacity of Palestinians to control their own political and economic activity;
- that these two processes are sustained over a long period of time.

One example of this in practice would be sustainable, bottom-up Palestinian economic development occurring as a result of Palestinian-owned private sector growth rather than foreign investment or under the control of monopoly elites or the – donor-dependent – public sector. Another might be the freedom of movement for people, goods and services within the West Bank and across its borders without any interaction with Israeli control mechanisms beyond that normally associated with international trade (that is, not debilitating or unusually costly).

Thus, if these concrete criteria were being met, then this would, by definition, mean that Palestinians would have: (a) taken greater control of their political and economic activity; (b) would have greater access to political rights; and therefore (c) would have, in an important way, undermined the structures that have maintained their oppression and thereby begun the formation of a new 'historic bloc'. Further, in a more practical sense, greater control for Palestinians over their own political and economic activity is likely to improve the Palestinian bargaining position in relation to Israel in any context (Khan 2010).

Therefore, in the context of this book's discussion, the basic frame of reference for measuring success or failure is defined in concrete terms that relate to greater Palestinian autonomy over their own basic political and economic activity. Such a change would represent a real improvement in the Palestinian bargaining position, the basic conditions for Palestinians and a genuine shift in power. As such, it is not limited to an artificial notion of 'peace' or 'resolution' that is essentially the captive of the 'statebuilding' as 'peacebuilding' framework and the conceptual horizon that is inherent to those discussions.

3 The fragmentation of Palestine

Direct negotiations between Israeli and Palestinian officials began at the Madrid conference in 1991. In the wake of the Soviet Union's collapse and the US-led war against Iraq (1991), the George H. W. Bush administration sought to establish a new order in the region. The White House's insistence that Israel would have to conform to a new regional order or risk being ostracised by its closest ally is often seen as the primary reason the then Israeli leadership adopted a change in policy and began negotiations. However, this narrative depends on a favourable interpretation of US motives. It suggests that it was always the intention of the US to bring peace to the Middle East and pursue justice (to a certain extent anyway)[1] in the case of Israel-Palestine. With the end of the Cold War, it seemed, the US finally had the opportunity to pursue that agenda.

This interpretation is too simplistic. Certainly, US pressure played a role in pushing Israel to the negotiation table, but there were other factors – many from within Israeli society itself – which also drove decision making at the time. There were three significant structural incentives for Israel's change in direction towards a limited form of engagement with the Palestinians. These were: (a) the incomplete nature of the original ethnic cleansing of Palestine, which left a major demographic threat to Israel's (self-awarded) status as a Jewish democracy; (b) the Arab boycott which had stunted Israeli economic growth since the state's inception and threatened to retard the expansion of Israeli businesses in the post-Cold War era; and (c) the immediate impact of the First Intifada.

Zionism's promise unfulfilled

Even in the immediate aftermath of the 1948 war, Israeli policy makers understood that to secure their long-term goal of a predominately Jewish state, with *prima facie* democratic characteristics, it was necessary to deal with the fact that the ethnic cleansing of Palestine had been incomplete.[2] However, concerned with cementing the combined mythologies of an Israeli (but not a Palestinian) right to self-determination and denial of the Nakba, the issue of demographics had been (at least in public) studiously disregarded by Israel for the first 20 years of the occupation.³ Yet the events of the mid-1980s to early 1990s helped establish conditions where confronting concerns of a growing Palestinian population through an alternative means seemed more appropriate. This would be the idea of sacrificing land to maintain a Jewish demographic superiority rather than Palestinian population transfer. The three critical events were the economic crisis that hit Israel during the mid-1980s; the First Palestinian Intifada (1987–93); and the Gulf Crisis (1990–1). All three of these events can be understood as transformational to the environment in which Israeli policy makers and elites made and prosecuted their decisions regarding the Palestinians.

Israel's economic crisis in the mid-1980s, also known as the kibbutz crisis, fundamentally re-organised the structure of power relations within the state. It was brought about as a result of the Labor government's Economic Stabilisation Plan (ESP or New Economic Plan, 1985) that had been designed to help stimulate the economy and end rapid inflation that had developed throughout the decade since the 1973 war. The plan cut government spending, enacted wage and price controls, and devalued the currency significantly (see Fischer 1993; Bruno and Minford 1986). The impact of this crisis and the rolling back of government spending had a significant impact on the basis of Israel's kibbutz movement and re-oriented Israeli society towards more traditional capitalism.⁴

The crisis also had an effect on an ongoing dispute between Palestinians working for Israeli employees, and Israeli labourers. The disagreement, which had begun in 1979, pitted Palestinians, who demanded to be represented by Arab trade unions, against Israeli labour and the government, who were aligned to the Histadrut (the powerful Israeli labour union, which – through holding companies – also owned various major Israeli companies). The row flared up into violence, and the Israeli military got involved to suppress popular dissent and deport labour leaders.⁵ The crisis raised tensions between the Palestinian and Israeli working classes and demonstrated to the various Israeli parties that the Palestinian labourers in Israel represented a significant political threat that could not necessarily be contained indefinitely (see Palumbo 1990, Chapter 8).

This fact was drawn into particularly sharp focus during the First Palestinian Intifada of 1987–1993. Many of the political activities by Palestinians designed to confront the occupation did so through direct attacks on the economic infrastructure of Israel. These included strikes, demonstrations, boycotts and refusal to pay taxes. Israel's response, which included the huge mobilisation of military force, restrictions on movement and curfews, compounded the damage to Israel's economy (see Razin and Sadka 1993; Fielding 2003a, 2003b). Finally, the Gulf crisis of 1990–1 had a major psychological impact on the Israeli elite. For the first time in its existence, Israel deliberately abjured the role of defending itself against a hostile Arab threat. The US pressured Israel to stay out of the conflict with Iraq so that it could maintain its broad coalition that included other Arab states. Instead of being able to protect itself, Israel endured the effect of SCUD missile strikes against Tel Aviv while depending on American troops and patriot missile batteries for its defence. The humbling psycho-emotional impact of this on both policy makers and the general population was significant in that it demonstrated the profound level of dependence of Israel on American support (see Ben-Ami 2006).

The cumulative impact of these three events was that for Israelis – both the general population and the elites – it severely reduced the appeal of trying to maintain the status quo. The Gulf War demonstrated the weakness of Israel relative to other forces in world politics. In particular, the US insisted that Israel be kept out of the war and allow others to defend it. Moreover, at the domestic level, both the economic crisis and the Intifada shook the very core of the notion in Israeli exceptionalism. In some ways the radical dream of Zionism had begun to fade and it looked like it might give way to a reality requiring difficult choices. In other words, Israelis could no longer pursue a kind of semi-socialism, represented by the kibbutzim, at the same time as they enjoyed the benefits of an otherwise capitalism-oriented economy. Furthermore, the idea that Israel could continue to colonise and exploit the Palestinians in the same way without consequence was no longer believable. Israel was paying a price that it had otherwise avoided since 1948. The incomplete ethnic cleansing of the Palestinians combined with the incomplete normalisation of the state left Israel with severe weaknesses.

The significance of Israel to the US during the Cold War had translated into more-or-less uncritical American support since 1967. For the Israelis, this had meant that it was possible to hold together (or postpone dealing with) the issue of normalising itself in the region. However, the Soviet Union's decline and the apparent dawn of a new post-Cold War age brought this certainty into question. If the Middle East was no longer to be an arena where superpower rivalry would be played out, then it would no longer be assured that Israel would enjoy unfettered American support. Therefore, at the same time as domestic tensions were rising, international dynamics were aligning to make the prospect of pursuing a favourable compromise more appealing.

Israel and globalisation

The 1980s was also the period where a more hardline philosophy of neoliberalism grew to prominence internationally, particularly in Western Europe and North America. Further, with the decline of communism and the apparent triumph of liberal democracy, it appeared that globalisation was the inevitable path to prosperity in the new era. Thus, Israeli capitalists, too, sought to take advantage of the advancing tides of globalisation. It was those Israeli capitalists – all of whom had achieved dominant positions within their sectors of the economy by the mid-1980s – that had pushed the government to adopt a raft of market-oriented reforms. In the wake of the economic crisis, the Israeli capitalist elite sought to shift from a phase of inward-looking development to an outward-looking phase of expansion (Nitzan and Bichler

2002). As this taste for internationalism snowballed and material links between the capitalists and the state weakened, nationalistic and reactionary politics became less salient, at least at the elite level. This changing environment would soon come to frame Israel's response to Palestinian demands for self-determination (Nitzan and Bichler 2002). However, a major obstacle remained for Israeli businesses seeking global expansion. This was the Arab Boycott. The reason why this was such a problem even in terms of expanding into markets outside the Arab world was that it effectively combined three boycotts into one. The boycott had begun before 1948 and it effectively made it impossible for any foreign company to do business with an Israeli business while at the same time dealing with firms based in the Arab world.[6]

Domestically, the ESP was the threshold event. It effectively privatised several of Israel's largest and most powerful conglomerates and enabled the first serious wave of international investment in Israel to take place. Yet while some sensitive parts of the economy remained under the state's control and protection, the privatisation of other aspects was managed carefully by the government to serve the interests of Israel's capitalist elite. The most important aspect of this change was that it allowed the capitalist elite to look internationally for partnerships to expand into foreign markets. This involved lobbying foreign governments for more favourable conditions for Israeli businesses internationally. This created two major outcomes: (a) the upgrading of Israel's Preferential Treatment Agreement with the European Economic Community to a full Free Trade Agreement; and (b) the launch of a similar agreement with the US. In 1985, Israel became the only country in the world with a Free Trade Agreement with both the Europeans and the US.

Investment also flowed the other way. The ESP also loosened some state restrictions on foreign investment into Israel. This meant that just as Israeli capitalists were to expand overseas, at the same time the domestic market began to be diluted with foreign money. The 1980s also saw the splintering of the system of monopoly control that had dominated the domestic market until that point. The internationalisation of Israel's economy – and globalisation in general – had a knock-on effect on the political and social discourses that contributed towards Israeli, and Zionist, self-identity (Ram 1999). This challenged the hegemony that had been enjoyed by a particular form of Zionism within Israeli popular and elite forums.

While there were certainly potential direct benefits to be found through normalising Israel's status in the Middle East – for example, the prospect of importing fresh water from Turkey via Syria – Israel's capitalist class was actually looking at its potential interests outside the region. In particular, this meant Asia. In the late 1980s and early 1990s, foreign products surged into the Israeli market and a series of trade conferences in Israel, attended by delegations from across Central and East Asia, promised more of the same. Unlike the Europeans and Americans, who had taken measures to manage or even counteract the impact of the boycott, Asian businesses and governments remained either ignorant of or apathetic towards such restrictions. Therefore,

Israel's motivation for engaging in negotiations with the Palestinians was not solely based on a desire for meaningful peace; rather – to some extent at least – negotiations were a way of opening the door to globalisation.

Political leaders in Israel's Labor Party were the most vocal in articulating this agenda. According to Shimon Peres, who had also been responsible for bringing the ESP into law, the logic of peace negotiations and economic liberalism went hand-in-hand (Peres and Naor 1993). Events at the time appeared to support this logic. By 1994, merely as a result of engaging in negotiations, Israel achieved recognition by several Arab regimes – including the PLO – and a formal peace with Jordan.[7] Eventually, by 1997, the economic integration between Israel, Jordan and Egypt manifested itself in the establishment of major joint Arab–Israeli ventures, such as the Qualified Industrial Zone (QIZ) projects with Jordan and Egypt. However, importantly, Israeli businesses achieved the goal of diluting the Arab Boycott merely as a result of engaging in negotiations. Their commitment to actually establish an independent Palestinian state or arrive at any other more permanent solution to the Palestinian problem as a trade-off for these peace dividends was never really tested. In fact, the globalisation of Israel's capitalist elite would eventually lead to a much more profound disconnectedness between those traditional powerbrokers and the Israeli state in the 1990s and 2000s.[8]

Israel's elite was then only interested in dealing with the Palestinian question inasmuch as it was a means to an end. This was one factor that would resurface throughout the negotiations during the 1990s and into the 2000. Furthermore, divergence of the elites' goals from those officially recognised by the other parties (including a reactionary element within Israeli society itself) goes some way towards explaining the talks' degradation, the stalemate and the return to prominence of the reactionary political 'strongman' in Israel beginning with Benjamin Netanyahu in the late 1990s (see Bouillon 2004, Chapter 7).

The First Intifada

However, beyond its impact on Israel's domestic economy, the First Intifada was also very important as a demonstration of Palestinian rejection of Israeli rule. It caught Israelis off-guard. The military and political infrastructure was unprepared and was slow to come to terms with the nature of the crisis. Moreover, as a spectacle observed by outsiders, the uprising and the Israeli military's response was particularly damaging to Israel's image abroad.

Images of Israeli troops beating or otherwise oppressing young Palestinians, who in a generally non-violent popular uprising seemed to embody the spirit of emancipation advocated in Western rhetoric, were broadcast globally (Abunimah 2011). This was particularly detrimental to what had been the prevailing narrative in the West, which had presented Israel as a weak and vulnerable actor resisting the irrational, racist aggression of the Arab world.[9] Instead, these images suggested that it was Israel itself, with Western support, which was acting as the belligerent. The resulting international disquiet (which to some extent was replicated by observers within Israel) made clear the virtue of pursuing policies in the West Bank and Gaza that went beyond overt coercion.

However, the Intifada also struck at the self-confidence of Israel's political and military command structures. The fact that the Intifada was not predicted and the Israeli response was poorly managed, particularly in its early phases, pointed to a systemic failure in Israel's existing structures and its ability to contain the Palestinian population within the oPts. This strategy had been rooted in the traditional colonial methodology of divide and rule. Israel had attempted to co-opt Palestinian elites inside the oPts and create power bases that would act as alternatives to the PLO.

Particularly during the late 1970s, the military government in power over the oPts cracked down on the existing urban-based elite by outlawing the National Guidance Council and promoted alternative nodes of power. The most well known of these was the Village Leagues, a system of representative councils promoted by the military government in the rural West Bank. The intention behind it was to promote divisions between those in rural areas and Palestinians in the larger towns who were served by more nationalist oriented organisations. This was combined with Israeli promotion of an Islamist alternative to the PLO, particularly in the Gaza Strip, and the assassinations of a number of prominent Palestinians overseas.[10] For the PLO, this coincided with the aftermath of the Jordanian Civil War (1970–1971) and was a period of extreme strain for the PLO leadership.[11]

Occupation policy

At the beginning of the 1980s, Israel had shifted its policy towards establishing more permanent structures of occupation throughout the territories. This became known as the 'Civil Administration', which, despite its name, depended more overtly on a direct form of rule by the military establishment. Israel had already used forcible land seizures as a method of containment and disenfranchisement of Palestinians since 1967. However, a legal change in 1981 made it possible for the state to seize land by claiming that it was property belonging to the state of Israel (Gordon 2008, 120). This change demonstrated that Israel had adopted a new approach to dealing with the Palestinians. This was characterised by the different modes of power being employed by the Israeli authorities to deal with the Palestinians and took various forms of legal-bureaucratic apparatus as intermediaries in dealing with the Palestinians, while maintaining a clear hierarchy between them and Israelis.[12] Thus, the shift from direct military rule to dealing with Palestinians through intermediaries and the more permanent structures of legal procedures demonstrated that the hierarchical relationship between Israel and the Palestinians in the oPts had entered a new phase. Israel was establishing a new framework that simultaneously distanced the state from its direct responsibilities to the Palestinian population and at the same time extended Israeli colonialism within the oPts.

When it came to dealing with the Intifada, Israel had already started down the path of managing the Palestinians indirectly. As the more traditional and often brutal methods of handling resistance failed to quell the uprising, it also became clear that a great cost was being incurred by Israel through pursuing this line. The appeal of an alternative logic through establishing more and more layers of bureaucratic-legal apparatus between the Palestinians and the Israelis was hard to resist.[13] Through bringing the PLO into negotiations, the Israeli government found a way to outsource the occupation – in particular, the most burdensome responsibilities to the occupied population – to the Palestinians themselves. This arrangement would ultimately be supported financially by international donors who were ostensibly drawn in by the promise of investing in a 'peace process' and broader regional stability.

The Palestinian backdrop to negotiations

In 1982, Shlomo Argov, Israel's ambassador to the Court of St James, was nearly murdered by the Fatah Revolutionary Council, a splinter group from Fatah (otherwise known as the Abu Nidal Organisation, after its founder). Though the Revolutionary Council was far from being an ally of the PLO leadership, the event provided Israel's hawks with a sufficient pretext to launch an assault on the PLO in Beirut. The war began on 4 June 1982 and ended, for the PLO leadership at least, with the negotiated exodus of somewhere between 8,000 (Cobban 1985, 3) and nearly 15,000 (Bregman 2002, 175) of its cadres in August that same year. Israel's invasion had inflicted catastrophic damage on Beirut and on the Palestinian refugee population. It also fundamentally altered the political, social and military landscape of the northern Levant in such a way that its repercussions would last into the following century. The PLO left a number of institutions and some 2,000 members in its wake in Beirut, but its ability to operate with autonomy[14] or conduct military operations against Israel and its interests was crippled. After losing Beirut, the PLO leadership scattered. Having been violently expelled from two of the countries neighbouring Israel (they had been expelled from Jordan in 1970) and being unwelcome in Syria, for political reasons, and Egypt, since the 1979 peace treaty, the PLO needed to look further afield for a new home.

When Tunisia's President, Habib Bourguiba, offered Arafat and a contingent of the PLO leadership a new base at Borj Cedria near Tunis, it was gratefully accepted in spite of the significant distance between the new headquarters and occupied Palestine. This Tunisian era was a sustained period of decline for the Arafat regime. Although it continued to conduct military operations against Israel,[15] the fact that the PLO was now based over 1,000 miles away from the focus of its concern began to undermine its image as an effective resistance organisation (see United Nations 1990, 285). In this context, the outbreak of the First Intifada produced two effects simultaneously.

First, it helped restore support for the PLO – particularly within the oPts – by re-igniting a direct conflict between Palestinians and Israel. The uprising immediately demonstrated to both the PLO's critics and the rest of the world that, at least in terms of rhetoric and ideology, Palestinians in the oPts still expressed a strong affinity for the PLO.[16] Further, the collaborative relationship of all the PLO factions was enhanced with the establishment of the Unified National Leadership and its first call for a general strike in early January 1988.

Second, by contrast, the fact that open hostilities had broken out in the territories beyond the PLO's control and without coordination with it meant that in the first phases of the Intifada, the PLO's top ranks could only follow the direction of the movement rather than leading it. Yet even this was not a smooth process. On several occasions, the gulf between the PLO leadership on the outside and the movement's *de facto* leadership in territories widened and some misalignment between the outlooks of the two became more apparent. As Khatab (2009, 46) puts it:

> In order to survive ... the PLO outside made some political concessions that were not echoed by the inside leadership, especially concerning the agreement with Jordan – that in any negotiations the PLO would represent Palestinians within a Jordanian delegation – which ultimately compromised PLO representation of Palestinians.

Therefore, in the early stages of the Intifada, its ultimate direction remained undefined. This was particularly evident during the fierce debate that developed around a document detailing the Palestinians' demands – the 'Fourteen Points' – that had been submitted to the US Secretary of State by prominent members of the Palestinian intelligentsia in January 1988.[17] Among other more specific demands, such as the release of prisoners held captive by Israel, the document demanded an international force to be established in order to assume responsibility for controlling the territories in lieu of the occupation forces. The dispute over the significance and the timing of the 'Fourteen Points' document took place within various intellectual circles, but came to an end when the Intifada's leadership endorsed the document and it became the *de facto* reference point for the political agenda of the uprising (Hunter 1991, Chapter 3). According to later interpretations, the 'Fourteen Points' constituted an effort to add impetus to the political negotiations with Israel or to 'capitalise politically upon the uprising' (Hunter 1991, 73).[18]

The PLO's agenda achieved two further victories in the summer of 1988. First, King Hussein of Jordan formally relinquished Jordanian claims to sovereignty over the West Bank (Pineschi and Kassim 1988, 247). Second was the circulation of documents at the Algiers summit of the Arab League by one of Arafat's deputies, Bassam Abu Sharif. These declared the PLO's intention to engage in direct negotiations with Israel on the basis of a two-state solution (Braizat 1998, 185). This shift to pursuing a two-state solution as an ultimate goal was effectively made irreversible in November 1988, when, again in Algiers, Arafat declared independence for Palestine in the oPts, denounced terrorism and recognised the state of Israel. He repeated this message at a meeting of the United Nations General Assembly in Geneva in December 1988 and, as a result, the PLO achieved a major goal of winning – in principle at least – international support for the prospect of direct negotiations.

Uprising

The first two years of the Intifada took a significant toll on Palestinian society and by 1989, it had effectively reached a stalemate (Qumsiyeh 2010, 153). But the PLO had undoubtedly attained something of a victory, at least in the sense that it had re-asserted itself and its agenda despite the vulnerability it had faced at the beginning. As Sayigh (2000, 632) explains:

> Two models of Palestinian political organisation confronted each other in 1988: the voluntary, grass-roots activism, social mobilisation, and decentralised leadership that typified the intifada in its first year, and the contrasting bureaucratiziation, patronage, and centralizing institutions through which the PLO extended its state control from exile. For a brief moment the former model appeared to pose a serious challenge, but the triumph of the latter was perhaps inevitable.

At this point, the PLO turned its attention to international diplomacy and attempted to engage directly with the two global superpowers. In the case of the USSR, which was at that point disintegrating, the PLO's concern was focused primarily on avoiding the possibility of mass Jewish emigration from behind the now permeable Iron Curtain (Weiss 2011). However, Arafat failed to extract any concession on this front, although the PLO was awarded the nominal honour of an embassy in Moscow and a full Soviet ambassador based in Tunis (Sayigh 2000, 639). But more important than the ailing USSR was the US. American insistence on discussing the end of terrorism (which in this context was a term used to incorporate any form of armed resistance to Israeli occupation) as a precondition for any support of further negotiations helped re-affirm the uneven power balance. However, these efforts would soon be overshadowed by the escalation of the crisis in the Gulf.

Viewed with the benefit of hindsight, Arafat's decision to align the PLO with Saddam Hussein's Iraqi regime during the Gulf Crisis in 1990–1 can be seen as an unqualified strategic blunder. More important than the loss of public sympathy internationally that resulted from this decision was the fact that by siding with Saddam, Arafat alienated many of the PLO's most important sponsors in the Gulf monarchies and provided Israel with yet more rhetorical ammunition with which to demonstrate to its own public, and to international audiences, that the PLO was not interested in genuinely pursuing peace. When the PLO participants arrived at the Madrid conference in

October 1991 as part of the Jordanian delegation, their strategic position was significantly weaker than it had been just a matter of months before.

Yet Israel initially failed to take advantage of this weakness. Yitzhak Shamir's opening speech looked backward with hostility to Arabs in general rather than forward to the prospect of peace and joint prosperity. It appeared parochial and not in keeping with either the spirit of the conference or the new, post-Cold War world order. It even implied that Israel still rejected the entire premise of dealing with the Palestinian issue as a matter of principle. In contrast, the Palestinian delegation proved more than capable of crafting a favourable image, which appeared distant enough to be disassociated from the Tunis-based leadership not to be tarnished by recent history, despite the close working relationship that persisted behind the scenes (Shlaim 2010, 157–61).[19]

The official bilateral dialogue that began in Madrid continued in Washington, but in December 1992, a secret backchannel was established between the two parties and a second track of negotiations began based at the Fafo Foundation in Oslo. The arrangements had been made by Norwegian academics, most notably Terje Rød-Larsen, to organise meetings, initially between Ahmed Qray, a senior member of the PLO and Fatah, and Yair Hirschfeld, a history professor at Haifa University.[20] These negotiations continued unofficially, but with the support of Arafat and Shimon Peres, the Foreign Minister in the new Israeli government. In May 1993, the negotiations won official sanction from Israel, and on 20 August, both parties secretly signed an interim agreement that included mutual – albeit lopsided – recognition, allowed for Palestinian autonomy in the Gaza Strip and the West Bank town of Jericho, a town in the East of the West Bank, and established a framework for future talks. The agreement was then made public and an official ceremony to sign a Joint Declaration of Principles (DOP) took place in Washington on 13 September 1993.

Divisions

However, the Oslo Accords were highly divisive among the Palestinian leadership. Several of the PLO's most well-known supporters, including Edward Said and Mahmoud Darwish, publicly rejected the plan, and it faced stiff resistance both within the Fatah Central Committee and the PLO executive (Sayigh 2000, 658). Nonetheless, further details were formalised between Arafat and Israel's Prime Minister Yitzakh Rabin with the signing of the Cairo Accord on 4 May 1994. The PA was officially established later that month in Gaza and with jurisdiction over Jericho. Arafat himself returned to the oPts for the first time since 1949 and was embraced by cheering crowds on 12 July 1993.

Despite the various internal conflicts and evident discontent within the PLO, Arafat had secured his position as national leader at the beginning of a new phase in Palestinian history in the 1990s. This had been achieved through: (a) bold and sweeping political manoeuvres culminating in the peace talks with Israel; and (b) the monopolisation of the finances of virtually all the Palestinian movements associated with the PLO. However, also out of the Intifada, various Islamist groups arose as new potential competitors to the Arafat–Fatah domination of the Palestinian political landscape.

Although both Hamas and the Palestinian Islamic Jihad had strong historical roots, particularly in the Gaza Strip (see Jamal 2005, Chapter 5; Gunning 2007, Chapter 3; Milton-Edwards and Farrell 2010, Chapters 1, 2 and 3; Roy 2011, Chapter 2), the First Intifada (1987) was their first real opportunity to prove themselves in direct resistance to Israel and a means to demonstrate that they offered an alternative to the PLO. Hamas launched its charter, which, among other things, tied the prospect of territorial concession to sacrilege, in August 1988, at the same time as Arafat was preparing to endorse a two-state solution at Algiers in November (Jensen 2008, 19). Further, at times, particularly during the later years of the uprising, it was unclear as to whether the hostilities between Fatah and Hamas were in fact a higher priority to each party than was unified resistance to Israel. For example, according to Milton-Edwards and Farrell (2010, 62): 'Throughout the spring of 1991 the two [Hamas and Fatah cadres] regularly engaged in clashes – some armed – in major West Bank cities such as Nablus'.

Further, the Islamists had rejected American invitations to Madrid and had denounced the PLO for attending. As a result, an awkward *de facto* alliance developed between Hamas and the older leftist parties (Milton-Edwards and Farrell 2010). However, while these leftist groups had been badly weakened by Arafat's gambit, Hamas, by virtue of remaining on the outside of the PLO framework, was able to grow. It also benefited from independent sources of revenue and material support from outside,[21] and a developing a network of associated civil society and social welfare organisations within the oPts which operated outside the PLO's control (Roy 2011, Chapter 4). In an effort to wreck the peace talks, Hamas and its allies stepped up the level of violent attacks and proved resilient in spite of Israel's clampdown and reprisals. It organised popular protests and orchestrated coordinated attacks to coincide with the signing of the DOP in Washington. The threat that the Islamists posed to the PLO was clear. Having gambled virtually all that was left of its political capital on a strategy of engagement with Israel, which also involved putting a significant level of faith in the ability/willingness of the US to act as a relatively honest broker, the PLO was in danger of being outflanked.

Hamas was effectively impervious to the kind of traditional methods at Arafat's disposal to attack his internal enemies. Furthermore, the fallout from the disfavour Arafat had incurred by supporting Saddam at the expense of the PLO's main financial backers in the Gulf had grown into a crippling financial crisis for the PLO. By the time of the DOP, the PLO was struggling to fund its civil society networks in the territories and refugee diaspora (Sayigh 2000, 656–7). On the other hand, Hamas in particular offered the Palestinian public the kind of unambiguous rhetoric of resistance and the consistent provision of social services that demonstrated that it could genuinely rival Fatah and the PLO if left unchecked (Jamal 2005, 115–19).

The Oslo process

The Oslo process is best understood not as a single transformative event, but as a series of interactions between the two primary antagonists with the frequent input and involvement of powerful third parties. Like any period of significant political change, it was not necessarily very clear at the time to anyone involved how the next phase in the development of events would play out.[22] Such were the structural constraints on agency – particularly for the Palestinians – and the enormous power differential between the main antagonists that the production of a Palestinian sovereign entity with genuine independence was highly unlikely from the beginning. Based on the assumption that the Israeli government more or less constitutes a rational actor and that, as such, it was unlikely to voluntarily change a power differential that tended to serve its interests, this conclusion should not be surprising. The incentive-disincentive calculus that confronted the Israeli leadership throughout this period simply did not create a contextual environment where progress towards a genuine two-state solution was likely to result in the most rewarding outcome.

The fact that the Oslo process started with the signing of two critical agreements (the DOP and the Paris Protocol) that entrenched the power differential rather than challenging it and then continued on the same route (by signing of the Interim Agreement on the West Bank and the Gaza Strip (Oslo II), the Hebron Agreement and the Wye River Memorandum) demonstrates that even allowing for the serious and important differences between the five different Israeli leaders between 1993 and 2000, it is possible to identify a general trend in policy during that period and analyse it. This general trend is best understood with the use of Hilal and Khan's (2004) terminology of 'asymmetric containment'. This means 'the retention by Israel of strategic points of control all over the oPts, and the rapid construction of a system of checkpoints' (Hilal and Khan 2004, 6) within the West Bank and the Gaza Strip. Simply, 'asymmetric containment' describes a policy of asserting control over important strategic assets and locations to establish and maintain order over the population within those spaces and the use of those spaces.

Hilal and Khan (2004, 6) use a metaphor to explain this idea more eloquently: 'Palestinian negotiators frequently pointed out that in a prison, the prisoners control 95 per cent of the space. The 5 per cent they do not control make it a prison'. Further, because the PA took over responsibility for the day-to-day management of Palestinians in Area 'A', the 'asymmetric containment' policies pursued by Israel effectively produced the equivalent of prisoners both policing themselves and organising their own welfare services (Gordon 2008). One can supplement these conclusions with reference to the rapid expansion of Israeli settlements in the oPts that occurred throughout the 1990s.

Clearly, the Palestinian position in relation to Israel during this period had been one of weakness following on from weakness. The PA/PLO leadership was unable at any point to assert true authority over the situation. The format of this discussion of 'asymmetric containment' follows, more or less, the chronology of events created by Israeli agency, while at the same time discussing what impact these changes had on the structural framework of Palestinian politics and economics. Aside from the inequalities inherent in the DOP – that the PLO recognised Israel's right to exist as a state while Israel merely recognised the PLO as the sole representative of the Palestinian people – by far the most critical outcome of the early period of negotiations was the signing of the Protocol on Economic Relations that existed between Israel and the PLO in Paris, 1994. According to Sara Roy (1999, 68), the three critical outcomes of the Paris Protocols were:

> The retention of Israeli military law (and the economic restrictions therein) during the interim phase ... Israel's full control over key factors of production, such as land, water, labor, and capital ... Israel's complete control over external borders and the perimeters of Palestinian areas.

For the Palestinians, then, the upshot of these agreements was that they remained trapped in an intermediate phase between statehood and lack of it.

In practical terms, the most important and pervasive outcome came in the form of restrictions on movement. Also known as 'closure', this practice had begun during the 1991 Gulf War, when, still in the midst of the Intifada, Israel's military revoked previous military orders that allowed Palestinians general access into Israel. However, following the conclusion of the conflict, the structures of the closure policy remained in place. The creation of the PA in 1994 advanced this policy rapidly. Israel's military and security establishment had found that it occupied a position of significant strategic advantage that it could exploit through having the PA act as its mediator. In this way, it could both satisfy its apparent security concerns and also inculcate the stratification of Palestinian society through using differently graded permits as rewards for cooperation or behaviour it approved of (see Halper 1999, 2000, 2001).

When Oslo II was implemented in 1995, it created an additional level of complexity. It further fractured Palestinian territory. Again, according to the logic of the 'Peace Process', Oslo II established Palestinian control over mostly urban areas as another interim phase towards statehood. What this meant in practice was that according to three levels of gradation, the PA would be handed responsibility for the majority of the Palestinian population in the oPts, while Israel's control over the majority of the West Bank would be granted a veneer of legitimacy. Officially, Area 'A' fell under full Palestinian control in terms of administration and security, while Area 'B' was to be administered by the PA, although Israel would maintain responsibility for security. Area 'C', some 70 per cent of the West Bank, remained under full Israeli control (for a much more detailed account of the history of the closure and permits schemes, see Hass 2002; 2010; 2012; Roy 2006; Ophir, Givoni and Hanafi 2009).

According to 'asymmetric containment', the logic of Oslo II made perfect sense. In no way was Israel's access to anywhere in the oPts genuinely challenged, even in Area 'A', where Palestinians were supposed to exercise control over security matters. The ease with which Israel entered and re-occupied those areas later during Operation Defensive Shield in 2002 demonstrates that little genuine power was actually transferred. Furthermore, by signing Oslo II, the Palestinian leadership effectively gave a stamp of approval to Israel's continued dominance. The agreement stipulated that it was the PA's responsibility to fight terrorism and satisfy Israeli security concerns as a precursor to moving forward to the next phase of negotiations. For Israel, as long as it could hold, reasonably convincingly, to the line that the PA was not satisfying those criteria, then it would have *de jure* rights to continue to exercise control over the majority of the West Bank (Khan 2005). Israel's task of holding to this line was made easier by the activities of the rejectionist groups such as Hamas and the Palestinian Islamic Jihad. Various acts of violent resistance to the occupation within the territories and the employment of terror tactics against civilians inside Israel proper gained popular attention worldwide. The use of suicide bombers in particular helped establish an international image that was associated with irrational radicalism and anti-Semitism.

The spark that led to Hamas' use of extreme violence was the Hebron massacre in February 1994.[23] But Hamas and the other rejectionist groups took the opportunity of retaliation as a means to pursue their own political interests. For Hamas particularly, this meant exposing the gap between the PA's endorsement of negotiations with Israel and a strong element within Palestinian society that favoured escalating violence. These acts of terrorism had a serious effect on Israeli society; Hamas and other rejectionists (primarily the Palestinian Islamic Jihad) carried out some 21 attacks, killing 63 Israelis, between the signing of the DOP and the end of the 1990s.[24]

Israel's elections of 1996 were dominated by the topics of terrorism and the future of the occupation and was a threshold event in the course of the Oslo process. Rabin's assassination had made Shimon Peres, one of the architects of the DOP, Prime Minister. Peres was certainly a weaker candidate than Rabin. In particular, he lacked the strong military qualifications that had been critical to Rabin's ability to sell the discourse of peace to the Israeli public.[25] Through exploiting this space, Benjamin Netanyahu, the head of the revisionist Likud Party, ran on an overtly hawkish platform and triumphed. The combination of Israel's closure policy and the net result of the various agreements established a number of islands of Palestinian autonomy, which were surrounded by areas under Israeli control. This process has been called cantonisation, or bantustanisation (after a similar policy implemented in South Africa under the apartheid regime). In practical terms, the result of this policy was to produce around 64 different Palestinian cantons throughout the territories (Applied Research Institute Jerusalem (ARIJ) 2008). The effect of doing so on Palestinian society, politically, economically and socially, has been enormous. It divided 'already small economic units into even smaller ones' and 'den[ied] Palestinians control over their borders, both internal and external, to the West Bank and Gaza' (Roy 2004, 369). When, during the Second Intifada, these restrictions were tightened even further, they would have drastic consequences that Roy has described in particularly stark terms as 'ending the Palestinian economy' (Roy 2002).

Socially and politically too, the increased restrictions on movement created a new structure for Palestinian lives. This comprised further stratification in terms of the quality of life for Palestinians in the oPts. The prospect of an improved standard of living compared to the hardships of continually confronting direct Israeli rule encouraged Palestinians to move towards urban areas and to remain there. This was because urban areas enjoyed renewal and development projects, and the provision of various services by both the PA and a new network of foreign and Palestinian NGOs, while Israeli restrictions made it extremely difficult to undertake infrastructural development in Areas 'B' and 'C' (see Tabar and Hanafi 2005). Virtually all major institutions were affected from political organisations to higher education.[26] However, a further critical development was that the PA's agency was itself organised around this process of cantonisation.

The birth of a bully

Soon after it was formed, the PA quickly took on many of the qualities of authoritarianism, or became what Henry and Springborg (2010, Chapter 5) call a 'bully praetorian republic'. According to the DOP, the PLO was obliged to establish a monopoly on the use of force by Palestinians in the areas it controlled, while respecting Israeli rule outside those areas. Arafat combined the Fatah militias with the structure of the PA and compensated his closest supporters with well-paid positions. The agreement with Israel also allowed for the return from exile of other large groups of armed fighters to the territories, including a 7,000-strong contingent of the Palestinian Liberation Army, which was re-organised and became the Palestinian National Guard.

This vast swelling in the numbers of armed cadres loyal to the new administration certainly had the effect of intimidating any domestic opposition, although it did not prevent them from engaging in further armed actions and terrorism inside Israel. The establishment of this bulging security structure that was based on patronage and personal loyalties accounted for an enormous proportion of the PA's resources and as such reflected the governmental style of the PA more broadly – this might actually have been on Arafat's agenda all along. According to Khalidi (2006, 160), under Arafat, the PA replicated some of the worst elements of the corrupt, nepotistic and at times brutal 'para-state' of the PLO that had been run from Beirut when both Arafat's influence within the PLO and the PLO's independence were at their peak.

However, the PA of the 1990s was not the same as the organisation that, in Beirut, had brandished its revolutionary credentials with pride. By the 1990s, the PA had become a vehicle for crony capitalism, clientalism and corruption. This was perhaps an inevitable product of Palestine's governmental and economic structure. Part of this equation was certainly Arafat himself. He thrived on disorder, so much so that his personal dominance of both Fatah and the PLO was predicated on his ability to be at the heart of all decision making, allowing him to show favouritism to his allies and exploit divisions between rivals (Crisis Group 2009b). The weakness of any other forces within the PA's structure capable of checking his power enabled such behaviour to occur on a massive scale. Arafat built a vast public sector, providing jobs to nearly 200,000 Palestinians, approximately one-half of them in the security services, while at the same time the PA remained dependent on foreign aid to plug the approximately $75 million annual budgetary shortfall (Samara 2000). The fact that many of these jobs were within the security sector and that many had also gone to returnees (refugees allowed into the oPts as part of the Oslo process) meant that, by default, new jobs tended to be located within Area 'A' and, as such, they created a strong incentive for internal migration from rural to urban areas. Yet another vicious cycle was established, where the PA effectively supported its own encirclement by rewarding those who came to, or stayed within, the confines of its archipelago, policed its population and did little or nothing for those outside.

The Palestinian elites

Palestine's fragmentation was not only a product of Israel's occupation or even the political divisions between various factions, but was also an outcome of the fact that Palestinian society was also divided along class lines. In this respect, Israeli and Palestinian societies share some similarities with each other. Both can be characterised by an extremely powerful central core, growing ever more distant from a weaker and poorer periphery. In both, the core combines political connections with economic might and has frequently demonstrated its strong influence over the direction of domestic and foreign policy. During the Intifada, however, it became clear that while both the Israeli and Palestinian elite withstood the conflict without losing a great deal in terms of relative position within their respective societies, they did so through adopting very different management techniques.

As we have seen, throughout the 1980s and 1990s, the Israeli capitalist elite became more globalised, shifting the main base of many of its operations to the US, diversifying its broader portfolios and incorporating a wide range of international assets. The Palestinian elite was already broader than a single national identity. The main base for its businesses had always been outside Palestine, often in the Gulf or elsewhere. For the Israeli government, the driver for its participation in the 'peace process' issue was to repair the 'rupture in the controlling structure' (Gordon 2008, 171) that took the form of the

First Intifada. The PLO, on the other hand, was brought to Oslo in the wake of its disastrous mishandling of the 1990–1 Gulf crisis, which put it on the wrong side of both most of its Gulf allies and the US at a time when its role in the region was expanding, while at the same time it was acting out of a crisis of its authority within Palestinian politics. But for more business-oriented elites in both societies, their incentives were later supplemented by the prospect of handsome 'peace dividends' and – particularly for the Israelis – access to emerging markets at the apparent dawning of a new age of liberal democracy and globalisation. As negotiations got under way in 1991 and the Oslo process surfaced in 1993, Palestinians themselves, or at least a small group of elites based in the diaspora, also began looking towards the prospect of the 'peace process' in terms of its creation of new opportunities for business and other peace dividends.[27]

Yet by the end of the decade, it had become clear that what 'peace dividends' had resulted from the Oslo process were actually enjoyed almost exclusively by elites who became crony capitalists on both sides of the Green Line. While for ordinary people in Israel, Palestine (and, to a lesser extent, Jordan) had in fact seen its socio-economic conditions worsen during the period of the 'peace process'. Whether or not it is entirely fair to reduce the causes of this growing social stratification and the development of crony capitalist elite to the 'peace process' alone is unclear. As discussed above, the groundwork for these kinds of social structures in both Palestine and Israel was already set in place before the 'peace process' began. However, Oslo clearly enabled them to flourish and gave elites on both sides the opportunity to entrench the structure of domination through both the legal-bureaucratic means and new internationalised apparatus.

Furthermore, particularly in the Palestinian context, the 'peace process' enabled the emergence of other, intermediate-level elite groups. Broadly speaking, these elites fell into two camps. The first was the NGO-globalised elite, which tended to be more supportive of the Oslo process, both for the sake of ideology and interests. The second was the Islamist rejectionist elite represented politically by Hamas (see Roy 2011). This group also owed its position to a network of social welfare and political programmes. However, as we have seen, it remained strongly opposed to the 'peace process', rooted in ideological opposition to the PA.[28] Throughout the 1990s, these two intermediate elite groups pulled society in opposite directions. The NGO-globalised elite used the language and methodologies that were transposed, often directly, from other international organisations and either found themselves pursuing those goals set out by the main sponsors of the 'peace process' or at least navigating the apparatus that donors had set up, while the Islamists simply rejected them and sought to ground their power in more direct charitable and community work.

These differences would become accentuated more and more towards the end of the 1990s and become drastically obvious during the Second Intifada, where the *modus operandi* of the NGO-globalised elite – which was based on a particularly strong interpretation of the concept of risk management – essentially immobilised its outreach and relief work, leaving room for the Islamist social welfare network to extend into that gap (see Gordon and Flic 2009). Beyond this intermediate level, however, significant power remained concentrated in the hands of the crony capitalist elite. This group was to grow in significance throughout the Oslo process and withstood the devastation of the Intifada, then later the violent schism between Hamas and Fatah in 2007, far better than either the NGO-globalised elite or the Islamists.

What was lost in this mix then was the ability of a single narrative, or even a common set of principles, to take root and become hegemonic. What this meant in practical terms was that the political leadership did not have the ability to articulate convincingly the intellectual framework through which it wanted its agency to be understood. (Instead, over time, it grew more reliant on the overt use of force.) In particular, the PA leadership had lost the ability to govern through consent because the general public lost confidence in its ability to achieve two interconnected goals: the first was to progress in the 'peace process' and the second was to improve the general welfare of the population.

The reasons for this loss of confidence can be reduced to three categories of factors: (a) that the promise of general prosperity resulting from the 'peace process' was demonstrably a façade; (b) the conflicting agenda of the NGO-globalised elite and the Islamists made it difficult for any single discourse to dominate popular consciousness; and that (c) visible transformations in the domestic political-economic environments had occurred whereby apparently more and more power was being centralised within a small group of elites. By the time the peace talks had clearly finally fallen apart, the PA was unable to manage the increased fragmentation of society effectively. Thus, it turned towards more coercive means to maintain control.

The façade of peace dividends

The most basic and most important conclusion that can be drawn from an analysis of Palestine's economy during the Oslo years (1993–9) is that during that period, it actually grew weaker and even more dependent on external support. Roy (1999) argues that in reality, the Palestinian economy was 'de-developed' during this period. According to Roy, Palestine is unlike other examples of dependent relationships between economic systems where underdevelopment is evident.[29] Yet in the case of Palestine, the label 'underdevelopment' does not fit. This is because the prospect for any development of the dependent party (Palestine) had been completely undermined as a result of the basic rules of the relationship (Roy 1999, 65). Roy attributes much of the blame for this to Israeli policy. In particular, it was the policy of closure and the disarticulation of Palestinian territory that it produced that was responsible for: (a) the inability of the economy to develop out of the malaise that 30 years of direct occupation had left it in; and (b) the manifest worsening of economic conditions – in other words, the reduction in productive economic activity – which had led to the increase in severity of conditions. However, since the adverse effect of closure has been accepted virtually universally and has been discussed above, and in great depth elsewhere (see, *inter alia*, Ishac and Radwan 1999; Fischer, Alonso-Gamo and Von Allmen 2001; Hilal and Khan 2004 Roy 2006; Gordon 2008; Khalidi and Taghdisi-Rad 2009), it is sufficient to state that the deleterious effect of closure has, in Roy's words:

> Not only mediated the economic transfer of Palestinian resources to the Israeli economy but delinked local economic activity (employment, trade, personal income) from market forces, making them increasingly dependent on demand conditions in Israel. The result was the steady weakening and disablement of Palestine's economic base an eroding productive capacity, and the growth of the service sector as the largest domestic employer.
>
> (Roy 1999, 65)

Beyond the impact of the occupation, there were other factors that contributed to the failure of Palestinian economic development during the 1990s. In particular, this was the cumulative impact of the class-based stratification of society,[30] corruption throughout the PA, over-reliance on damaging rents and the adoption of various policies in line with a 'good governance' economic framework by the PA.

Each of these factors was interlinked with the others and together they form another vicious cycle. In particular, this was a process whereby the PA grew more corrupt and more reliant on damaging rents (largely based on money it extracted from international donors), which it used to maintain the political support it needed from both the top-ranking elites and, via the bulging public sector, from the employed middle classes. In the short term, this had dual effects. First, it meant that the existing gaps within the class strata were widened and, second, it weakened the PA's position politically, reducing the political capital it could exploit either domestically or (because of the acknowledgement of its corruption) internationally.

Further, the more important longer-term impacts were that this cycle stifled the possibility for growth in the private sector and made the PA even more subservient to the demands of its benefactors.[31] In the case of the private sector, there was simply no room to develop. Trapped between the swollen public sector, the rent-seeking monopoly elites and the crippling impact of the occupation's closure policy, it was not possible for the Palestinian economy – particularly for the non-services sectors – to function effectively, let alone grow. What further compounded the problem was that, without developing a sustainable tax base, the PA was forced to borrow even more in order to support its outgoings year-on-year and thus it continued to dig itself into a hole.

As the PA's debts mounted, there seemed to be no way out other than to hope for the international donors to forgive its arrears, perhaps gambling on the fact that 'peace' was itself a valuable commodity (Samara 2000). Yet, in the meantime, unemployment grew, employment conditions worsened and for the PA, the political cost of this enterprise only grew even more exposed though the rejectionism (and terrorism) of its rivals.

Crony capitalism

Yet while the middle and lower classes were growing more disillusioned with the PA's performance, the rent-seeking elites continued to do very well out of the arrangement. The members of this group would prove to be important players in shaping the direction of Palestinian politics in the 1990s in such a way that tended to favour the perpetuation of the 'peace process'. Yet, beyond the stifling of the private sector, the fact that power and decision making seemed to be concentrated within this group in a way that was clearly disconnected from the lives and experiences of ordinary Palestinians, the continued development of this crony capitalist elite can be seen as another major factor that contributed to the failure of the 'peace process' discourse to establish hegemony.

The group was made up of a number of particularly powerful families that included the Masri, Nuqul, Salfiti, Khoury and Shouman families (Hanieh 2011). Most had become very successful through investing in the Gulf oil industries soon after they were expelled from Palestine in 1948. Yet their ties to the regions' monarchies in the Gulf and Jordan had oriented them politically. However, at the same time, all of them had remained tied in one way or another both to the oPts and to the PLO. By the beginning of the 'peace process', all of them were still potentially powerful actors in the Palestinian political scene, but the announcement of the DOP was divisive and the group split. Some members, such as Abdel Majid Shouman, the head of the Arab Bank, rejected the agreement and suspended their financial backing to the PLO, while others, such as the brothers Subih and Munib Masri, lent their support to the process. As a result, they grew closer to the so-called moderates within the PLO.

This support was manifest both rhetorically and, importantly, materially through large investments in the PA's infrastructure. This main avenue for this process was a network of holding companies that were established to help build and develop the Palestinian state. They were based on the assumption that the peace talks would encourage investment. The Palestinian Investment and Development Company (Padico) launched with a capital base of $1.5 billion. Its role and the roles played by its subsidiaries in supporting the PA's initial waves of institution building were indispensable. Just seven years after its launch, at the end of the 1990s, Padico boasted an impressive portfolio (Samara 2000, 24; Bouillon 2004, 38–41; Robson 2008), including the Palestinian Telecommunications network, Paltel (27 per cent owned by Padico), the Palestinian Securities Exchange (70 per cent owned by Padico) and Aquarian (Palestine Real Estate Investment Company). According to Padico's website, it is unique 'compared to other Palestinian and international corporate entities for many reasons, including its diverse board of directors and their seasoned experience across various economic sectors'. In addition in its submission to the UN Global Compact Communications on Progress Report (Padico 2014), it claims:

> The company invests in leading large-scale projects that assure sustainability in earnings and cash flows. The company has employed a shrewd, longterm investment strategy since its establishment, premised on sector and investment diversification, allowing it to adapt to the challenging circumstances in Palestine.

However, Hilal and Khan's (2004, 103) assessment attributes Padico's success less to its inherent characteristics and notes the rent-seeking/attribution relationship with the PA:

> Some of these companies [subsidiaries of Padico] were natural monopolies; others were not ... In each case, monopoly rents were not taxed away by the state but could be retained provided the investment was sustained and performance was acceptable. The PNA was also ready in its tax code to grant additional tax exemptions to investors for different periods depending on the capital invested and the labour employed. This further enhanced the rents of selected larger companies dominated by expatriate capital. In addition, informal mechanisms were also reported for enhancing the rents of vital companies, such as arrangements to defer utility or tax bills, often in exchange for kickbacks, but sometimes simply in response to special pleading.

While, as Hilal and Khan argue, not all rent-seeking behaviour is necessarily always a bad thing – especially in complex contexts such as Palestine – the appearance that the state is allocating favours to its friends can be very damaging. The image that the PA was effectively acting as a predatory state on behalf of its cronies caused harm to the Palestinian private sector and it is worth noting that the impact of this was widely known at the time. Roy (1996, 38) cited an example of a foreign government employee who estimated that: 'According to the US Department of State, there are at least 13 known monopolies under the control of no more than five individuals who are members of Yasser Arafat's inner circle'. Yet it was also acknowledged by leading figures in the Palestinian intelligentsia that society in general was suffering from an overall process that seemed to be serving the interests of a very few (Giacaman 1998).

Furthermore, it was not just that this small group of elites existed in an apparently different world from the rest of society that harmed the notion that this 'peace process' was for everyone. Rather, it was apparent that while the general population suffered from a sinking economy and, indirectly, the continued effects of the occupation, members of this elite appeared to be using their influence to pursue greater integration with Israel and the further entrenchment of the occupation.

Even when the peace talks collapsed, despite the widespread trauma and myriad existential changes that took place in the lives of Palestinians throughout the oPts during the Second Intifada and its lawless aftermath (particularly on the streets of Nablus), this same network of elites remained relatively unharmed by the violence. The majority of private enterprise in the West Bank that existed during the late 2010s could still be traced through a series of holding companies to the Masri and Khoury families (Hanieh 2011). These two families directly owned a considerable range of property and organisations operating in the West Bank. Even ten years after the Second Intifada began, this collection of capitalists 'completely dominate the political economy of the Palestinian territories' (Hanieh 2011, 95) to such an extent that it is 'almost impossible to find a large- or medium-sized company in which they do not own a significant stake' (Hanieh 2011, 95). There was clearly a concentration of wealth and power for some elites, yet at the same time ordinary people were not experiencing much in the way of benefits from the promised peace dividends. These factors contributed the fact that no pro-negotiations camp would achieve hegemony.

Globalisation of the mid-level elites

At the same time, a further change in the social dynamics of the oPts was taking place. In this case it was not a product of the PA's dependence on the donor community, but rather it occurred partly in spite of that relationship. From within the Palestinian middle classes, a new wave of institutionalisation was taking place. This largely took the form of a dialectical process between what has been called NGO-isation and a rejectionist reaction to it.

NGO-isation describes a process 'through which issues of collective concern transformed into projects in isolation from the general context in which they are applied without taking due consideration of the economic, social and political factors affecting them' (Jad 2007). The term describes a more complex process than simply the proliferation of NGOs in society. In fact, this distinction was particularly relevant to Palestine, where there was a long history of NGO activism operating in the oPts. They were behind a number of significant campaigns, including a boycott of Israeli products in the 1980s and a powerful campaign to 'buy Palestinian' (Tabar and Hanafi 2005, 49).

However, during the 1990s, the landscape of the NGO network was very different. Many were funded directly by foreign sources and pursued agendas that were framed by, or based on, this experience. One manifestation of this difference is that they tended to represent an interpretation of social issues crafted in an international context and therefore, in contrast to the work of NGOs in Palestine prior to Oslo, not specific to the experiences of Palestinians

The fragmentation of Palestine 57

in the oPts. As a result, many would champion social activism in such a way that seemed irrelevant or at least disconnected from the actual ecosystem of Palestinian society under occupation. As Islah Jad explains, where youth activism groups, for instance, would offer the opportunity to attend workshops or gatherings, they would do so in a way that was socially exclusionary for many in the working classes: 'many of the NGO events are held in expensive hotels, serving fancy food, distributing glossy material' (Jad 2007, 178).

Linda Tabar and Sari Hanafi (2005) argue that such changes in the behaviour of the Palestinian NGOs during the 1990s are likely to be products of the fact that those NGOs that were in the ascendency during this period were so because they were well connected and supported by foreign donor organisations. This had occurred partly because of the fact that international donor organisations often saw supporting Palestinian NGOs both as a means to circumvent the corruption of the PA and as an opportunity to support the development of a pro-peace civil society environment in the oPts, which was considered essential for the 'peace process'. However, the unforeseen consequences of this were that instead of developing Palestinian society in general through the promotion of these NGOs, the impact of this relationship was that it created a number of well-funded, Western-looking civil society organisations that were largely disconnected from the real world in which they were supposed to act. They became enclaves within educated, urban Palestinian society, often operating in English rather than Arabic and promoting their agenda in the terms of the target-setting mentalities of their foreign sponsors (Tabar and Hanafi 2005).

In other words, they had become globalised. This is not to say that they were in any sense transnational entities in their own right, but rather that they tended to advocate agendas and methodologies that were rooted not in Palestine, but in the meetings, seminars and workshops of foreign organisations, where priorities were set and policy was formulated under conditions very different from those actually experienced by people in the oPts. Both as a result of this and the fact that their funding was often dependent on particular political constraints, these organisations tended to be inclined to take the 'peace process' at face value and advocate support for it in general society, albeit perhaps indirectly.

At the same time as this development was forging a new dynamic in the Palestinian middle classes, there was dialectical response emerging. This was a rejectionist agenda usually associated directly or indirectly with Islamist politics. This rejection tended to be much more representative of the roots of the pre-Oslo Palestinian NGO movement and, because they operated outside the parameters of donor-based funding streams provided to the globalised NGOs, they were able to maintain a greater level of independence (Milton-Edwards and Farrell 2010; Roy 2011).

This period produced a number of alternative nodes of power, authority and wealth, and various other minor hierarchies, wherein legitimacy was derived from appealing to and replicating different, but ultimately parochial, discourses. The globalised NGOs justified their actions and continued existence by demonstrating their modernity and the extent to which they were different from traditional seats of power. Yet at the same time rejectionist movements opposed them, citing their capitulation to a Western imperialist agenda. The result was a mix of polarisation and a stagnating political morass. As Jad (2009, 15) summarises:

> The role of NGOs in the West Bank and Gaza shifted under the influence of the state-building process initiated by the Madrid Conference in 1991 ... the dual dynamics of state building and NGOization led to the demobilization of all social movements.

Yet there were other factors at play within Palestinian society that also added to the burden of hardship endured by the general population inside the oPts. The PA developed along authoritarian lines, which rested on an unsustainable cycle of rent-seeking and crony capitalism. The dual products of this process were the mounting debt burden endured by the PA and a languid private sector.

This meant that while ordinary Palestinians suffered from the absence of opportunities and prosperity that were meant to be the cornerstones of Oslo's appeal, a small network of already powerful elites was conspicuously successful. Further, due to their close ties to the weak PA, it seemed as if they had to some extent hijacked the national political agenda, pushing it more towards integration with Israel because it served their own agenda. Simultaneously, the involvement of international donors more directly in Palestinian society introduced a network of globalised NGOs and a rejectionist reaction to it. The competition between these two wings of the institutionalised middle class was both polarising and sclerotising for political activism at that level.

In essence, then, under these conditions, it was impossible for the peace discourse to become hegemonic. The disconnectedness that most ordinary Palestinians felt from the powers that were shaping their own lives was palpable and, when the façade of this 'peace process' collapsed in the early 2000s, the true nature of those forces was revealed as 'asymmetric containment'.

Notes

1 The significance of the George H. W. Bush Administration's decision to make $10 million-worth of loan guarantees to Israel conditional on the suspension of settlement expansion in 1991, particularly in the context of large-scale immigration from post-Soviet republics to Israel, should not be overlooked.
2 Various mopping-up operations continued in the wake of the war, and Ben Gurion's ambition to expand Jewish-controlled territory into the West Bank, towards Nablus, was only restricted by the prospect of confronting resistance from the British Army – which had a defensive pact with the Jordanian monarchy – rather than any moral concern over the continued transfer of the Palestinian population. Yet when the West Bank and further territory was acquired in the 1967 war, the fact that population transfer was not an option in the same way had been 20 years before meant that Israel faced a much more urgent concern of losing its demographic advantage in the territory between the Mediterranean Sea and the Jordan River. See Morris 2001; Pappe 2007.

The fragmentation of Palestine 59

3 Although documents circulated internally to policy makers do address Israeli concern over this issue. See Koenig 1976; Zayyad 1976.
4 Until that time, the kibbutzim had been able to depend on government credit guarantees to cover their debt; however, as a result of these changes, many of the advantages the kibbutzim enjoyed were watered down or removed altogether. While the kibbutzim maintained an advantageous position relative to the rest of society, the impact of these changes was clearly dramatic. See Brod 1990; Zilbersheid 2007.
5 For instance, Ali Abu Hilal – a labour leader – was deported from Israel in 1986. See Palumbo 1990, 208.
6 The boycott worked in the following way: beyond the obvious first level of boycott, which banned Israeli-Arab trade outright, it also: (a) banned companies from trading in the Arab world if they also traded with Israel; and (b) blacklisted those companies that did business with companies doing business with Israel. The cumulative cost of this was significant, between 1948 and 1994, it was estimated at around $40 billion in lost opportunities. The boycott had already been challenged in 1979 with the signing of the Israeli–Egypt peace, but the benefits from this paled in comparison to what could potentially be achieved if the boycott were to be more comprehensively undermined (see York 1994; Retzky 1995).
7 The impact of this on the boycott was to dilute its first layer (the ban on Israeli–Arab trade). Yet it also nullified the crippling effect of the boycott's second and third layers (the ban on companies that traded with Israelis and the blacklist of companies that did business with companies doing business with Israel).
8 For instance, various companies that were Israeli, at least in name, remained unaffected by the economic consequences of the Second Intifada. This was primarily as a result of the fact that most of them were registered in the US and did much of their business there. See Bichler and Nitzan 2007.
9 This was embodied in the minds of many Western observers by the examples of the Baathist figureheads such as Gamal Nasser, Saddam Hussein or Hafez al-Assad, who in their public appearances would often conflate anti-imperial, anti-Western rhetoric and anti-Zionist and sometimes anti-Semitic statements (Cleveland and Bunton 2009, Chapters 16 and 19).
10 This included Zuheir Mohsen, a prominent member of the pro-Syria As-Sa'iqa faction within the PLO who was murdered by the Mossad in Cannes, southern France in 1979, Naji Al Ali, a prominent artist and creator of the 'Handala' cartoon, who was shot to death by Mossad agents in London in 1987, and Khalil al-Wazir, a high-level PLO official, who was killed by the Israeli military in Tunis in 1988.
11 The PLO had been forced to relocate from Jordan to Beirut in 1970–1. However, in 1982, the Israeli military invaded Lebanon in extremely controversial circumstances. Yet while the war in Lebanon proved extremely costly for both sides, in one respect it was a dramatic failure for Israel. Driving the PLO out of Lebanon failed to weaken the organisation's ideational presence in the territories and instead added to the mythology of 'resistance-at-all-costs' and condensed the spectrum of political choices facing Palestinians within that context. In other words, in the polarised climate after 1982, Palestinian politics developed along the axiom that to resist was to support the PLO and to reject the PLO was to reject resistance. In practical terms, though, the PLO was now no longer able to operate effectively from the close proximity to the oPts and instead was forced to depend more heavily on the support and activism of its members and allies within the territories themselves. This created pressure on other elites to either conform or risk being seen as anti-resistance. This pressure was particularly manifest in the fear of being outflanked by supporters of the PLO that were prepared to act radically. The best example of this was the assassination of Zafir al-Masri, the interim Mayor of Nablus, in 1986

60 *The fragmentation of Palestine*

by agents of the Popular Front for the Liberation of Palestine (PFLP), who had inferred his collaboration with the occupation (see Sahliyeh 1986).

12 The shift to this mode of rule-through-intermediaries was enabled by a closer alliance between Israel's executive and the judicial system. It allowed for the utilisation of particular interpretation of existing Ottoman laws as a pretext. The rate of forcible appropriation of land accelerated throughout the 1980s and reached its peak in the seizure of some 14 per cent of the West Bank by 1984, and by the beginning of the Intifada in 1987, some 125 settlements in the West Bank and the Gaza Strip had been built in these areas, representing an investment totalling over $8 billion (Gordon 2008, 120).

13 Gordon suggests that the notion of bringing more Palestinians into the running of these intermediate bureaucracies as a means of outsourcing responsibilities without losing power had been floated in Israeli governmental discourses throughout the history of the conflict. He cites examples of the Palestinian Farmers' Party created by the Jewish Agency in the 1920s, informal power-sharing agreements with the Kingdom of Jordan, the creation of the Village Leagues in the late 1970s and the establishment of the South Lebanese Army in 1978 (Gordon 2008).

14 Which had been enabled by the 1969 Cairo Agreement and had blossomed into an effective state within a state in Lebanon.

15 The most notable of these was the murder of three Israelis in Cyprus by the Fatah affiliate Force 17, which resulted in an Israeli bombing raid and the killing of tens of PLO cadres.

16 The text of the first joint leaflet issued on 16 December (a mere week into the uprising) in Gaza states: 'The rulers of Israel deluded themselves into thinking that they had come closer to creating an alternative to the PLO and that with their empty talk of direct negotiations with Jordan' (Khatib 2009, 47).

17 These were: Hanna Sinyura, the editor of East Jerusalem's *Al-Fajr* newspaper, and Gazan lawyer Fayiz Abu Rahm (see Cobban 1985, 220).

18 For the full text of the Fourteen Points, see Laqueur and Rubin (2008).

19 The full text of both the speeches by Shamir and Haydir Abd al-Shafi – the leader of the PLO delegation – are available in Laqueur and Rubin (2008).

20 According to Benny Morris (2001), Hannan Ashrwawi had previously met with Hischfeld in 1989 and suggested talks between him and Qray.

21 Its sponsors included Iran, Syria and the Lebanon-based Hizbollah (see Chehab 2007, Chapter 7).

22 Therefore, although looking back on the Oslo era with hindsight might allow us to make *prima facie* judgments that damn the behaviour of particular parties, or assumptions that particular individuals had illicit motives from the outset, this is probably not a very helpful approach in the long run. Indeed, in doing so, it is likely that some of the more important subtleties of the situation would be lost. To take a dramatic example, it is of course unlikely that the then Israeli Prime Minister Yitzakh Rabin would have had any knowledge that his pursuit of the negotiations would lead to his assassination in Tel Aviv on 4 November, 1995.

23 The Hebron massacre refers to a mass murder of worshippers at the Ibrahimi Mosque by American-Israeli military surgeon Baruch Goldstein, who was subsequently beaten to death.

24 The impact of this on the Israeli economy is less easy to determine, although it is likely that terrorism severely hampered Israel's tourism industry and further encouraged many Israelis with dual citizenship to leave the country. Nonetheless, there was also a political consequence of this terrorism which helped strengthen Israel's case, which was that the PA was unable or unwilling to combat terrorism and was thus unworthy of advancing to the next phase of negotiations.

25 Some historians, particularly those with more sympathetic perspectives towards the Oslo process as a whole and often the Israeli Labor Party in particular, are

keener to criticise Netanyahu's belligerence, which they blame for retarding the natural progress of the 'peace process' (see Ben-Ami 2006; Shlaim 2010). Yet, viewed through the lens of an analysis of 'asymmetric containment', a reasonable assessment could find that the Netanyahu government was only marginally different in its approach to the 'peace process' than the Labor administration that preceded it – although it certainly used more bellicose language – and based on the measure of settlement expansion alone, the Likud government actually slowed the rate of colonisation in the oPts.

26 See the records of Birzeit University's Right to Education Campaign at: http://right2edu.birzeit.edu.
27 A good example of this is the launch of Padico, a vast holding company with interests in numerous sectors including construction, telecoms and various other services, under the chairmanship of Munib al-Masri.
28 There also remained further political groups not accounted for in this simple division, most notably those parties of the left which, while remaining opposed the Oslo process, were also ideologically opposed to the political agenda adopted by the Islamists. For the sake of clarity and because their power to influence the political landscape in Palestine was extremely limited at this point, these groups are not discussed in depth here.
29 'Underdevelopment', according to dependency theory, is often a product of the relationships of extraction that occur between developed and less developed economies, and it tends to mean that the weaker party is unable to fulfil its economic and social potential. The symptoms of this are generally high unemployment or mass employment at very low wages, poorly organised services and amenities – which do not necessity serve the needs or interests of the domestic population – and a limited capacity for home-grown private sector development. This, in case studies from Africa, Latin America and South Asia, for instance, is the result of the impact of: (a) large foreign companies that tend to extract wealth and, because of their size and resources, make competition impossible; and (b) the weak regulatory powers of the state. However, even in cases where underdevelopment is evident, it is possible for the weaker party's economic system to change and develop over time, and conditions may improve even if the broader hierarchical relationship remains fundamentally unchallenged.
30 A particularly interesting and useful breakdown of the impact of the occupation on the different socioeconomic classes in Palestine, both before the DOP (1993) and how it laid the groundwork for what followed, is presented in Samara's article 'Globalization, the Palestinian Economy, and the "Peace Process"' (2000, 22).
31 These were in fact often directed against the expansion or maintenance of rents in the economy, regardless of whether their impact was potentially positive (see Hilal and Khan 2004).

4 Making plans

With Arafat's death in 2004, it was the beginning of the end for the Intifada. Israel had inflicted a crushing defeat on the armed Palestinian resistance and laid siege to most of the urban centres in the West Bank. The former Prime Minister, Mahmoud Abbas, took over as leader of the PLO and disavowed further acts of terrorism and the cession of armed resistance to Israel. Abbas, whose political approach had always been considered more compatible than Arafat's with both American and Israeli interests, was extended international support as a response to these statements.

Abbas was officially elected to the presidency in 2005 with an overwhelming majority; it is likely that this contributed to the belief in Washington that further democratic elections in Palestine would return a Fatah majority. When the US pushed Israel to allow Palestinian legislative elections in 2006, it was taken by surprise when it was Hamas that was swept to power. The US and Israel totally rejected Hamas' right to govern and led the EU, and other major donors, in an international embargo of aid to any Palestinian government that included Hamas. Domestically, this pressure meant that initial efforts to run the PA through a unity government fell apart after less than a year and a violent schism between Hamas and the PA establishment caused the political separation of the Gaza Strip from the West Bank. It emerged later that US and UK clandestine forces had also worked with the PA security forces to bring about this collapse.

In many ways the Israeli and American reaction to Hamas' victory replicated the same logic that had been applied to the Palestinians throughout Israel's invasion during the Intifada. It juxtaposed the use of coercive methods – in this case the curtailment of aid – with a promise of improved conditions if Palestinians accepted the leadership of those approved by Israel. In the end, this is what happened and aid did return in even greater amounts when the PA establishment was returned to power in 2007 after an armed conflict – a schism – with Hamas. Therefore, when – out of the collapse of the unity government (and the demise of meaningful Palestinian democracy) – the PA was resurrected, it was into an environment where Israel, the US and its allies were determined to re-affirm their control over Palestinian politics and enforce structures of a new security agenda and a neoliberal economic model in order to ensure that there could be no return to the politics of the Arafat era. President Abbas appointed Salam Fayyad as Prime Minister and under Fayyad's leadership, the PA launched what it described as a renewed effort to re-order Palestinian society and build the institutional framework for a state.

It was at this point that the PA began to propagate a new message to explain its actions. This narrative promised that, through institution building and accepting the political direction that was *de facto* imposed by Israel and the rest of the outside world, Palestinians could finally achieve independence. However, by late 2011, when Fayyad distanced himself from the PLO's efforts to obtain statehood at the UN – which was being blocked anyway by the US's threat of a veto – it was evident that the promise of independence was as implausible as it had sounded at the outset. In view of this, this chapter and those that follow focus on examining the political dimensions of this period. They inquire into why, and by what means, the PA, with external support, re-asserted its control over domestic politics in the period after the Intifada failed and the unity government collapsed. Further, it investigates the ways in which the PA and donors propagated a myth of progress towards independence in order to justify these actions. It argues that from this point onwards, the PA's goals and the goals of foreign actors were inextricably linked. Moreover, there are two further general observations to be made. First is of an overall pattern of entropy within the PA's statebuilding framework. This began with a more-or-less clear alignment among the interests and agenda of the main allied actors – the US (and other foreign donors), Israel and the PA – in the immediate aftermath of Hamas' election in 2006, which became more diverged as time went on. The second point is that, though there was some crossover between the popular will and the PA's goals at the beginning of the process, many of the changes and developments undertaken as part of PA policy – especially in terms of the domestic conditions of the West Bank or to the infrastructure of the PA – did not end up aligning with the best interests of the general Palestinian population.

This chapter introduces the overall framework of policies and rhetoric that dominated Palestinian politics between 2007–11. It explains the dynamic of the post-Second Intifada context within the West Bank. In particular, it looks at how power was manifested and distributed between Palestine and the other relevant actors, particularly in the period 2007–9. It discusses what each side's real intentions were behind the statebuilding agenda and it exposes the very important distinction between the real impact that these changes have had on Palestinian society in the West Bank and the rhetoric that was promoted, primarily, by a team of technocrats – headed by Fayyad – that ran the government of the PA during that time. Finally, through outlining this broader political framework of the PA's post-2007 agenda, this chapter lays the groundwork for more detailed analyses of the PA's security and economic development agenda discussed in the following two chapters.

64 *Making plans*

This chapter presents this discussion in the following subsections. First, it outlines the context of extraordinary violence during the Intifada. Second, it looks at the dynamic nature of Israel's occupation policies in the 2000s. This focuses on the re-organisation of its structures of power and control in Gaza – in what has become known as 'disengagement' – and how that same logic was transferred to the West Bank. Third, it concentrates on the overall political framework offered by the Fayyad-led government in the wake of the schism. This exposes the gulf between reality and the PA's narrative of statebuilding, and also discusses the deep relationship between the PA's institutions and the input of foreign governments. Finally, this chapter introduces the specific topics for discussion in the following three chapters: the 'security' and 'development' agenda and the pervasive role of foreign agents.

The Second Intifada: four forms of coercion

From the outset of the Second Intifada, both extreme violence and attacks on civilian targets were the norm (Amnesty International 2001; Catignani 2008a, 2008b; Whitaker 2002). However, following a particularly vicious attack by Hamas, which killed 30 people in an old people's home in the city of Netanya on 27 March 2002, the Israeli Prime Minister Ariel Sharon ordered the launch of Operation Defensive Shield, which was effectively the full re-invasion of the West Bank. In this context, the Oslo II divisions between Areas 'A', 'B' and 'C' were totally ignored and Israel's mechanisms of 'asymmetric containment' came into full force. Israel imposed severe restrictions on movement across the West Bank. Effectively surrounding all urban centres within the territory and putting them under blockade, Israeli forces also besieged the PA's *moqata'a* (headquarters) in Ramallah, which kept Arafat enclosed for two years (March–May 2002, then September 2002–October 2004). There followed two pitched battles that attracted global attention: the Israeli invasion of Jenin refugee camp (early April 2002) and then the siege of the Church of the Nativity in Bethlehem (April and May 2002).

In Nablus, the fighting was focused mostly in the Old City and in the refugee camps. The major battle was fought between 2 and 21 April 2002. Israel used new tactics that blurred the line between civilian and military environments. It further integrated its invasion forces with aerial bombardment that devastated some structures in the Old City. Approximately 80 Palestinian fighters were killed and 300 were injured, while on 9 April, the Israeli military sustained 13 fatalities through a deadly suicide attack.

Let us define violence in a broad sense: as the instrumental use of force intended to expand or maintain a power hierarchy. In occupied Palestine specifically, the violence represents mechanisms of coercion that serve the interests of Israel through regulating and disciplining Palestinian society. This apparatus is actuated with greater intensity in order to meet the need of producing and reproducing greater acquiescence among the subject population. In essence, then, the violence of the Palestinian experience during the Intifada can be categorised into four subgroups. The purpose of the categories is not to provide an exhaustive explanation of the Intifada experience or to justify counter-violence. Rather, it is to help make the different forms of violence experienced by ordinary Palestinians more comprehensible and therefore elucidate its meaning for the political context of the following years.[1]

Spatial violence

Spatial violence constituted the disruption of existing patterns of life through the appropriation and re-assignment of space. Obvious forms of this on a broad scale were the sieges of the cities in the West Bank that began in 2002. These comprised restrictions on movement between urban centres and between urban and rural areas. In Nablus, this was what is generally meant when referring to the siege that began in 2002 and lasted in full until 2007, when it was gradually dismantled (although its apparatus is still present). This form of coercion also redefined access to what were normally considered public spaces through the imposition of curfews or the establishment of checkpoints. These curfews were often targeted discriminately on different areas in Nablus and were focused particularly on the Old City and the refugee camps. This discrimination served to enflame hostilities already present as a result of the social and political stratifications in the city, and this contributed to further political violence (see below).

However, a further manifestation of spatial violence that was particularly significant during the Intifada was the invasion of private spaces. Until 2005, one element of this practice was the destruction of homes as a punitive measure against the families of suspected terrorists. According to B'Tselem (2011b), there were 664 homes destroyed under these conditions between 2001 and 2004. This left more than 4,000 people homeless.

More widespread in Nablus was the rupture of Palestinian lives through direct incursions into private homes as a means of navigating dense urban environments without entering the streets (particularly in the Old City and Balata refugee camp). This consisted of using explosives to create holes in the walls of houses and generate alternative passageways while avoiding the main streets where the soldiers would be potentially exposed to hostile fire. As Eyal Weizman (2007, 185) explains: '[The Israeli soldiers] were punching holes through parting walls, ceilings and floors, and moving across them through 100-metre-long pathways of domestic interior hollowed out of the dense and contiguous city fabric'.

Further, this kind of abrupt and overt incursion into private spheres was not the only way in which the Israeli forces imposed a coercive power into the home environment. During the siege of Nablus, electricity supplies were often cut and gas was restricted, along with access to other basic supplies. That this can be interpreted as a form of Israeli coercion is confirmed by this tactic's repetition following the election in 2006, when, in describing similar tactics but transferred to the siege of Gaza, Israeli commanders stated that it was their objective to 'put the Palestinians on a diet' (*Agence France Press* (AFP) 2006).

Kinetic violence

Certainly some of the actions taken by the Israeli forces described under the category of spatial violence also qualify as violence directed against the person. Clearly, in the cases of house demolitions and home invasions that led to the death of inhabitants, or examples where individuals were killed during the enforcement of curfews or at checkpoints, or died as a result of lack of access to healthcare, spatial violence led directly to the death of individuals. What is meant by kinetic violence were the acts of violence specifically designed to kill particular individuals (Bishara 2009). The most obvious examples of this were the targeted assassinations undertaken by Israeli forces against specific Palestinian leaders.[2] Again, the tactic of targeted killings had been used prior to the Intifada and even prior to the Oslo process – for example, the bombing of PLO headquarters in Hammam Chott, Tunisia in 1985 – although Israel did not acknowledge its use of a targeted killing policy until 2000 (Office of the United Nations High Commissioner for Human Rights 2010).

However, the additional impact of the targeted killings during the Second Intifada derived not only from the fact that their numbers increased, but also from the fact that they were directed against political figures who were well-known and often killed civilians as well. As Kimmerling (2003, 163) explains: 'the murder victims were public figures, many of whom were admired by the Palestinian people; secondly, the operations are often not clean, and killed other, innocent, individuals along with a targeted person'. Examples included the founder of Hamas, Sheikh Yassin, who – along with nine others – was killed by a rocket from a helicopter gunship in 2004 (he had survived a similar attempt on his life in 2003). According to B'Tselem (2015b), between 29 September 2000 and 26 December 2008, a total of 384 people were killed in the process of targeted killings (some 232 Palestinians were the objects of targeted killing and the remainder were collateral damage). Across all aspects of Israel's tactics during the Intifada, the intention to kill was implicit from the outset. Israel's policy during this time was expressed as 'the policy of targeted frustration' in a ruling of the Supreme Court of Israel (2011), although according to observers, it was designed not only to suppress resistance but also to 'compel the Palestinians to admit defeat' (Kimmerling 2003, 163). Yet according to a leaked CIA report (2009, 2), Israel's targeting killing policy was counter-productive: 'Israeli [High Value Targets] efforts from 2000 to 2002 strengthened solidarity between terrorist groups and bolstered popular support for hardline militant leaders'.

This, according to the CIA, was because such strikes:

> may increase support for the insurgents, particularly if these strikes enhance insurgent leaders' lore, if noncombatants are killed in the

attacks, if legitimate or semilegitimate politicians aligned with the insurgents are targeted, or if the government is already seen as overly repressive or violent. Because of the psychological nature of insurgency, either side's actions are less important than how events are perceived by key audiences inside and outside the country.

(CIA 2009, 2)

This argument would appear to be backed up by the results of a survey conducted by An-Najah University, which at the time noted that '67 per cent of Palestinians supported a ceasefire', but it also showed that 92.7 per cent of Palestinians saw Palestinian military operations as 'a natural reaction to Israeli military operations' (quoted in Bishara 2009). Nonetheless, Israel's display of force was overwhelming. During the first few months of the invasion, the army fired over one million bullets. Further, while Palestinian militant organisations were prevented from re-arming by the interception of several supply ships, the Israeli military issued an emergency appeal to the US government to re-supply its munitions (Laor 2002; Catignani 2008b).

The scale of death and destruction was striking. According to B'Tselem (2012a), nearly 5,000 Palestinians were killed during the Intifada. Israel also increased the number of Palestinians captured and detained under a variety of extra-judicial arrangements, such as administrative detention. The detention of minors, indefinite detention and torture were regular occurrences under these circumstances (Cook, Hanieh and Kay 2004).

Systemic violence

The systematic violence of the Israeli invasion was the most direct product of the policies of 'asymmetric containment' that preceded it. It describes the denial of services, the destruction of the Palestinian economy and the use of pseudo-legal bureaucratic mechanisms to wage war on Palestinians. Examples of this are numerous and most could be tied directly to a biopolitical interpretation of Israeli tactics designed to subjugate the Palestinian population *en masse*. Obviously, some examples of this have already been discussed, particularly restrictions on movement checkpoints and the indiscriminate use of kinetic violence. However, what is distinct about this form of violence is that it took the form of both creating and destroying institutional mechanisms that regulated Palestinian life.

Examples of how systemic violence was used can be seen in Israel's creation of a pseudo-legal bureaucratic regulation of Palestinian life. There are two main examples of this that are important to note with regard to the creation of the political conditions that followed the Second Intifada. The first of these was the permit system, which had been established in a different form prior to the Oslo process. Of course, the express point of any permit system is to impose controlling measures on a population. These were implemented and extended through Palestinian society during the Oslo period and because they did not at the time cause immediate disruption (any more than was usual), the full effect was not known until the crisis of the Second Intifada. Permits were also used to accentuate pre-existing divisions in Palestinian society. They were used to reward good behaviour, according to Israeli definitions, and to make life difficult for those who did not behave in the way in which the occupier desired.[3]

Political violence

Political violence describes the methods by which Israel and its allies sought to challenge the legitimacy of the Palestinians' basic rights in order to provide political cover for its own actions. This kind of violence is deeply linked to the other forms discussed above. In Kimmerling's (2003, 3) words, politicide 'is [a] process that has, as its ultimate goal, the dissolution of the Palestinian people's existence as a legitimate social, political, and economic entity', and in this case it was the attack on the question of legitimacy of the Palestinian cause overall that was at issue.

In some cases this was obvious and manifest in terms of misrepresentation, such as the conflation of Palestinian terrorism with Al-Qaida, invoking uncritical international support that saw Palestine as another frontline in the so-called 'War on Terror' (Wines 2002). Israel also negotiated with the US to unilaterally redefine its territorial ambitions and the status of particular areas of occupied land. This was done while at the same time the US and Israel conspired to present the Palestinians as the 'unreasonable' party that was unwilling to negotiate without preconditions. The culmination of this was an exchange of letters between Sharon and President Bush in April 2004, wherein Bush offered unprecedented recognition for 'the permanence of major Israeli settlements in the occupied territories' (Khalidi 2006, 211) and endorsement of the Israeli position on the possible future return of Palestinian refugees (Bush and Sharon 2004). Both of these concessions were made by the US on behalf of the Palestinians without consultation and outside any framework of negotiation.

The most significant aspect of political violence, which is particularly relevant to Nablus' experience of the war, was that through its 'spatial' and 'systemic' forms of violence, Israel created conditions where internal Palestinian strife became nearly as destructive as the conflict between fighters and the occupation. In this case Israel could claim that Palestinians were responsible for their own suffering, regardless of the context. This was the period of lawlessness that consumed the streets of Nablus between the height of the fighting between Israeli and the Palestinians in 2002 and 2003, and the re-assertion of the PA's authority after the schism in 2007.

The legacy of criminality and lawlessness that was cultivated by Palestinian gangs while the city remained under siege was the hardest for most people to bear. While Palestinian security forces were banned by the Israeli military, armed Palestinian gangs – not necessarily comprising the same people as those who orchestrated the resistance, but including a mix of criminal gangs and resistance groups that turned to criminality as conditions worsened – took advantage of the conditions, extorted from businesses and ruled the streets through violence and intimidation.

Palestinian responses to the violence

The violence of the Second Intifada was therefore ubiquitous and oppressive in ways that were unlike anything that had preceded it in the history of the occupation. In an important sense, violence became a normal part of everyday life and Palestinian responses became transformed as well. Death became normalised. In reference to the ubiquity of posters commemorating those who had been killed in action, Lori Allen (2008, 468) explained at the time that 'space and life are filled with the destiny of remembered death'.

In contrast to popular resistance during the First Intifada, which had manifested in behaviour that was exceptional to the norm – for example, public protests and strikes – for the majority of Palestinians, resistance was shown in the simple desire to continue with their lives in spite of Israeli obstruction. Many Palestinians found that they were forced to prioritise immediate concerns, such as the welfare of the family, over broader political or moral judgements regarding the right course of resistance against Israel. However, at the same time, this pursuit of an *ordinary* life could be justified in terms of resistance, particularly for young men, when it was tied to the concept of sacrifice for the sake of others or one's family. In this case, sacrifice meant overcoming the desire to confront Israeli force directly. Instead, priority fell on actions and behaviour that would sustain as much as possible the notion of an ordinary life in spite of Israeli efforts to wreck it (see Kelly 2008).

However, the elections in 2006 provided Palestinians with an opportunity to express the dissatisfaction with the performance of the PA. As discussed above, Israel and the other international actors refused to deal with Hamas at all. Even a compromise unity government – despite the fact that it grossly over-represented Fatah and third party representatives (such as Salam Fayyad's 'Third Way' party that received a mere two per cent of the vote) – was unacceptable.

Disengagement

The keystone of Sharon's policy towards the Palestinians was the programme of 'disengagement' from the Gaza Strip. Above all, this policy was driven by the realisation that Israel must act in order to maintain its strategic, diplomatic and demographic superiority over the Palestinians. It was necessary to radically alter the structure of Israeli and Palestinian relations on the ground (Rynhold and Waxman 2008). It took place in August 2005 and involved the removal – including in some cases by force – of Israeli settlers from 21 colonies in the Gaza Strip and four smaller colonies in the West

Bank. The operation was widely supported within both Israel and among the Palestinians. It also achieved virtually unanimous support from Israel's allies overseas (Morley 2005).

According to the official description of these events by the Israeli Ministry of Foreign Affairs (Government of Israel 2005), the rationale for the disengagement was that 'it constitutes a practical test of the possibility for peaceful coexistence with the Palestinian Authority. It contributes to the renewal of peace talks and to the establishment of a Palestinian state alongside Israel as envisaged by the Roadmap, provided the Palestinians fulfill [sic] their obligations to end terrorism and incitement'.

The policy was also described as 'bold and courageous' by the Bush administration (*The Guardian* 2004). This praise, though not surprising, had been hard won by Sharon, for whom one of the intended outcomes of the policy was to gain some form of 'reward' from the US. According to a biography of Sharon by his son, the Prime Minister had added the four West Bank settlements to the withdrawal with the express intention of gaining favour with the US:

> What had become clear from those talks was that if the Disengagement Plan did not include parts of Judea and Samaria, the Americans would not offer any type of reward for the initiative, nor would it receive their backing. Therefore, already at that point my father had realized that the Disengagement Plan would have to include four isolated settlements in Samaria.
> (Sharon 2011, 684)

Similar suspicions were expressed in secret correspondence between Bannerman Associates, a Washington-based international consulting firm, and a number of the PLO's top leadership, which outlined a coordinated strategy by Sharon's government designed to use disengagement in order to win support from the US. However, according to Bannerman Associates, Sharon failed to win his primary goal of tacit US endorsement for unrestricted expansion of the large West Bank settlement blocs of Ariel, Maale Adumim and Gush Etzion, he did achieve his secondary goals. These were, from an Israeli perspective, constructively ambiguous regarding the nature of any final status agreement between Israel and the PLO, specifically on the question of borders:[4]

> In contrast to the Clinton Administration, President Bush and his advisors have been noticeably silent on final status issues ... The Bush Administration may agree ... to new and ambiguous language that refers to Israel's demographic and security concerns.
> (Bannerman Associates 2004)

The letter also outlined the fact that the US Administration had moved closer to Israel in accepting its position on a number of issues, including refugees, language over terrorism and the existence of the separation barrier. However, perhaps most importantly, the letter notes the apparent dissonance between Israeli and US commitment to the 'Road Map' of 2003 and disengagement. Yet this inconsistency was apparently overcome due to the fact that both the US and Israeli governments more or less agreed on the necessity of isolating the Palestinian leadership. Though the Israeli government had threatened to have Yasser Arafat 'removed' (McGreal 2003) in 2003 and Sharon again threatened his life earlier in 2004 (Benn 2004), the letter suggests that a 'leadership trap' was more likely:

> What Sharon probably has in mind is to keep President Arafat imprisoned in the Muqata for the rest of his life ... Keeping Arafat imprisoned ensures there will be no serious internal political evolution so long as the symbol of Palestinian nationalism is held captive in humiliating circumstances. Thus, Sharon or his successor can argue that there is no Palestinian political leadership committed to fighting terrorism and no reasonable party with whom Israel can negotiate.
> (Bannerman Associates 2004)

As it turned out, Bannerman Associates' predictions were quite accurate. Arafat did remain in the Muqata'a almost all the way up to his demise, and was only allowed to leave for Paris as a result of special lobbying by the French government.[5] Moreover, the claim that Israel was carefully manoeuvring the Palestinian leadership in such a way that it could neither take part in negotiations nor reasonably object to them is supported by further evidence released by WikiLeaks (US Embassy Tel Aviv 2004d, 2004e, 2004g).

Prison

As 'disengagement' took place, both the Israelis and the Americans were acutely aware of the possibility of potential spoilers. A short series of cables from the US Embassy in Tel Aviv outlined the potential military, political and economic consequences of the Gaza pull-out. Overall, these cables outlined a broad assessment that Israel's withdrawal would not significantly improve the security situation in Gaza and it would be unlikely that any appreciable change in the economic or political conditions would follow either. The cables go on to outline the assessment that a 'full withdrawal' could expose Israel to greater risks and, further, make it less capable of executing military exercises within the strip. Thus, we can deduce that Israel would never have realistically allowed for full authority in Gaza to be passed to the Palestinians (US Embassy Tel Aviv 2004a, 2004b, 2004c;).

By examining Sharon's first public explanation of the disengagement plan in 2003, it is clear that, rather than a transference of full sovereignty over the Gaza Strip to the PA, his intention could be better understood as a redeployment of military assets to a more defensible posture. Sharon (2003) said: 'The relocation of settlements will be made, first and foremost, in order to draw the most efficient security line possible, thereby creating this disengagement between Israel and the Palestinians'. The then Prime Minister went on to explain that the so-called 'security line' would not constitute a 'permanent border' for Israel, but would, if peace talks stalled, comprise a unilateral, militarised threshold between settlements and the Palestinian population. The overall goal was that 'Israel will strengthen its control over those same areas in the Land of Israel which will constitute an inseparable part of the State of Israel in any future agreement' (Sharon 2003).

In a practical sense, the implications of disengagement were at least threefold. First, it meant that Israel's strategic withdrawal would allow for some greater Palestinian freedom, but within a tightly restricted space. The second was that it effectively re-asserted Israel's claims over some areas within the West Bank (the major settlement blocs mentioned above). Finally, the disengagement plan created a new ambiguous 'norm' for the status of Palestinian territory and its inhabitants. This was somewhere between occupation and self-determination.

This conclusion was well-understood across Israel's political spectrum, as the following extract from a cable demonstrates. The then junior minister Tzipi Livni (who would go on to become Foreign Minister and then Leader of the Opposition) articulated some concerns about the complicated implications of this compromise. She explained that while Israel would continue to exercise control over Gaza in a range of important ways – for example, through controlling its boarders, its airspace and curbing the presence of any forces that it considered undesirable – there was no desire to take on any of the burden of government for the local population:

> 'So in these senses', she said, 'the occupation will continue', and the evacuated territories would not constitute a sovereign state. On the other hand, Israel does not want to have responsibility for the economic and humanitarian situation of the Palestinians.
> (US Embassy Tel Aviv 2004e)

Shimon Peres, another prominent figure within Israeli politics, also noted this ambiguity in conversation with the US ambassador. He stated that the 'GOI's [Government of Israel's] disengagement from the Gaza Strip would be incomplete until agreements were reached on the passage of people and goods. Until then Gaza would remain a prison' (US Embassy Tel Aviv 2004f).

Clearly, in spite of the reservations of some of Israel's leadership, the ambiguity created by the disengagement was a strategic asset for Israel. Because of the lack of clarity over Gaza's status, Israel avoided the necessity of having to deal with the evident contradiction between its goals of maintaining Israel's unassailable strategic advantage and the attainment of acceptance from – most importantly – the US, which was demanding progress on the 'peace process' in exchange for continued support. This was clearly successful as a significant proportion of Western support was redirected towards facilitating the withdrawal.[6] For the Palestinians themselves, the ambiguity of disengagement served a slightly different purpose. Certainly, it can be interpreted as a mechanism that was designed to leverage Palestinian compliance; for example, Israeli officials frequently insisted that the PA maintain quiet in Gaza during the pull-out. Sharon himself apparently told visiting US Senators that it was 'imperative for the PA to understand that disengagement should not occur under fire, for if the IDF and settlers are fired upon, Israel will have to react in a very harsh way' (US Embassy Tel Aviv 2005a). But the consequences were broader than that.

The ambiguity of the status of Gaza served as a practical example of a model that could be broadened out to the whole oPts, preferably with the PA in the role of acquiescent elite rather than Hamas' hostility. Under this model, the PA could be granted the appearance of state-like powers that merely veiled Israel's real control. In Gaza this strategy was tested in the management of the Rafah crossing between Gaza and Egypt, which was redesigned as part of Sharon's plan. The agreement between the PA and Israel over the Philadelphia corridor, a narrow strip of land along the border between the Gaza Strip and Egypt, stipulated that both Israeli and European observers would oversee its security remotely. However, there was a role, too, for the PA. This was in terms of staffing the international border crossing at Rafah.

The operation of the terminal was particularly curious, as it involved the actual work being done by PA security forces on the ground, yet *de facto* control was maintained by the Israelis, who monitored the entire proceedings via video link:

> The control room receives constant live video streams from a network of CCTV cameras operating at the terminal. The face of each passenger standing in front of the Palestinian border police is thus transmitted to the control room as well as real-time video feed from the machines X-raying luggage. From the control room the Israeli and European observers can communicate with the on-site Palestinian security, demand a rescan or a search in this or that bag, or halt the transit of suspected passengers altogether.
>
> (Weizman 2007, 153)

The European observers would officially maintain the right of arbitration between the Israelis, the Palestinians or the Egyptians should a disagreement arise. But in practice, ultimate power lay with the Israelis, who could – and eventually did – deny the Europeans access to the facility and, as a consequence, shut down the entire terminal.[7]

It is worth noting, however, that despite the international acclaim, the disengagement policy was not universally supported even within Israel. Benjamin Netanyahu, the hawkish former leader of Likud, resigned from Sharon's government in opposition to disengagement, despite the fact that he acknowledged that he would not be able to prevent it from happening.[8] Netanyahu would go on to lead Israel into a later, large-scale assault on the Gaza Strip in 2014. Yet the disengagement plan was also opposed from the left. Shlomo Ben-Ami, Israel's former Foreign Minister and chief negotiator at Taba, called it a policy of 'scorched earth' (2006, 277) and stated: 'Sharon is the first prime minister since Oslo who did not aspire to solve Israel's conflict with the Palestinians' (2006, 287). In Ben-Ami's view, Sharon even surpassed Netanyahu's own hawkishness during his first term in office (1996–9).[9]

Rebranding the occupation in the West Bank

Obviously, disengagement was not directly transposed to the West Bank. The presence of half a million settlers, a large number of sites important to Jewish tradition, stronger economic ties between the West Bank and Israel, and the belief that a military presence must be maintained in the Jordan Valley (Schiff 1989) meant that it would always be unlikely that the Israeli military would resort to either the kind of military redeployment and/or extraction of settlements from the West Bank, as it did in Gaza. Nor, on the other hand, would it be likely that Israel would utilise the level of widespread and ruthless violence against the Palestinian population in the West Bank, as it has been able to in Gaza since disengagement (this is discussed in more detail later).

However, there were certainly elements of the underlying philosophy of Israel's policy towards Gaza that can be found in the nature of the methodologies of control that were used in the West Bank. Examples such as a greater emphasis on the value of air power – particularly evident during the Second Intifada – serve to illustrate this. Similar to Gaza, airpower was not only utilised in the form of bombardment from above, but also in the use of permanent surveillance airships deployed above Nablus and Jenin, presumably providing a real-time visual feed for the direction and assistance of the invading forces.

Further, the construction of the separation barrier and the shift to other hi-tech means to maintain surveillance was another sign that the occupation's West Bank policy was intended to shift more towards replicating that of the occupation of Gaza (Tawil-Souri 2012). The route of the barrier suggests that the *de facto* border it created is intended to separate the larger, higher value Israeli settlements from what may at some point become Palestinian territory. Moreover, Israel's military has also developed a similar dependence on the use of immediate lethal force to particular locations within the West Bank, such as the area between the wall and the Green Line (the 1948 armistice line, recognised generally as Israel's *de jure* border) known as the 'seam zone'. Yet this philosophy would evolve differently for the West Bank in other respects. Essentially this comprised two main dynamics. The first was Israeli and donor support for the militarisation of the PA security forces and their imposition of order on the West Bank, which could be interpreted as a key element in a kind of counterinsurgency strategy (see Turner 2015), while the second was the privatisation of Israel's apparatus of occupation.

The first of these dynamics was, as we have seen, evident in Israeli support for the PA security forces' role as a proxy against Hamas (legitimised through broader rhetoric). Research interviews with a political analyst from a major international think tank and a representative from the British government's DFID confirmed that the Israeli security establishment was both: (a) an important driving force behind the overt and covert training programmes for Palestinian security forces run by foreign actors; and (b) extremely pleased with how they had progressed.[10] The second similar dynamic revolves around Israel's privatisation of its occupation apparatus in the West Bank. Following various rounds of consultation and planning in the 2000s, the Israeli military began a long-term process of reform that would see its uniformed presence diminish greatly from within the oPts, instead being replaced by a range of private military contractors.

According to Daniela Mansbach, this forms part of a broader programme to 'normalise' some of the checkpoints by renaming them as – more humane-sounding – 'terminals'. The idea is to alter their appearance and structure to give the appearance of 'civilian border-crossing points, identical to any other international terminal used around the world' (Mansbach 2009, 261). This, Mansbach argues, is a development that has been undertaken through a number of different processes. The changes were administrative, conceptual and architectural, and these changes are intended to normalise the experience of invasive Israeli monitoring (Mansbach 2009, 263). Moreover, the authority over the so-called terminals has been shifted from the military to either non-military institutions, such as the Israeli Airport Authority Border Police, or private security companies. The Israeli NGO 'Who Profits?' (2009) presented the data for this in detail:

> The most direct and evident corporate involvement in the checkpoints includes five companies which provide security services to the checkpoints: Mikud Security, Ari Avtaha, S.B. Security Systems, Modi'in Ezrachi and Sheleg Lavan ... Apart from these security firms, many other companies have been involved in the operation of the checkpoints by supplying dedicated equipment, such as specialized scanners and surveillance technologies.

Who Profits? goes on to list 18 companies, including well-known brands such as Hewlett Packard and Chevrolet, which were involved in some form or other in providing support for the occupation mechanism:

> These companies, and some of these are large multinational firms, are aiding in the construction and maintenance of a system of military checkpoints which was condemned by human rights organizations as a brutal repressive system, which violates basic human rights.
> (Who Profits? 2009)

76 *Making plans*

An interesting example of how this worked is presented in an independent review of GROUP4SECURICOR (G4S) a British–Danish security company. While the report cleared G4S of any legal or ethical responsibility for human rights abuses in the oPts, it did detail some of the activities it was employed to undertake and the scale of use for these checkpoints, for example:

> At a number of OCA [Overland Crossings Authority] crossing points and checkpoints in the security barrier, G4S maintains baggage scanning equipment and metal detectors (like those used at airports). G4S does not own the equipment. It provides services to maintain the equipment. A total of 10.9 million Palestinian people came into Israel through crossing points and checkpoints in 2013. At Qalandia, for example, 6000 Palestinian workers cross into Israel each day with the busiest period being between 04.00 and 06.45.
>
> (G4S Israel 2014)

Importantly, the motivation for this programme of privatisation was not necessarily to reduce the costs of the occupation, but rather to take advantage of the assumed neutrality of the private sector. In such a scenario, Palestinians would, it is assumed, learn to accept the presence of these checkpoints as a natural part of daily life, just as one essentially consents to the particular security constraints imposed at an international border crossing. The appeal of privatisation was that it would demilitarise and even depoliticise the occupation.

There are three additional aspects of this discussion that are worth noting. These are first that – like disengagement from Gaza – international donors bought into the logic of this rebranding. In particular, donor funds were used to facilitate the transformation of checkpoints in the West Bank into terminals. Examples of this include the USAID-funded upgrade of 'crossing points' between Jenin and Nazareth at Jalama (Government of Israel 2009). The second was that this logic was applied more broadly than just at checkpoints; indeed, donor-supported developments that were intended to create similar zones of highly securitised ambiguity were evident elsewhere, including the development of new industrial zones (this is discussed in more detail later). But, in addition, the structures of the occupation were being redesigned and re-organised in such a way as to progress towards a kind of three-dimensional network of control. For example, as Alesandro Petti (2010) notes with reference to the road and highway system:

> By observing the transformations of the regimes imposed on the use of roads in the Occupied Territories, the evolution of the strategies aimed at the control and surveillance of undesired population flows becomes clear. Over time, although built in the name of 'public interest', the bypass roads that allow Israeli colonies to bypass the Palestinian villages became increasingly exclusive in character, transforming into 'sterile

roads' – Israel military jargon for roads that have been decontaminated of Palestinians.

Yet, as Mansbach argues, these efforts to 'rebrand' the checkpoints as terminals have not altered their inherently violent logic, 'the adoption of what appears to be a modern, legal and, thus, legitimate order, while continuing to employ violent, oppressive, and undemocratic methods of control' (Mansbach 2009, 270). Moreover, the integration into daily practice signifies that – rather than being considered an exception to the norm – violence itself becomes an embedded part of normal.

Similarly, we can see how this logic is also evident throughout the other changes in the occupation policy. This means that, ultimately, any/all progress towards greater Palestinian autonomy that could take place in the context of economic development or reductions in the size and depth of Israel's military presence in the West Bank would remain confined by a political-military envelope that demands Israeli strategic superiority. The same logic that allowed for disengagement from Gaza – without ending its occupation – and transformed checkpoints into terminals demanded that while the Palestinians might enjoy some progress towards independence-like status, there would be no real Palestinian state. As Khan argues, Israel's resistance to the formation of a Palestinian state is based on a strategic analysis that concludes that even a state with limited sovereign capacity would be too great a potential threat to the Israeli view of its national security. Instead, any concessions made to Palestinian autonomy must be 'reversible' (Khan 2005, 4). As such, Israeli decision makers remain assured of their military's own reserve capacity to re-instigate control over the oPts if they wish. Furthermore, it is clear that the PA establishment and the external third parties would have known this from before Fayyad's government took office. As Khan (2005, 10) soberly explains, 'many of the discussions and debates on which this analysis is based are public – in the Israeli media, political parties, think tanks, and universities. The relevant documents are easily available, including on the Internet'.

Statebuilding

Given that the statebuilding documents are discussed in the previous chapter, it is appropriate that this section draws on additional material – primarily interviews – in order to embellish that overview. Importantly, it discusses how the PA's statebuilding plans would interact with the kind of restrictive envelope imposed by Israel. According to a former senior minister in the PA, the reform and statebuilding plans were framed by the context of the devastation of the Intifada, which he characterised in the following way:

> It was quite clear that in the Intifada there was a total lack of law and order ... many investors were very worried about their assets here and their capacity to continue to do business in Palestine. Many factories

78 *Making plans*

> were closed and where things remained working there was often the added expense of bribes here and there ... it was really our first task to clean up.[11]

According to this perspective, the major concerns that informed the planning for the PRDP and the statebuilding plan were, first, to re-establish order and, second, to assert the PA's role as the only real centre of political power – at least in the West Bank. The PA's vision for reform and development therefore began with a security agenda, which is discussed in greater depth in the following chapters.[12]

Officially, the PRDP's longer-term aims were for improvements across four categories of public policy. In the language and order presented in the PRDP itself, these were: 'Safety and security'; 'Good governance'; 'Increased national prosperity'; and 'Enhanced quality of life' (Isseroff 2002).

Furthermore, the PA's efforts would also be put into the development of rural areas in particular in order to attempt to redress the inequality between them and urban centres. According to the PA narrative, cities like Nablus would 'get a good share'[13] of the reform budget, but this would be carefully managed by the central government in order to maintain control. The PA leadership, which was sensitive to any potential challenge to its authority after the debacle of the 2006 elections, considered it important that traditional elites should not be seen to provide any kind of opposition or an alternative to the PA's agenda. Where possible, they would be encouraged to support it.[14]

The four areas of reforms outlined in the plans were 'in a delicate balance [yet] consistent with preparation for statehood'[15] and were intended to re-orient the Palestinian labour market in such a way that it was better equipped for integration into global/regional markets. To this end, education and social development would be advanced in such a way as to prepare young Palestinians for knowledge-based industries – for example, high-tech services. This was intended to build on the advantage provided by Palestine's relatively high level of education and its strong links with both the Arab world and the West. The PA's commitment to an open market was seen as a natural and essential part of plans. The World Bank's Economic Monitoring Report to the Ad Hoc Liaison Committee (2011, 9) made the rationale for this explicit in 2011:

> As a small open economy, the future Palestinian state will depend upon increasing trade, especially the export of high value added goods and services that exploit its comparative advantage arising from a relatively low wage but well educated workforce ... The Palestinian market's small size means that, without access to the world market, Palestinian producers will not be able to achieve minimum efficient scale.

This also meant that the domestic economic environment would have to be flexible. Some traditional Palestinian industries, such as textiles, were unlikely

Making plans 79

to be able to survive in the current global climate. The rationale for this was simple: there had never been a domestic market of any significance and the export market (subcontracted to Israeli companies) suffered from its inability to compete with cheaper imports. Israeli merchants were no longer interested in buying from Palestinian factories, particularly while labour costs elsewhere were lower. The impact of QIZs in Egypt and Jordan had been particularly damaging to key Palestinian industries such as textiles (which at the time was the second-largest employer in Palestine's industrial sector).[16] Following from the free market model, the PA embraced efforts to replicate these zones with the establishment of their own versions of the QIZs in the form of the Palestinian Industrial Estate and Free Zone Authority (PIEFZA). Plans for similar zones had circulated since the late 1990s, but gained new impetus in the late 2000s (these zones are discussed in more detail later; see also Kanafani and Taghdisi-Rad 2012).

Although it was couched in terms of supporting the private sector, the PA also restricted the level to which Palestinian banks could invest abroad to 60 per cent of their total capital. Finally, through the language of the reform programme, the PA emphasised its commitment to the Oslo agreements and particularly to the Paris Protocol (1994). Yet this was largely motivated by an acknowledgement that it could not realistically act in any other way given its relative weakness. However, the plans were certainly intended to be interpreted as preparation for establishing statehood and the deadline of September 2011 was highly important as it represented a 'political horizon' and Palestinian ownership of its own political future: 'after 19–20 years of peace talks the world should find another way. We [Palestinians] should be ready to take it'.[17]

In order to achieve this goal, the PA was forced to become even more financially dependent on foreign aid, mostly from Western governments and Gulf regimes (Bahour 2010; Silver 2012). At the Paris conference, donors had promised $7.7 billion (some $2.2 billion more than the PA had asked for). Approximately $1.7 billion in donor aid had been in the form of direct budgetary support for the PA (spent, for instance, on payroll) and, overall, approximately 50 per cent of the West Bank's GDP was dependent to some extent on foreign aid. This 'miserable situation'[18] was seen by the PA as a necessary evil in the short term, but was expected to give way to better conditions soon, as the plan came to fruition and the private sector developed. Even in accepting its dependency, the PA had aimed to assert the appearance of Palestinian ownership over the process. It had planned to establish a single gateway for aid funds to the PA controlled by the Ministry of Finance (headed by Salam Fayyad, who was both Prime Minister and Finance Minister). Accordingly, all other ministries would be forbidden from dealing directly with donors and were required to submit all applications to the Ministry of Finance, which would apply to the donors on their behalf.

This, according to the PA, would lead to the concentration of those civil servants most skilled in obtaining funds from donors in one ministry, which would make all the applications and would also allocate the funds more fairly and evenly across all government departments according to an agenda set not by the donors, but by the government. The former official stressed that significant progress had already been made towards this goal: 'planning and budgeting is not as united in many countries around us [in close proximity to Palestine]'.[19] However, it is telling that this process had been managed with the direction of a donor agency, the DFID, which was a department of the British government, and that other donors had resisted the process, preferring bilateral relationships in particularly sensitive areas such as security.

'Statebuilding' strategy

The PA statebuilding project also included particular policies ostensibly designed to resist continued Israeli occupation and settlement expansion in the West Bank. These are discussed in more depth later, but this discussion serves as an introduction.

According to the official explanation, the main objective of this resistance agenda was to demonstrate that Israel, not the Palestinians, was the main reason for the blockage in further progress towards a two-state solution. Broadly speaking, this strategy comprised two parts. First were the high-level, diplomatic efforts by the PA leadership intended to demonstrate the PA's commitment to the two-state solution. For example, the PA outlined plans to build a Palestinian airport in the east of Jerusalem in what is currently designated 'Area C' and under full Israeli control according to the Oslo agreements. Further, Fayyad undertook public relations visits to numerous villages in the West Bank. This, while initially treated with scepticism by some locals, some elements in the diaspora and foreign media, demonstrated a remarkable difference between Fayyad and the other senior figures in the PA.

The second element of the PA's resistance policy was its boycott against products built or made in Israeli settlements. This proved to be an intelligently planned and well-organised campaign. The PA passed a number of laws, such as those banning the use of fireworks (all of which are made in settlements). Further, yellow stickers reminding shoppers to avoid Israeli settlement products were ubiquitous in the old city of Nablus and an 80-page glossy booklet with pictures and names of Israeli settlement products were distributed by civil society organisations and students during the launch of the campaign.[20]

Foreign agenda

For international donors, the PRDP presented an opportunity to implement a good governance strategy that would restrict the prospect of obvious forms of corruption while also opening up Palestine to particular forms of foreign investment. This was high on the agenda in the PA's initial document outlining its reforms. The PRDP made good governance one of its four core policy objectives.[21]

Making plans 81

The UK government played a significant role in the planning and execution of the PRDP. In fact, it had seconded a small team of bureaucrats from the DFID to the PA's Ministry of Planning in 2008, following an invitation from Fayyad's government. According to an interviewee from the DFID based in Jerusalem, the team provided technical assistance during the initial planning of the PRDP and had continued to provide such support throughout the process, and its staff remained in place at the PA.[22] The presence of the DFID team was a great source of suspicion among some Palestinian groups, particularly organisations on the left of the political spectrum that were already distrustful of the PA's motives.[23] However, as expected, the DFID denied any undue influence over the PA. Rather, it stressed that the reform programmes had originated with the Palestinian leadership and that, as a result, its own role was confined to assistance and was initiated following an invitation by Prime Minister Fayyad.

In response to a written request for more details, the DFID's head office in London stated that:

> The UK recognized there would be issues of providing funding to a Hamas led government which would not meet the Quartet conditions. But at the same time the UK wanted to maintain contact, for example working at a low technical level with ministries without Hamas Ministers, so that the UK would not be seen as abandoning the Palestinians. The UK decided to continue technical assistance to non-PA institutions (mainly the PLO's Negotiation Affairs Dept and the President's office); redirect financial assistance to support basic services and humanitarian provision through non-PA channels; and continue assistance to refugees through UNRWA. (During 2006, the UK provided £1.1m for the negotiations support unit; £1.8m for civil service reform; £0.45m for governance support; and £0.26m for various small projects, and in addition to £16.54m for UNRWA.)[24]

Further, according to the official line presented by the DFID's head office, the main role played by the DFID was in helping the PA establish an effective system of centralised control over: (a) finances; (b) security; and (c) essential services (for example, UNRWA and water services). However, my interviewee, an employee overseeing the DFID's work in the West Bank, explained that the central element of this was the framework, which was described as core governance. This focused on:

> Helping with the drafting process and the development of the fiscal framework; linking budget planning to the development of the Palestinian Reform and Development Plan ... but from our point of view – we certainly responded to a request. We supplied the expertise and that expertise was utilized by the ministry in order to develop the PRDP.[25]

82 *Making plans*

According to the DFID, the rationale behind this kind of intervention was never to control the reform agenda per se. Rather, it was to empower the PA as the government of a potential state in the long term and, in the short term, in its relationships with other donors. The DFID intended that the *core governance* programme would work by ensuring that an appropriate fiscal framework was in place to curtail both corruption and, for the sake of donors, the appearance of it. The DFID, then, offered a narrative that was complementary to the PA's. In particular, its political language was strongly supportive of the PA's statehood ambitions within the framework of a two-state solution. Further, it identified Fayyad's role as essential to future progress. According to a DFID employee:

> Fayyad has bravely ... pointed out to the international community that 'you are financing it', this is your investment and it might well go up in smoke at some point. The cost of failure is enormous [it] is much greater than all the aid that's already come into Palestine. [Fayyad has] created the recognition in the international community [that] this is not only the last chance saloon in terms of politics. This is also the last chance in terms of creating a solution that we can afford ... What is the cost of failure in Palestine and Israel? Just look at the figures of UNRWA at the moment – how do you keep on looking after an ever-growing Palestinian refugee community? How do you look after all those people in the seam zone and 'Area C' – whose position is so precarious ... they are already totally dependent on aid.[26]

According to the DFID, then, the PA's political strategy was two-pronged. The first prong was to take advantage of the international donors' growing need for an urgent two-state solution. The second was to remove the opportunity for Israel and its allies to convincingly blame the Palestinians for further failures in the progress of the 'peace process'. According to the representative of the DFID, the PA was demonstrating that it was implementing the will of the international community as seriously and professionally as possible and that it was therefore Israel that was to blame for obstructing progress – or, in other words, 'the blockage to peace therefore is not the Palestinians it's the Israelis'.[27]

Given the British government's close ties to Israel and the fact that any foreign involvement with support for the PA could only have taken place with the (at least tacit) approval of the Israeli government, such an objective – that of demonstrating Israel's culpability for the lack of progress in the 'peace process' – is remarkable. However, even if this was the case, the British government's official stance has been strongly in favour of a two-state solution since the 1990s and it has regularly condemned Israeli actions that it views as damaging to that prospect, such as the expansion of Israeli settlements in East Jerusalem and the West Bank. It is unlikely that this would have escaped the notice of the Israeli government. Therefore, it is possible to deduce that, in

Israel's view, the DFID's role in creating a 'good governance' framework for the Palestinians must not have constituted sufficient assistance to the PA to enable it to progress towards genuine independence, or that the genuine independence was not the real objective of these institutional development plans.

Further, the DFID's real role was not that it had taken over the PA from the inside, but that through supporting the PA's statebuilding rhetoric, the DFID was involved in promoting a somewhat unbelievable myth that institution building was directed towards challenging the broader strategic envelope that Israel maintained. On the other hand, the project had proven successful because the PA had implemented the appropriate strategy and reforms that, according to the DFID's standards (in the sense that its governmental structure was functioning to a particular level of efficiency), should have allowed it to attain statehood. But this did not mean that the PA was ever going to be in a position where it could demand genuine independence from Israel.

By looking at the DFID's role in terms of the broader agenda of the Western involvement in Palestine, it becomes clear that sacrificing the pursuit of genuine independence was an essential element of the equation. According to the DFID, in order to demonstrate that it was Israel that was unwilling to make the reasonable and appropriate political steps towards Palestinian statehood, it was necessary for the PA to give up any and all semblance of serious resistance. Instead, the PA's own policy agenda would have to reflect the interests of donor organisations – like the DFID – and it would have to adopt a good governance policy framework. In other words, the PA was encouraged by the DFID and other allies to outflank Israel by demonstrating that Palestinians appeared as committed as possible to the West's own vision of a two-state solution. This would emphasise the lack of political will on the part of Israel. Therefore, in the personal view of a DFID employee interviewed for this project, the Palestinians were now in the strongest possible position for negotiations, which would – based on the urgent financial needs of the international community – be likely to force a more permanent resolution in the near future:

> In my honest assessment there isn't any real reason why there should not be a state. If there was a graduation test for a state, most states would fail it and Palestine would probably pass it by now. That's not a reason to hold off on statehood. All the reasons to hold off on statehood have been shown to be overtly political now. [Fayyad] has been putting it into starker relief that the problems are not necessarily on the Palestinian side.[28]

If nothing else, this final comment demonstrates the fact that through the eyes of DFID employees, the British government's role was supportive of the PA's own agenda. However, the fact that, from the perspective of this interviewee, the criteria for 'graduation' to statehood evidently did not entail commitment to respect the results of democratic elections leads to a different – but equally

84 *Making plans*

important – conclusion. This was that the British government had established a deep connection with the PA and helped plan and implement the PRDP precisely because that agenda was in alignment with its own interests and the interests of its partners, and was not in alignment with the general will of the Palestinian population as it had been expressed in 2006.

One of these interests was clearly identified in terms of a good governance framework to help reduce corruption. However, the other major shared interest for the PA, Israel, the British government and its allies – which was to exclude Hamas from government and to strengthen the PA in order to curtail Hamas' influence – was only discussed through the euphemistic language of 'the decision of the International Quartet'. Evidently, the apparent generosity of the British government did not extend to all branches of its work or to all Palestinians. As discussed above, leaked documents to the *Al Jazeera* news network and *The Guardian* newspaper in 2010 revealed that the British Secret Intelligence Service (SIS) had formulated a covert plan designed to destroy or disrupt Hamas (which included the application of torture and other criminal activity).[29]

The envelope

It was in this context of a 'rebranded' occupation that the PA's statebuilding plan was launched. Though the following chapters look in more depth at other key drivers for the statebuilding agenda – including the threat to the PA from Hamas, the lack of legitimacy enjoyed by the PA and PLO leadership, and the moribund state of the Palestinian economy – the fact that this chapter introduces the Palestinian plans after a lengthy discussion on both the impact of the Second Intifada and the changing nature of Israel's occupation policy is deliberate. While the following chapters discuss the complex interplay of various drivers and impediments to the statebuilding agenda, it is essential to note two important conclusions: (a) that the strategic envelope imposed by Israel (discussed above) represented the basic framework for limiting Palestinian agency in this context; and (b) that international donors were extremely keen to play a supporting role in this programme, just so long as Palestinian agency would remain confined by the envelope.

In other words, Palestinian statebuilding represented a particular political programme involving a range of policies that – like any wide-ranging political project in any context is likely to be – evolved, stumbled over its various internal contradictions and served as a site for political conflicts. But, critically, this plan in this context suffered from a distinctive weakness. This was that in the face of Israeli opposition to genuine Palestinian independence – which was backed up by both the potential for overwhelming military force and a compliant international community – this plan's promises to work towards genuine independence from Israeli control were impotent.

It is of course likely that the leadership of the PA understood this fact. (several examples cited above and in the following chapters demonstrate that some of the PA's leaders did in fact acknowledge this – at least to some degree – at various points during their period in office). But it is perhaps too much of a stretch to suggest that the plan was deliberately misleading. Though this author has – on previous occasions – criticised the Fayyad leadership harshly for effectively integrating with Israel's occupation, it should not be inferred that this argument rests on asserting that there was any willingness to comply with Israel's demands beyond what appeared necessary to achieve those political goals. It is important to differentiate between the roles and intentions of the various different top figures in the Palestinian leadership. While there is certainly evidence to suggest that some top figures within the PLO developed a relationship with Israel's leaders that became an embarrassment – including President Abbas, Ahmed Qurei and Saab Erikat – when it was made public, there was no evidence that has become available thus far to suggest that it would be fair to tar Fayyad and the so-called 'technocrats' with the same brush.[30]

Yet no matter what the intentions of Fayyad and the other technocrats were – compared to the intentions of the PLO's 'old guard' or international donors for that matter – the sombre reality is that they largely did not matter. As the discussion in this chapter has outlined, the various different layers and contests within Palestinian politics during the period 2007–11 may have been interesting, intriguing and important in various different ways, but essentially at no time did they challenge the strategic envelope imposed on the Palestinians by Israel. In other words, there is no evidence to believe that the 'technocrats' did not fully believe in the plan they were pursing or that the majority of their actions were undertaken in anything other than good faith; rather, the point is simply that the plan itself was profoundly flawed.

Notes

1 Other interpretations of categorising violence during the Second Intifada include Azouley and Ophir's division between 'eruptive violence' and 'withheld violence'. In some respects, it is possible to overlay these categorisations with theirs in the sense that *political* and *systemic violence* can roughly be overlaid by 'withheld' violence, while *spatial* and *kinetic violence* align more closely with 'eruptive' violence (although some elements of spatial violence can be interpreted as 'withheld' violence, particularly with regard to the use of checkpoints and siege; see Azouley and Ophir (2009, 99–140).
2 A useful definition requires that: 'lethal force is intentionally and deliberately used, with a degree of pre-meditation, against an individual or individuals specifically identified in advance by the perpetrator. In a targeted killing, the specific goal of the operation is to use lethal force. This distinguishes targeted killings from unintentional, accidental, or reckless killings, or killings made without conscious choice. It also distinguishes them from law enforcement operations, e.g., against a suspected suicide bomber. Under such circumstances, it may be legal for law enforcement personnel to shoot to kill based on the imminence of the threat, but the goal of the operation, from its inception, should not be to kill' (Office of the United Nations High Commissioner for Human Rights 2010, 5).

86 *Making plans*

3 Amira Hass (2010, 2012) has provided a detailed history of this permit regime.
4 Israel would also pursue US support for development in the Negev as a 'price' for the disengagement (US Embassy Tel Aviv 2005b).
5 There is some suspicion that Arafat was in fact murdered by polonium poisoning, presumably either by Israel or by rivals within the Palestinian leadership. This claim has not been proven, however. Moreover, a government-backed assassination of Arafat would not be consistent with the framework of Israeli during this period that can be drawn from the evidence presented (Swisher 2012).
6 In particular, the United States Security Coordinator for Israel and the Palestinian Authority (USSC) found its role almost entirely absorbed by the disengagement. This is discussed in more depth in later chapters.
7 The terminal was closed by Israel in 2006 following the kidnapping of the Israeli soldier Gilad Shalit. However, the European mission was suspended and moved out in 2007 following Hamas' takeover of the Gaza Strip (European Union External Action 2014).
8 Though according to the argument articulated by Rynhold and Waxman, Netanyahu had accepted the necessity of a disengagement-like plan in the late 1990s (see Rynhold and Waxman 2008; Verter 2005).
9 Ben-Ami argues that the Sharon–Peres partnership saw the Second Intifada as proof that the Palestinian leadership could not be trusted to keep control of Palestinian military forces, who would seek, if they were given the chance, to re-assert Palestinian claims to all of historical Palestine. Yet Ben-Ami's interpretation is also based on the conviction that the PLO leadership, and Arafat in particular, had rejected a good opportunity to make peace during the negotiations at Camp David (July 2000) and later the next year at Taba, which is hardly a point beyond dispute (see Ben-Ami 2006, 293; and Agha and Malley 2001).
10 Research interviews, July 2009.
11 Research Interview with former official in the PA, Ramallah, 12 July 2010.
12 For example, the 'Israeli-Palestinian Ceasefire and Security Plan' proposed by the then CIA Director George Tenet (13 June 2001) required the unilateral cessation of Palestinian violence as a prerequisite to any further progress in negotiation. See Isscroff (2002).
13 Research interview with a former official in the PA, Ramallah, 12 July 2010.
14 Ibid.
15 Ibid.
16 'Before the onset of the qualified industrial zone in Jordan and Egypt, around 85 per cent of the Palestinian textiles industry subcontracted for the Israeli textile sector. However, the Palestinian economy started to lose this source of revenue, as the qualified industrial zone provided not only cheaper sources of labour in Jordan and Egypt, but also allowed the Egyptian and Jordanian textile industries to receive preferential treatment in the United States market' (Kanafani and Taghdisi-Rad 2012, 30).
17 Research interview with a former official in the PA, Ramallah, 12 July 2010.
18 Ibid.
19 Ibid.
20 Interview with a representative of the PA Boycott of Settlement products, Ramallah, 1 July 2010.
21 The PA's definition of good governance was: 'A system of democratic governance characterised by participation by citizens [sic], respect for the rule of law and separation of powers, capable of administering natural resources and delivering public services efficiently, effectively and responsively, and supported by a stable legal framework, a robust legislative process and accountable, honest and transparent institutions which protect the rights of all citizens'. See Palestinian Authority (2007, 5).

22 Research interview with a DFID employee, Jerusalem, 16 July 2010.
23 For example, in a response to the Palestine Investment Conference Bethlehem in 2010, which was sponsored by the DFID (*inter alia*) and supported by Tony Blair, a letter authored by a several left wing organisations stated: 'The projects proposed in the PRDP have been developed under the supervision of the World Bank and British Department for International Development (DFID), on terms set by them. The extent to which they have determined the agenda has in effect made them a "shadow government", setting out the development and economic priorities of the Palestinian Authority'. See BDS Steering Committee and National Committee for the Commemoration of the Nakba (2008).
24 The letter also listed the following areas of the DFID's work with the PA: (a) establishing and maintaining a reform trust fund managed by the World Bank; (b) technical assistance for public sector reform, including development planning and public financial management, civil service reform and support to the President's office; (c) technical assistance for Palestinian negotiations; (d) security sector reform; (e) core funding to the UNRWA; and (f) water sector reform.
25 Further, the interviewee stated that this kind of assistance followed the standard of the DFID's work in many other contexts, where the emphasis was on improving the host government's relationship with donors in order to resolve the major social and political problems associated with the immediate problems of underdevelopment or poverty: 'It's fairly bog-standard governance type work ... In another country it would be similar to a poverty reduction plan [addressing the question] how do Palestinians go about strategizing, in order to tell the donors what their needs are across different sectors?': interview with a DFID employee, Jerusalem, 16 July 2010.
26 Interview with a DFID employee, Jerusalem, 16 July 2010.
27 Ibid.
28 Ibid.
29 It is of course impossible to know to what extent DFID staff knew of the secret plans or cooperated with them. Further, it is also not possible to know who in the ranks of the British government authorised the SIS to undertake such a programme. The DFID indeed denies any direct responsibility for the activities of the SIS and states that its only engagement with the Palestinian security services during that period was limited to the civilian police. However, given that the DFID employee I interviewed had stressed the close working relationship between the DFID, the Ministry of Defence and the Foreign Office (which is responsible for the SIS) and that the DFID was coordinating with the Special Envoy of the Quartet, Tony Blair – who was British Prime Minister in 2006 when this plan was orchestrated – it is easy to see how activities undertaken all branches of the British government operating in the Palestinian territories may be seen to be tainted by these events.
30 For more details on the embarrassing relations between Abbas, Qurei and Erikat, see the coverage of the so-called 'Palestine Papers' by *Al Jazeera* (wwwwww.aljazeera.com/palestinepapers) and *The Guardian* (wwwwww.theguardian.com/world/palestine-papers) in 2011 and more recently leaks from the South African intelligence agency, particularly regarding the suppression of the Goldstone Report; see Swisher (2015).

5 Palestinian authoritarianism

The concept of security was at the heart of both the Palestinian statebuilding agenda and the concrete nature of the PA's post-2007 policy making. It is the most obvious focal point where Israeli, international and the Fatah-dominated PA's interests converged. While all sides contributed to different extents to this broad consensus of interests, the PA was the primary conduit through which it was condensed into policy and put into practice. From the outset, this agenda's primary objectives were to rid the West Bank of Hamas' influence and to re-assert order in the wake of the Second Intifada. This programme won support from Israel because it also served the purpose of maintaining Israeli dominance over the West Bank. But Salam Fayyad also promoted it – in both public and in private – as the first, essential stage of statebuilding.

Further, another important trend was also developing during this time. This was that, despite the close association between Fayyad's leadership and the PA's re-assertion of authority in cities such as Nablus (beginning in 2007), the power of the security forces would not remain subject to his will. As splits between Fayyad, Fatah and Mahmoud Abbas came more obviously to the surface towards the end of the former's premiership, it also became clearer that a dangerous trend of even more unbridled authoritarianism was emerging with Abbas and the security forces at its centre. This chapter provides both a brief background to the PA's security forces and looks at how Fayyad attempted to exert his influence over them. The goals of this chapter are threefold. First, it looks at what these changes meant in terms of what they tell us about the nature of the statebuilding project. Second, it looks at the build-up and implementation of the 'surge', the crackdown on Hamas and the re-assertion of order across the West Bank, beginning in Nablus. Third, it examines how these changes helped set the stage for Palestine's shift into an accelerated form of authoritarianism at the end of Fayyad's premiership.

Contradictory views on security and policing in Palestine

Since the formation of the PA, Palestinian security forces have been targets for opprobrium from all sides. For the most part, this has focused on their reputation for corruption and brutality, and the implication that they have been too closely tied to Fatah's armed wings. Yet, conversely, the creation of the PA security forces was written into the Oslo agreements and it was made clear that they were intended to be a bulwark against terrorism or other violence against Israel. This contradiction was brought to the fore on a number of occasions throughout the 1990s, particularly as the Oslo process began to crumble. But it was highlighted during the Second Intifada when – in response to attacks by Palestinian militants – the Israeli military directed its response at the infrastructure of the Palestinian security forces.

Yet for international actors, particularly the US and the UK, the PA security forces were not seen in the same light. While the Bush and Blair administrations were harshly critical of the conduct of the PA security forces during the Second Intifada, their response was to advocate for reform rather than demolition. Again this disagreement could not be hidden for long and it came to the fore at the height of the Second Intifada when the US-sponsored 'Road Map to Peace' initiative was launched in 2003. While the Road Map called for reform of the PA security forces and an end to terrorism as a prerequisite to Israel's withdrawal, Israel rejected it and demanded:

> The Palestinians will dismantle the existing security organizations and implement security reforms during the course of which new organizations will be formed.
>
> (Government of Israel 2003)

The difference of opinion between the Israelis and international actors would continue throughout the 2000s and ultimately conclude with a kind of victory for the reformers. The British government directly involved itself in the question of Palestinian security in 2005. Initially this was brought to public attention when Israel protested about secret meetings between the British secret services and Palestinian militants in the Gaza Strip (Coughlin 2005). However, this soon developed into a more detailed and comprehensive plan for reforming the security forces and repurposing them as a mechanism to combat Hamas and other militant organisations (Black and Milne 2011, 6).

A former MI6 officer turned commentator on the Middle East, Alistair Crooke (2011), explained how this project or 'surge' against Hamas would grow to dominate the agenda:

> The 'surge' sucked in everything: aid, economic assistance, institution-building – all were reoriented towards the counter-insurgency project. Ultimately, the Palestinian state-building project, and the Coin [Counterinsurgency] surge, were to become one.

The Fayyad government too was deeply engaged in this project. From the outset of his premiership, Fayyad had embraced both the prospect of security reform and the opportunity to challenge Hamas. Fayyad also made a point of demonstrating how committed his government was to challenging Hamas, especially when his audience comprised important international actors. In an example revealed in the WikiLeaks 'cablegate' archive, Fayyad made it clear how the nexus of security sector reform, combating Hamas and the statebuilding project fitted together:

> On West Bank security, Fayyad said he wants to deploy several hundred security personnel in all major West Bank cities to control the streets. 'If we start to regularly patrol the streets of Nablus', he explained, 'we'll be able to keep the bad guys away'.
>
> (US Consulate Jerusalem 2007)

Yet after leaving office as Prime Minister and establishing his own NGO, 'Future for Palestine', Fayyad himself had become a target for the PA security forces. Most dramatically, in August 2014, the Preventative Security Service raided his office (they claimed to be investigating alleged financial irregularities relating to a campaign to support needy children in Gaza). Fayyad later issued a statement offering his compliance with any necessary investigation, but media reports noted that it was unusual for the Preventative Security Service to investigate such allegations, a task normally undertaken by the civilian police. It was implied that the PA security forces were engaged in deliberate efforts to intimidate their former leader (Ravid and Khoury 2014).

Simultaneously, the PA security forces were growing more powerful on the streets of the West Bank and fewer checks were being effectively imposed on their actions by the government. Numerous examples of abuses of human rights – particularly in cases involving suppression of protests – began to give the impression that 'regardless of continuous declarations of respect for human rights, including the rights to freedom of assembly and expression, by the PA, police officers and Special Forces officers, the reality has [been] made clear that a culture of respect for citizens' rights and freedoms is in fact absent among these bodies' (Ravid and Khoury 2014).

So how and why did it come to this? In the space of ten years, the PA security forces were transformed. At the end of the Intifada, they were a collection of organisations that were completely distrusted by Israel and Western governments and were on the verge of extinction. Yet through a process of reform, they became the effective vanguard for statebuilding – at least in the eyes of the Fayyad government – only to liberate themselves from Fayyad's grip and reveal their truer authoritarian selves, eventually turning on both their former leader and on the basic rights of ordinary Palestinians. In order to address this question, it is necessary to provide a contextual background of the Palestinian security forces.

Background on PA security services

The Palestinian Basic Law 1997 officially established the PA security services. Prior to this, a *de facto* paramilitary presence had accompanied the PLO in returning to the West Bank earlier that decade. Further to the Basic Law, the legal framework established by the PA to govern the security forces is extensive and has developed significantly over time, though it has never been completed. A collection of Palestinian legislation pertaining to the security forces compiled by the Geneva Centre for the Democratic Control of Armed Forces (DCAF) spans more than 500 pages, including 'laws, executive decisions, and administrative decisions of security sector institutions', which for the most part have been created in a 'piecemeal' process (Friedrich, Luethold and Milhem 2008, 12). Moreover, the DCAF notes that:

> Palestinians deserve to be commended for the progress they have achieved in establishing a legislative framework for their security sector. Nevertheless, the legal system still contains many gaps and internal [in] consistencies, which call for harmonization and further codification.
> (Friedrich, Luethold and Milhem 2008, 11)

The incompleteness and piecemeal nature of this legal framework is at least partly a product of the complex environment inherited by the PA in the early 1990s. The PA's legal structure was built upon a hotchpotch of different legal structures left over from periods of British, Jordanian, Egyptian and Israeli rule. Yet the vagueness also served a political purpose for the Palestinian leadership at the time of the organisation's formation.

By way of example, the Basic Law stipulates that 'the President is the Commander-in-Chief of the Palestinian Forces' (Friedrich, Luethold and Milhem 2008). While not unusual in comparison to similar legal structures in other countries, the legal structures designed to oversee the executive branch were particularly weak in Palestine.[1] The combination of a strong executive branch, a weak legislature and a vague legal framework would serve two purposes for the PA's leadership. First, it allowed many of the PLO's existing paramilitary forces to attain a semi-official status while ensuring that they were in practice accountable only to Yasser Arafat himself as supreme commander.

The second purpose served the interests of Israel and the US (as the main sponsor of the 'peace process' in the 1990s). It was hoped by Israel and the US that, by allowing the PA security forces to become officially recognised bodies, they would be encouraged to align their own interests with those of Israel. As such, they would be more reliable in terms of using coercion to prevent Hamas, or other agents, acting as spoilers to the peace process. Since their inception, the role of the security forces has always been as the servant of two masters. Under Arafat, they were used as a means to maintain his, and his cronies', power domestically and, through them, to serve the interests of Israel and the US.

Arafat's regime took full advantage of the available ambiguity. Through the liberal allocation of jobs, he used the security forces to develop a cliental relationship with elements of the population that might otherwise have voiced discontent. At the same time, the regime established a massive domestic military force and that could, in theory at least, defend against any potential challenge from Fatah's rivals. Yet Arafat did not exert quite as much control as he had hoped. The overall product of his methods was that the security services became bloated and unreliable. They were staffed by masses of poorly trained troops who were, though in principle loyal to Arafat, not necessarily subject to any meaningful chain of command (see Luft 1998). At the very least, they had become 'unwieldy', 'unaccountable' and disorganised, but they could also be described as more dangerous 'fiefdoms' ruled by powerful security chiefs (Crisis Group 2010, 1). The results of this situation were exposed during the Second Intifada, when virtually all pretence of control exercised by the PA's high command over the security forces collapsed. Some members of the Palestinian security forces turned against the Israeli military – with which they had been collaborating[2] – and engaged in both armed resistance against the occupation and terrorist attacks on Israeli civilians.

As discussed above, this breakdown of the relationship led to the realisation in Israel and the US that major changes were needed in the PA in order to secure their agenda. This meant that Arafat was to be abandoned and another leadership structure would be promoted for the PA. It was in this context that the Basic Law – the PA's *de facto* constitution – was modified in 2003. A National Security Council was established in order to try to dilute Arafat's influence and to bring some order to the security forces, but in fact little meaningful change was achieved until Arafat's death. When Abbas took over the presidency from Arafat, this was seen as an opportunity by both Israel and the US to begin working with the PA again to challenge domestic threats.

In line with the Road Map and other related statements, Abbas set about re-organising the security apparatus. He made several high-level changes – including bringing in some prominent opponents of Arafat – and oversaw significant modifications to the structure of the security forces.[3] Further, the Abbas government openly broke some of the patronage links that had been established under Arafat and imposed various employment regulations that were in line with the demands of international donors.[4] Finally, the National Security Council was re-structured and the 12 different security forces were re-organised into three broad areas of jurisdiction. These are represented in the following table.

While all of these security forces were legally accountable to the executive branch, various aspects of their *de facto* remit still remained outside any legal framework (Crisis Group 2010). Israel responded positively to the changes by gradually returning control over Area 'A' to the PA. This began with Ramallah and Bethlehem soon after the end of the invasion. The Israeli military continued to enforce a full ban on all police forces in Nablus until November 2007. Yet Israel's decision to return control of Area 'A' to the Palestinians was predicated on the assumption that the PA leadership, which was dominated by Fatah, would exercise *de facto* control over the security forces within permitted areas after the withdrawal. The security forces would return to the role they

Table 5.1 Structure of Palestinian security services c. 2005[17]

National Security	Interior	Intelligence
National Security Forces The PA's main military forces (approx. 15,000 officers). Designed to defend the borders of Palestinian Areas. Coordinated with Israel on joint security operations.	**Preventive Security Force** Effectively, but not officially, a major intelligence agency (approx. 5,000 covert officers).	**General Intelligence** Main intelligence agency (approx. 3,000). Responsible for espionage and counter-espionage inside and outside the oPts.
	Presidential Security Presidential and VIP bodyguard. Comprised an intelligence wing and a bodyguard unit (approx. 3,000).	
Coast Guard Intended to defend and police the Gazan coast (approx. 1,000).	**Civil Police** Lightly armed, day-to-day policing duties (approx. 10,000). Contained a small special rapid reaction force for emergencies (approx. 700).	**Military Intelligence** A smaller intelligence organisation than the General Intelligence. Focused on internal threats from opposition groups and from within the PA infrastructure.
Air Guard or **Aerial Police** Operated the PA's small number of helicopters, mostly used for diplomatic purposes.	**Civil Defence** Equivalent to fire and rescue services.	**Military Police** A semi-autonomous branch of the Military Intelligence focused on the emergency or high-profile situations.
	Governorate Security Bodyguard unit for governors and lower-ranked PA officials.	

were designed for – combating terrorism and maintaining order in Palestine – and any other potential threats to Israeli national security. However, under pressure from the US, Israel permitted the 2006 elections to take place and for Hamas to participate. But Hamas didn't just take part – it won.

Hamas' surprise victory created a profound challenge to the PA. This threatened to upset the hoped-for restoration of the pre-Intifada status quo ante. The US, Israel and the EU responded with an economic blockade against the oPts and channelled clandestine support to particular PA lieutenants, who had been brought in by Abbas and who were seen as particularly hostile to Hamas (Black 2011).

Culture and context of Palestine's security forces[5]

Another way of understanding the background to the security forces can be drawn from an analysis of the cultures of the police and security forces. These cultures tended to focus on partisan loyalty and self-interest rather than a more textbook ethos of 'public service and impartiality' (Lia 2006a). As an indicator of this, the 'Transparency International Government Defence Anti-Corruption Index 2013' rated the PA security services as a 'D-' and noted particular areas of concern in terms of secrecy and personal corruption (Transparency International 2013b). For the most part, efforts to confront this proved fairly ineffective (Transparency International 2013a). Furthermore, with the dawn of the new 'War on Terror', a sea change in donor-led policies meant the deprioritising of this issue (Lia 2006a, 2006b).

As well as these issues of corruption and the problems related to pre-existing policing cultures, the PA security forces operated within a unique context. In essence, the Oslo agreements had created highly unusual conditions for the PA security forces. In particular, these confined the security forces to Area 'A' and limited their powers, and in addition to being responsible for normal domestic policing and security issues, the Oslo agreements also held them accountable for ensuring Israeli interests. In effect, this included protecting the Israeli military and Israeli settlers within the oPts (Lia2006a, 2006b). One particularly brutal example of this precedent followed from the infamous 'Ramallah lynching' in 2000. In this case, when two Israeli army reservists were brutally murdered by a Palestinian mob, the Israeli military held the PA security forces accountable for failing to protect them (Philps 2000). It is interesting to note that by 2007, this lesson had clearly been learned by the PA. When a similar incident occurred – a lost Israeli soldier strayed into Area 'A' only to be attacked by an angry mob, which went on to burn his vehicle – the episode ended with his rescue by the Palestinian security forces. These actions were praised by Israeli ministers and were commended by the Fayyad government (Issacharoff and Associated Press 2007). Yet the broader lesson here is that the structural lopsidedness of this relationship effectively locked the PA into a position of inevitable and irrevocable weakness compared to Israel. As Khan (2005, 4) has suggested, this arrangement effectively created:

> An open-ended period of limbo in which the disengaged territories are neither truly sovereign nor technically part of Israel. Nevertheless, authorities 'governing' these regions with very limited autonomy are to be held responsible for delivering security to the occupiers, whose direct occupation of significant areas continues, without enjoying sovereignty or controlling their internal economy.

The schism and background on Hamas' rise

At one level, the schism between Hamas and Fatah established the backdrop for the PA's statebuilding agenda, but – less obviously – it also helped create

Palestinian authoritarianism 95

a situation where the PA security forces would be able to exert their power in the West Bank. This was because, once tensions between Hamas and Fatah developed into violent confrontation, Fatah was able to step away from the uneasy truce it had been forced into with its rival and, using the cover of an emergency situation, abandon its pretence of democracy. Though still confined by Israel's occupation in the wake of the schism, the different nodes of power (Fayyad, Abbas and the security forces) in the PA became more able to pursue their own agenda.

More specifically, the schism made it possible for the PA to confront its opponents and undermine the legitimacy of any criticism it was facing. In this case Fayyad and Abbas were in lock-step. Both opposed Hamas, but for different reasons. For Abbas and for Fatah, Hamas represented a grave threat to their historical dominance of the Palestinian politics. For Fayyad, this was an opportunity to finally achieve the political freedom he needed – from both Hamas and Fatah – to pursue his statebuilding agenda.

These events and motives are best understood in the historical context. Hamas had emerged as a significant force in Palestinian politics during the first major popular uprising against Israel's occupation (1987–93). Alongside its Islamism and fierce resistance to Israel, support for Hamas rested on the organisation's development of, and support for, a complex network of community and civil society institutions (Milton-Edwards and Farrell 2010; Roy 2011). When Palestinian and Israeli delegates announced the Oslo Accords in 1993, Hamas rejected them and engaged in various acts of resistance. The organisation's goals at the time were both to resist and reject Israel and also to undermine the PA, as it represented the culmination of Fatah's compromise with Israel (Milton-Edwards and Farrell 2010).

However, with the effective collapse of the Oslo process in 2000, both Hamas' armed wings and Israel's occupation forces escalated their violent campaigns and the PA effectively lost all control of the situation. Despite being militarily overwhelmed by Israel's re-invasion of the West Bank during the Second Intifada, Hamas' network of charity and community welfare organisations proved better able to serve the needs of a general population suffering under the strain of the unrelenting violence (Gordon and Flic 2009). The PA splintered and many of its security forces fell back into personal loyalties and organised criminality, failing to fulfil its role as service provider (Crisis Group 2010). It was in this context that the 2006 legislative elections took place and – participating for the first time[6] – Hamas won.

The elections in 2006 provided the Palestinian population with an opportunity to express its dissatisfaction with the performance of the PA and the situation overall. The outcome was conclusive, Hamas won 74 seats, compared to Fatah's 45 with a 3 per cent difference in their share of the vote (44.5 per cent for Hamas vs. 41.43 per cent for Fatah). Moreover, Hamas had achieved an overall victory in both the Gaza Strip and the West Bank, even taking control of Christian villages such as Taybeh – famous for its beer making – which had been assumed to be safe seats for the secular-minded Fatah. This suggested that the motivation for many voters was more frustration with the corruption and inefficiencies of Fatah and the PA than adherence to the Islamism of Hamas (Gordon and Flic 2009).

Yet despite the fact that Hamas achieved this overwhelming victory – and that the elections were recognised as 'free and fair' by international observers[7] – there was no smooth transition of power. Nor were the results of the elections respected internationally. Israel and the other international actors refused to deal with Hamas at all. Even a compromise 'unity government' – despite the fact that it grossly over-represented Fatah and third party representatives (such as Salam Fayyad's 'third way party', which received a mere 2 per cent of the vote) – was unacceptable.

Instead, in something of a post-election panic induced by the prospect of a recognised terror organisation in power, the US government had advocated a political and economic blockade. This was accepted – albeit reluctantly – by the EU and the PA's other major non-Arab donors. This, together with Israeli military operations in the Gaza Strip, only succeeded in raising the temperature, and brought further divisions between Hamas and Fatah. The situation grew more violent and continued to escalate into early 2007, despite Saudi Arabian-sponsored negotiations and an agreement signed on 8 February in Mecca. The unity government established on 17 March lasted only 99 days, coming to an end on 14 June, when Hamas cadres seized the headquarters of the Preventive Security Force in Gaza. Fatah forces responded with violence in Nablus and Jenin, Abbas dissolved the government and declared a state of emergency. He then appointed an alternative government with Fayyad at its head.

The Fatah establishment was clearly threatened by Hamas' rise, both as an indirect result of the international blockade and directly because Hamas' leadership had deputised its own brigade of supporters to form the armed Executive Force (which challenged the PA's supremacy in the Gaza Strip). In this context, then, the schism between Hamas and the Fatah-dominated PA can be understood as a moment when a crisis exposed the alignment of the interests and concerns of Israel, Fatah and the PA. This alignment was made even more obvious when press reports exposed the fact that Fatah's leaders had directly sought Israel's help in its battle against Hamas. According to *Haaretz*, in June 2007, Fatah leaders asked Israel to allow in 'dozens of armored cars, hundreds of armor-piercing RPG rockets, thousands of hand grenades and millions of rounds of ammunition for small caliber weapons' (Issacharoff and Harel 2007). Fayyad's position was slightly different and – to some extent – more cautious when it came to trusting that Israel would prop up the PA, even if Hamas could be removed. Throughout 2006 and 2007, Fayyad had made his opposition to Hamas clear, albeit with more nuance than the position taken by Fatah.

In a leaked cable from 24 February 2006 – just a month after Hamas' election victory – Fayyad outlined his view that it would be best for Hamas to be included in government as quickly as possible. This was not, however, out of any desire for Hamas leadership. Rather, 'Fayyad said that he would like to see Hamas alone in the government so that no one else would be blamed for its failures' (US Consulate Jerusalem 2006). Fayyad also shared his belief that if a power-sharing arrangement between Hamas and Fatah could be achieved, then there was a serious possibility of a reduction in intra-factional tensions, but also he expressed his concern that this would give Israel the pretext it was looking for to have a 'clear shot at finishing us off' (US Consulate Jerusalem 2006). Thus, neither Israel nor either party in the PA was willing to allow Hamas enough real power to undermine the status quo. For Fatah and the PA, this priority overrode any commitment to honouring the democratic process or allowing genuine resistance to the occupation. As it turned out, though efforts continue to be made to achieve a unity government among the Palestinian factions and are ongoing, and Israel certainly made several attempts to 'finish off' Hamas, none of these goals was achieved.

As the Intifada had been, the election of Hamas represented a threshold for Israel and the other external parties in terms of determining their commitment to depending on Palestinians to work as proxies. In the wake of the schism, all sides in this relationship prioritised the PA's survival. For Israel and Fatah, this was primarily out of a need to avoid any potential alternative. But for Fayyad and for the donors, the removal of Hamas represented an opportunity to pursue something new. This became known – somewhat derisively in the international media – as the 'West Bank First' model. Encouraged by Fayyad's launch of the PRDP, which put security sector reform at the heart of an apparently peaceful and responsible alternative to both the traditional dichotomy of Hamas or Fatah, donor countries offered vast amounts of aid to the PA and reinforced their rhetorical commitment to previous peace agreements. Furthermore, the apparent pragmatism of Fayyad's leadership in the aftermath of a crisis was also seen by donor states as an opportunity to encourage the PA to make changes in order to counter the corruption and patronage that had been seen as a major cause of the breakdown in security relations under Arafat. Evidence of these donor concerns could be seen in the outcome of the Fayyad government's reforms to the security services (the role of donor states is discussed in more detail in the next chapter). But it could also be seen in the way in which the PA security forces prosecuted their campaign against Hamas.

The events of the schism were easily the most violent intra-Palestinian confrontation that has occurred since the beginning of the occupation. Both Palestinian and international human rights organisations documented levels of violence that were even more severe than Israeli action during the same time period. It is also worth noting that although violence and human rights abuses occurred on both sides, the PA adopted many of the coercive methods that had been utilised by the occupation forces as recently as the Intifada while being supported by Israel, the EU and the US. In fact, according to Human Rights Watch (2008, 3):

Fearful of a Hamas takeover of the West Bank, security forces have detained hundreds of people arbitrarily, tortured detainees, and closed media and organizations that are run by or sympathetic to Hamas. The West Bank security forces have operated with significant support, financial or otherwise, from the United States, the European Union and Israel.

Moreover, Human Rights Watch (2008, 5) went on to describe the brutality of these actions, which included:

> Mock executions, kicks and punches, and beatings with sticks, plastic pipes and rubber hoses. The most common form of torture was forcing detainees to hold stress positions for prolonged periods, known in Arabic as shabah, causing intense pain and sometimes internal injury but no physical mark. Such positions include standing for hours with feet apart and hands tied behind the back, standing with one leg and one arm raised, or sitting on the edge of a chair with hands tied to the feet.

The PA's assaults on Hamas were not only manifest in this kind of direct paramilitary violence – they also took on the kind of sophisticated, multi-spectrum approach that characterises counterinsurgency strategies. The PA's plan was to go after Hamas at all levels, discrediting it politically, clamping down on its ability to propagate its political agenda and curtailing its fundraising and social support networks.

Hamas' independence had been its greatest asset. The fact it had remained beyond Arafat's grip over finances and outside his political control right from the beginning was largely the reason why it became a realistic rival to Fatah and to the PA in the 2000s.[8] But up until 2006, it had not been able to make the transition to electoral politics, meaning that Fatah would always have the advantage of legitimacy. Yet the 2006 elections exploded this paradigm. Hamas had shown itself to be a capable political machine that could also capitalise on the goodwill created through its activities during the Intifada. Hamas' rise was an embarrassment for both Fatah and for the PA's technocrats.

Hamas had demonstrated that it could act beyond the PA's reach and also showed that Fatah/the PA's approach, which rested on international support, was incapable of dealing with the concerns of ordinary people suffering from the effects of Israel's intervention. Beyond this, it appears that there was also some serious concern among the PA's top echelons regarding Hamas' ties with other Islamist groups, including Hizb al-Tahrir (US Consulate Jerusalem 2008b), a fiercely anti-Zionist salafist organisation that originated in Jerusalem in the 1950s and has expanded internationally (see Mackinnon 2007; Mustafa 2008). Hamas represented an intolerable threat to the status quo, and the PA swung into action.

First of all, this meant closing off Hamas' sources of funding, a task which was not as simple as it may at first have appeared. This was because much of Hamas' financing came in the form of small donations from expatriate Palestinians or through Zakat – Islamic Charity – committees within the oPts and was hard to trace (Hroub 2006, 137–8). The governments of various Western states had already targeted this supply of funds through various legal sanctions since the 1990s. But after the schism, Israel, the PA and the US worked together to crackdown on Zakat committees in the West Bank. On this issue, Fayyad was not entirely consistent in explaining his motives. In public he put this clampdown in terms of routine insurance against possible financial improprieties and left his criticism of Hamas to a mere implication that it was politicising poverty. Speaking in 2009, he told the *Journal of Palestine Studies* that:

> When we dissolved the zakat committees, I myself said that I wanted everyone to know why we were doing this. I said that we were dissolving and re-forming these committees because the needs of the poor must never be used for political gains by any party.
> (Farraj, Mansour and Tamari 2009, 66)

But in a private meeting with the US Deputy Assistant Secretary, Daniel Glaser, Fayyad appeared to make it clear that the moves against the Zakat committees were at least partly politically motivated. He explained that the fact that he had replaced the leadership of the committees with representatives 'had nothing to do with Hamas':

> Fayyad said his government has already taken 'courageous' steps to cut off Hamas' access to funds. In particular, he noted PA efforts to reorganize zakat committees and promised to provide any information requested ... Hamas, he said, is 'our problem much more than it's Israel's or the U.S.'s problem'.
> (US Consulate Jerusalem 2007)

At a practical level, the PA adopted its own form of systematic violence. With Israeli support, it targeted Hamas through its institutions.[9] Further, it extended its authority into mosques throughout the West Bank, ensuring that sermons were pre-approved and screened for any political language that could be interpreted as hostile (Crisis Group 2010). Hundreds of public sector workers who were seen to be too closely associated with the Islamists were also fired, including 400 teachers in one month, and possibly more than 1,000 in total (Crisis Group 2008). According to Crisis Group:

> Since June 2007, numerous Hamas-affiliated organisations – including charities, media organisations and cultural centres – have been closed by the PA or forced to appoint Fatah or PA loyalists to their boards. According to a source within the interior ministry, 187 organisations in the West Bank have been forcibly closed, the vast majority for political reasons.
> (Crisis Group 2010, 28)

The PA also engaged in political violence. Fayyad in particular promoted a view of the future of Palestinian politics with which Hamas was incompatible. He argued that the PA was the only body with the authority to impose order in Palestinian streets, regardless of election results and in spite of the fact that American and British clandestine forces were involved in planning the campaign against Hamas, and that it was common knowledge that the PA had coordinated its assault on Hamas with Israeli intelligence (see Rose 2008; Farraj, Mansour and Tamari 2009; Milton-Edwards and Farrell 2010, Chapters 9 and 14; Black and Milne 2011).

The PA also played an important role in maintaining calm in the West Bank during the Israeli invasion and bombardment of Gaza during Operation Cast Lead (2008/2009). Palestinian forces broke up demonstrations (for the most part) before they encountered any Israelis directly and used coercive methods to intimidate those who did demonstrate inside Area 'A'. The Palestinian forces also coordinated with the Israeli military throughout the public order operations. The result was that very few demonstrators took to the streets in comparison to protests that were occurring in Europe and elsewhere. Where protests did break out, the PA security forces prioritised their coordination with Israeli forces and resorted to beatings and other coercive measures in order to keep protesters in line. There was no doubt that the PA's priority at the time was to contain any popular expression of support for Hamas (Crisis Group 2010).

But the campaign went further. In 2008, human rights groups recorded that there were some 200–300 political detainees in the West Bank. Many of these detentions did not pass through the civilian legal system. Moreover, allegations of torture grew more widespread. While it is likely that senior PA officials knew about this kind of activity at the time (Crisis Group 2008) – and by 2010, Fayyad would publicly admit that torture had been used (*Maan News* 2010a) – the PA maintained its denials that any of this was officially sanctioned (Entous and Macdonald 2008). These events then perhaps give some indication that behind the scenes of this clampdown against Hamas, another battle was raging. This manifested itself in the form of a dispute between Fayyad and the security personnel over the standards of practice that would be employed by the Palestinian security forces, but ultimately this would escalate into a broader conflict over power in the West Bank.

Suppressing Nablus

Nablus was the primary focus for the PA's show of force. PA troops began their clampdown in Nablus in 2007, moving on afterwards to Hebron and other areas where Hamas had received large-scale popular support. Several hundred officers were brought in from outside the city to support the security forces based in Nablus. The PA forces' primary targets were Hamas cadres and a number of criminal gangs based in the Old City and the refugee camps.

They also shut down organisations sympathetic to Hamas and denied access to any public area for political gatherings from any party.

But Nablus could not really be called a stronghold of Hamas, though the group did operate there. During the Intifada, resistance in the Old City and in Balata Camp had been led by the Fatah-aligned Al-Aqsa Martyrs' Brigades, often cooperating with Hamas cadres (Bishara 2009). Nonetheless, the action to kerb the plurality of arms was clearly supported by both Abbas and Fayyad. Fayyad's goals were obvious, and they fitted into his larger plan of imposing order so as to create more opportunities for economic growth. However, for the President, moving against Fatah groups was more difficult.

While the brigades were nominally Fatah – and had endorsed Abbas for the presidency in 2004 (BBC 2004) – they tended to comprise a membership of the disaffected and those who felt alienated by the Ramallah leadership. While, like the Fatah mainstream, the brigades had certainly been opposed to an Islamist takeover, it was not clear what – if anything – else they were actually standing for other than, perhaps, taking advantage of disorder to pursue their own personal gain. In the words of a Crisis Group (2009b, 11) report:

> The militia-like Brigades became a principal element in the social breakdown that characterised the uprising's later years; with the PA security services destroyed – and in any event no small number of security service personnel moonlighting in the Brigades – they wreaked havoc.

With the surge into Nablus, then, Abbas risked aggravating political divisions within his own ranks. But given the international attention, the insistence by Israel and the prospect of losing control anyway, the President had no choice but to embrace Fayyad's plan. Between November 2007 and January 2008, the PA deployed around 350 troops to the city, set up checkpoints and went in search of illegal arms and stolen guns. Though some members of the brigades responded with rhetorical threats, media reports noted that the PA's access to the city was more or less unimpeded (Mitnick 2007). According to Nablus' governor, Jamal al-Mouhsen, the campaign was an unbridled success:

> Every decision we made has been carried out. We united the security forces and ended competition among them ... We confiscated 120 firearms from Hamas activists, along with explosives intended for attacks against Israel and the PA. Hamas has no more weapons in Nablus.
>
> (Issacharoff 2008)

However, it should be noted that in taking on Al-Aqsa Martyrs' Brigades, the PA's methods were not as harsh as they had been in the fight against Hamas. In fact, it was commonly understood among the inhabitants of Nablus that while some members of the Fatah-aligned forces had exploited the post-Intifada lawlessness for their own profit, they had not been the focus of the PA's assault in the same way.[10] It was suggested by several interviewees that the PA had returned to some of its older methods in relation to Fatah cadres, in the sense of buying support. Some of the same people who had operated in armed gangs during the crisis later returned to work for the PA forces themselves. In 2007, prior to the clampdown and in coordination with Israel, the PA had in fact adopted an amnesty programme for 178 members of the Al-Aqsa Martyrs' Brigades. This involved paying cash for the handover of illegal arms and a provision that members denounced terrorism (Council on Foreign Relations (CFR) 2012). The brigade members did not universally accept the proposal and the amnesty, and Fayyad later confirmed that the PA continued to monitor brigade members that were in the amnesty programme and to coordinate with Israel on their fate.[11]

The outcome of these actions was multi-layered. Both Abbas and Fayyad were heaped with praise in the international media, and even the Israelis seemed to be impressed with their ability to impose order, though this did not prevent the Israeli military from entering the city whenever it wished (*The Economist* 2012). For example, the pro-Israeli commentator Nathan Shachar (2009) declared 'Peace has broken out in the West Bank' in a 2009 article entitled 'The Good Cops of Nablus', while other commentaries that similarly praised the ostensible transformation of the West Bank, as a result of the Fayyad-government's achievements, appeared in the US and European media. For Fayyad, this was the beginning of a new chapter, within which his statebuilding agenda could really take off. In practical terms, this meant that three processes were effectively consolidated. These were: (a) the streamlining and re-organisation of Palestinian security forces (discussed in more detail in the next chapter); (b) the renewal of overt operational links with the Israeli military, the US and its allies after their curtailment as part of the blockade (though some ties had remained, particularly between Western intelligence agencies and the branches of the security forces personally loyal to Abbas prior to 2007); and (c) the imposition of order, which could be extended across the West Bank (see Zanotti 2010).

While for Abbas, the entire emergency-situation scenario did provide him with a useful argument to help justify extending his time in office, and further entrenching his powers, the splinters within Fatah would continue to haunt him. This would manifest itself in the form of rumours and discontent for the most part. Tensions occasionally came to the surface, such as an attempted assassination of Nablus' Governor in 2008, but would seem to resurface more dangerously in 2013 with protests in Nablus in January (Khoury 2013), followed by armed activity against Israel from both Gaza (*Reuters* and *Al Arabiya* 2013) and the West Bank (Khalil 2013) later in the year. For the ordinary citizens of Nablus, the difference was palpable. By the end of 2008, the police presence had become virtually ubiquitous within the limits imposed on it by Israeli forces, and the return of both foreign aid and direct investment from Palestinian sources allowed a range of infrastructural development projects to start and promotional commercial events to take place. Even in the refugee camps, which – given their distinct legal status – had traditionally been handled at arm's length by the PA, order had been restored, though the presence of police/security forces was not as obvious. However, until 2009–10, Palestinian forces would be required to leave the streets in the late evening in case the Israeli military returned in order to conduct night raids.

The meaning of the violence

The PA clearly saw itself as acting in the service of the general good by clamping down on Hamas. As stated above, on the issue of the necessity to restore order to the West Bank, there was broad alignment both from inside the PA – Abbas and Fayyad – and outside, including Israel, the US, the UK and the other donor governments. It is worth examining how the PA explained its role in this episode. In essence the PA's narrative explaining and justifying the violence can be summarised in the following four points:

- the objectives of the surge were not directly political – in that they did not target Hamas specifically – but rather they pursued persons and groups that were deemed to be a threat and potentially 'destabilize the situation';[12]
- the violence that occurred during the schism was actually the product of a decision to which the Hamas leadership was party – in other words, it was taken by the 12th government (the short-lived 'unity government' formed after the 2006 elections which collapsed with the coup);
- the use of the secret police (in this context implying the Preventative Security Forces and the General Intelligence) in enforcing order was in fact much more limited than public perception suggested; and
- where specific cases of torture and internment had been recorded during the assault on Hamas, these were isolated incidents and represented the 'misuse of authority by individual officers'[13] and were under investigation.

The main trope of the PA's narrative on the violence of the schism was predicated on a reaction to two threats to society. First was that various militias/armed gangs were causing great damage to society through both the open conflict amongst themselves and also through the exploitation of local businesses. Second was that the PA needed to re-assert its control and end the plurality of arms in order to deprive Israel of one of its main pretexts for retaliation and its continued presence in Area 'A'. The narrative presented here both reduced the significance of accusations of wrongdoing by the PA, while at the same time justifying an uncompromising security agenda with the pretext that any possible alternative would be very much worse.[14] Moreover, the culmination of dealing with these two threats, according to this narrative, would establish the building blocks for statebuilding.

By analysing this narrative in juxtaposition to the actual events that took place in Nablus and elsewhere in late 2007 and early 2008, we can see that there were of course aspects that did not align directly. Where there were mismatches between the narrative and the reality, the most important revolved around: (a) the methods used to prosecute this clampdown; and (b) the specifics of the narrative to justify it. For the most part, these gaps between the official position and the actual events are best understood in terms of the conflict between Fayyad and the PA security forces. Fayyad was the most articulate and dynamic advocate of the surge itself and – though he made his opposition to Hamas clear on occasions, particularly after the schism and the separation of Gaza – he frequently made extra efforts to appear non-political and to frame his justification of events in more technical terms.

However, with regard to torture and other repressive activities of the security forces, some of the statements by PA officials (Buck 2010) – and some of the information provided in interviews[15] – seemed to downplay it and/or disassociated the PA from it. This was despite the compelling level of evidence that the use of torture and abuse under the security forces, particularly in Palestinian prisons, was widespread (Al-Haq 2008) and that human rights groups had directly informed the PA leadership of their findings (Al-Haq 2010). Further, the organisation Human Rights Watch stated that the responsibility for these abuses rested ultimately with the political and military leaderships of both combatant forces.

Yet, it is important here to be fair to Fayyad and the other technocrats. While it is hard to believe that they were really as 'a-political' as they sought to present themselves, there is no evidence to suggest that they were particularly enthusiastic about a resurgence of Fatah in the West Bank either. Moreover, Fayyad did both speak out against torture and also take action against it. In January 2010, media reports noted that '43 officers had been jailed, fired or demoted for abusing prisoners' (Associated Press 2010). Fayyad also made personal apologies to the families of torture victims in order to send a message to the security forces. In a meeting with a US military representative, Fayyad apparently detailed his position in some depth:

> 'We cannot accept the abuse or torture of people', he said. 'It is a question of morality, not politics' ... he met with security chiefs following the Fatah Congress to underscore his standing order that there would be no tolerance for violent attacks of any kind.
>
> (US Consulate Jerusalem 2009)

The second claim, which cast the PA security forces in the role of acting purely in the interests of the general public through re-asserting order and ending the dominance of criminal gangs on the streets of cities like Nablus, is also problematic. This is because while it certainly is the case that the PA's actions did lead to an environment of greater stability – a consequence that can surely be interpreted as positive – the evidence suggests that it was clearly motivated by a political agenda to target Hamas. The fact that the PA security forces were targeting one specific armed faction, while cadres aligned to Fatah were effectively given a pass (or were even allowed to join the security forces and participate in the fighting) demonstrates that any claim that the agenda was a-political is absurd (Crisis Group 2010). Moreover, the fact that secret documents detailing the involvement of foreign intelligence agencies (discussed in more detail in the next chapter) have emerged, which outline the specific role of the PA security forces in planning the unilateral ousting of Hamas, casts serious doubt on the PA's assertions of an apolitical agenda and its claims to embody democratic legitimacy. This data suggests that the goals of Abbas and the PA security establishment were to inflict a military defeat on its political opponent and that Fayyad – who saw Hamas as an impediment to his vision of how the Palestinian state would be built – went along with this. Therefore, this invalidates the contention that the PA's security forces were acting purely in the interests of the general population. These measures were particularly focused on Bethlehem and Nablus, where Hamas had achieved strong popular support. While even if elements of the narrative can be accepted as true – that order was re-imposed so as to avert a genuine threat to public welfare through a conflict between Hamas and Israel – the PA's narrative is undermined by the fact that the end of the schism did not signal a shift to more democratic forms of governance in the West Bank, but instead became a starting point for further authoritarianism.

This should not necessarily be seen as a total indictment of Fayyad and the technocrats, at least not in terms of their intentions. Clearly, as emergency appointees who came to office in the aftermath of an annulled election, they did not exactly represent the embodiment of democratic governance. Yet it is clear from Fayyad's actions during this period, particularly in terms of his efforts to curtail human rights abuses, that the technocrats were not power-hungry authoritarians either. If anything, the major failure of the Fayyad government here was that it was not strong enough to truly assert power and maintain power over the security forces. Instead of shepherding the PA effectively towards a post-Intifada promised land of democracy (which, under these conditions, was an impossible task anyway), the Fayyad government acted more like a manager than a leader. It was able to govern and direct the security forces to a certain extent for a time, but never enjoyed a true grip over them.

Instead, over the long term, the civilian leadership of the PA became less relevant. As Sayigh noted, 'in the West Bank ... the security sector is increasingly called on to mediate between the PA government and society' (2011b). Further, 'in the West Bank, the intelligence agencies are emerging as autonomous power centres that acknowledge no higher, constitutional authority' (Sayigh 2011a, 26). This transition to authoritarianism would be accelerated after Fayyad resigned from the premiership, and the intimidation raid on his NGO's offices demonstrated just how far things had gone. In the end, there had been a clear shift in authority in the West Bank. In essence, Fayyad had managed the security forces as the head of the government – and, to an extent, had ridden on the crest of a wave of securitisation – for a time, but after his term was over, power was re-focused around Abbas and the ever more authoritarian security chiefs. As a former minister under Fayyad put it:

> Before [while still Prime Minister] Fayyad was the second most powerful man in the West Bank [after President Abbas]. Now the second most powerful man is Majid Faraj [the head of the General Intelligence].[16]

Of course, this authoritarian shift was not solely the product of events that took place in Palestine – there was plenty of help and encouragement from outside. The next chapter deals with the role of foreign governments in helping to create this situation as well as the reaction to and aftermath of this episode.

Notes

1. See Friedrich, Luethold and Milhem (2008).
2. During the late 1990s, some of the PA security services operated alongside Israeli forces on joint patrols. However, cooperation ended with the beginning of the Intifada and PA police stations and bases were primary targets of Israeli bombardment during the invasion.
3. This included Nasser Yousef, a prominent opponent of Arafat as Minister for the Interior; see Rubinstein (2005) and Eldar (2005).
4. This involved the firing of several senior officers, cutting over 1,000 lower-ranked officers and imposing various requirements on employment, such as the submission of extensive personal details to a central office, an age limit for recruitment and a standard retirement age.
5. Elements from this and the following section have also been published in my article 'After "Security First": An Analysis of Security Transition and "Statebuilding" in the West Bank 2007–11' (2014a).
6. Citing the PA as a product of an illegitimate compromise, Hamas had boycotted all elections, but in 2006, it pragmatically changed position and chose to participate; see Hroub (2006).
7. 'The conduct of the election was widely considered to be free and fair. Palestinians voted in one of 1,008 polling stations (754 in the West Bank and 254 in Gaza) and 132 seats were contested by 728 candidates (414 in districts and 314 on party slates). Initial observer reports stated that nearly all polls opened on time and the election was carried out in an efficient and orderly manner' (Pina 2006).
8. Arguably, this had at one time been seen as Hamas' virtue by Israel – which had sponsored and supported it in its infancy as a way of challenging the PLO's dominance during the late 1980s – a similar tactic to that used in regard to the Village Leagues (discussed in previous chapters).
9. Evidence of the kind of paramilitary campaign undertaken by the PA can be found through leaked documents available through *Al Jazeera*'s Transparency Unit. For example: 'Annex I – Palestinian Performance on Security' (2008). For more context, see also Associated Press (2012).
10. Research interviews, Nablus, 2009–10.
11. Indeed, 'the PA detained seven program participants on the basis of information provided to the PA by the Israel Security Agency (ISA) that they had broken the terms of the program, mostly due to failing to turn in weapons' (US Consulate Jerusalem 2008a).

12 Research interview with a representative from the Ministry for the Interior, July 2010.
13 Ibid.
14 Ibid.
15 Ibid.
16 Research interview with a former minister, 9 October 2014.
17 Information for the table gathered primarily from Madhoun (2006).

6 The 'State of Palestine'

The events of 2011–12 were both surprising and turbulent. The so-called 'Arab Spring' rocked the Middle East and confounded commentators, academics and policy makers,[1] many of whom had been pondering the apparent exceptional 'robustness' of the region's authoritarianism for quite some time. For a time, the region-wide unrest also seemed to overshadow the question of Palestine in international forums. This would not last, however. At the international level, the PLO forged ahead with plans to have Palestine recognised as a 'state'.[2] This project would turn out to be successful to some extent. Within the context of the UN General Assembly, Palestine won an elevation to 'non-member observer' status with a vote in November 2012. A number of friendly states and some parliaments – including Britain, France and Ireland in 2014, though this did not change their governments' position (Black 2014) – also recognised Palestine or upgraded its status. The final hurdle of acceptance by the UN Security Council had never really looked achievable, and in the end it was not.

But this hardly mattered. The PLO leadership was buoyed by the support it had won and, while this did not translate directly into enough leverage over Israel to win significant concessions, a new way forward was – apparently – being forged. This path led away from the negotiating table and, instead, towards challenging the legitimacy of Israel's occupation in independent forums. To this end, having endured the intense bombardment of Gaza in 2013 and further frustrations throughout 2014, the PLO took the step that had become known as the 'nuclear option'. This was to ask for an investigation into possible war crimes by the International Criminal Court (ICC). There are numerous ways to understand these events and what they meant. One perspective would have the putative 'Palestinian State' emerging from its chrysalis at the UN General Assembly in November 2012 and coming of age as it took its case to the ICC. In other words, this reading of events would have the Palestinian state as having been effectively 'built' – inasmuch as it achieved everything it could, bar full recognition from the international community – and actually bringing an end to the occupation, but it was pursuing those goals via measured and reasonable efforts through the forums of established international institutions.

It is important to note that this view – while in essence a paraphrasing of several of President Abbas' key speeches and public statements on the issue (in particular at the UN in 2011, 2012 and 2014) – is hardly representative of the PLO chairman's full view on the Palestinian statebuilding plan. According to PA insiders, who were closer to Fayyad than to Abbas, the President was far from eager to endorse the statebuilding project – that is, until it had almost run its course. They suggested that Abbas' public position could be best understood as fear-inspired opportunism. Abbas, like everyone else, was caught off-guard by a radically changing region – which brought about the fall of some of his key allies – as well as a troubling loss of public legitimacy.

Yet there is another way of looking at these events which views the processes that took the Palestinians to the UN and then to the ICC. Like the perspective furthered by the PA insiders, this view notes with some cynicism that the PLO's manoeuvres at the UN seemed to follow on very soon after a series of events that appeared to bring the PA's legitimacy very much into doubt. Yet some advocates of this more critical view go further than the position of frustration and anger at Abbas' opportunism, as expressed by the supporters of Fayyad. This chapter articulates a more critical analysis of the processes that brought the 'Palestinian State' into being. In particular, following on from the arguments in the previous chapters, this discussion seeks to put the so-called 'UN gambit' into a perspective that is both wider and deeper than the views articulated by either Abbas or the supporters of Fayyad.

The argument that is presented here and in the following chapter is wider than most similar versions of events because it takes into account the impact of radically changing regional dynamics in 2011–12, and it is deeper because it seeks to trace the evolution of three ongoing processes which – along with the acceleration of authoritarianism in the West Bank (discussed in the previous chapter) – contributed to the PA's declining stock among the general population: (a) the ever more obvious impact of foreign agendas in Palestine; (b) Israel's adoption of new tactics in its resistance to Palestinian autonomy; and (c) the implications of a deeply uncertain regional dynamic.

Layers of analysis

The 'surge' in the northern West Bank had proven extremely popular. According to the Palestinian Center for Policy and Survey Research (PSR), nearly 40 per cent of West Bankers polled in March and September 2007 stated that 'Law and Order' should be the government's top priority (see Table 6.1). Moreover, both public perceptions of safety and the approval rating of the Fayyad government rose steadily throughout 2008–10 among West Bankers (see Figure 6.1 below).

However, closer examination suggested that such a rosy picture was not quite accurate. While there was strong evidence to suggest growing public support for the Fayyad government and its prioritisation of 'Law and Order' in 2007, this (a) did not last and (b) did not translate into viewing the

Table 6.1 West Bankers: what should be the PA's top priority?[25]

	March 2007 (%)	September 2007 (%)
Law and Order	39.7	38.4
Boycott	25.3	15.1
Peace Process	14	17.5
Reform	19	21.6
Other	5	3.3
Don't Know	1	4.1

government as legitimate. Except for the short period immediately after the appointment of the emergency government by Abbas, the proportion of West Bankers who viewed the Abbas-Fayyad government as legitimate was more or less the same as that of the expelled Hamas government in Gaza and – perhaps more telling – the percentage of West Bankers who viewed neither government as legitimate also remained fairly consistently at the same level.

By the end of the Fayyad era in early 2013, the popularity of the West Bank government had dropped dramatically. Moreover, as the events of the 'Arab Spring' challenged or overthrew long-standing dictatorships across the region, the Palestinians took to their own streets on an unprecedented scale. In order to understand what caused this dramatic shift, it is necessary to look at the period 2008–13 – the final phases of the run-up to the declaration of the 'State of Palestine' – at a time when the various convenient alliances, which had served the security agenda during the conflict with Hamas, fell apart and the deeper meanings of the statebuilding project came into focus. *Prima facie*, it is possible to view this period in terms of revealing two different conflicts between the previously allied parties (the Fayyad government, Abbas and the security forces, and the international community).

As discussed above, there was an obvious conflict between the Palestinians and key players in the international community – primarily the US and Israel – over recognition of the 'State of Palestine'. And at the same time, the rivalry between Fayyad and Abbas intensified and – at the domestic level – ownership of the 'State of Palestine' became a battlefield between the President and Prime Minister. This was a dispute that Abbas would eventually win. But beyond this, a more critical perspective suggests that something more sinister was going on. In essence, this was that the entire push for recognition of the 'State' was a storm in a teacup, an ultimately irrelevant distraction from the reality that Palestine was well on the road to becoming what in 2008 Nathan Brown called a 'ward' of the international community (Brown 2008). Viewed from this perspective, the efforts by Abbas to seize the opportunity afforded to him by the prospect of a high level – but largely meaningless – confrontation with the US and Israel can be viewed very clearly as a move to shore up his own legitimacy, albeit in such a way that could be seen, in the broader

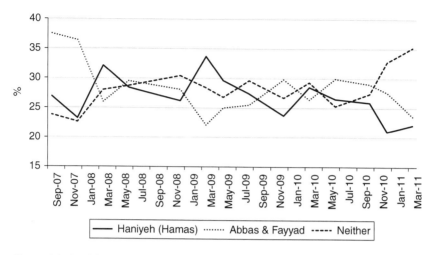

Figure 6.1 Legitimacy of governments[22]

context, as roughly equivalent to ensuring his authority at the helm of a sinking ship. This chapter discusses each of these arguments, before exploring Abbas' manoeuvring at the UN in the conclusion.

Public opinions[3]

In the aftermath of the 'surge', public perceptions of Fayyad and Abbas' leadership was relatively high. As evidence from public polling suggests (presented above), the people wanted safety and security, and their growing approval of the PA reflected an appreciation that an improved sense of safety and security is what they got, especially between mid-2008 and late 2011. The following graph overlays public approval ratings of the Fayyad government with data on the public perception of safety and security in the West Bank. As we have seen, this issue was a central pillar of the statebuilding plan. The graph shows a relatively clear correlation between perception of safety and security and the government's approval rating between the middle of 2008 and the beginning of 2010. The data on perceptions of corruption evidently remains consistently high throughout, though its initial drop from above 80 per cent to around 70 per cent may be attributable to some of Fayyad's efforts.

Data from research interviews conducted in Nablus in 2008–9 supported the conclusion that safety and security was the residents' primary concern. However, these data did not universally reflect the view that the PA (in general, not only Fayyad) could win back popular legitimacy through pursuing measures designed to improve safety and security alone. Closer analysis of these interviews suggests that there were apparently two broad narratives

112 The 'State of Palestine'

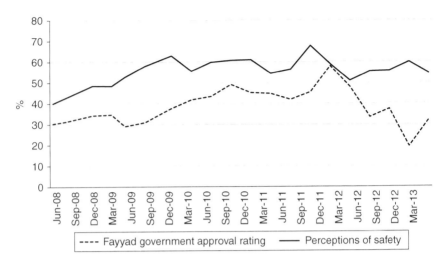

Figure 6.2 West Bank: public perceptions of safety and security compared to approval ratings for the Fayyad government[23]

evident in popular attitudes towards the PA, which can be categorised as consensual and rejectionist.

However, over time it became clearer that what distinguished these two camps were largely superficial factors and – as demonstrated by both the polling data and the outbreak of protests – the consensus in support of the PA would be overshadowed by the reality of the situation. Particularly relevant was the PA's lack of any real autonomy, especially in the context of the crippling fiscal crisis that hit the PA in 2011–12. Both the consensual and rejectionist narratives accepted that conditions in Nablus had improved. Yet both main narratives also expressed significant doubt that the PA could achieve its stated goals of Palestinian independence, or even a general long-term improvement in conditions through institution building.

Examples of the consensual narrative tended to accept that the 'surge' was a necessary means through which order and civil responsibility was restored to Nablus. It was seen as an effective operation even though allegations of human rights abuses, torture and maltreatment by the security forces were well-known, and it was also generally understood that the PA had collaborated with Israel and foreign governments during this period. The consensus held that the crisis was so bad that it warranted such a forceful response. In this respect the consensus did not distinguish on political grounds (between Hamas, the Al-Aqsa Martyrs' Brigades or any other group particularly) in its assignment of blame. It should perhaps be best understood in the same language as the polling data suggests: 'the desire for the restoration of law and order'.

Interview data

The following examples represent a narrow cross-section of research interviews conducted with a total of nearly 90 different interviewees across the West Bank during 2008–11. The examples presented here were chosen due to their relevance to the question of the PA's security agenda and because the interviewees were not overtly aligned to either Hamas or Fatah.[4]

A former civilian police officer – interviewed in Nablus in late 2009 – suggested that the security forces' actions should be seen as an essential moderating force in extreme circumstances. He stated that the police's role was to 'tame people and teach them to respect the law'.[5] Moreover, a senior business official at the Nablus Chamber of Commerce (interviewed at approximately the same time as the police officer) offered similar support for the PA security forces' actions based on the essential need for public order, so that a basis for development could be formed, and upon which businesses in Nablus could and should capitalise.[6] This interviewee's comments were generally in line with the parameters of the PA's narrative and essentially focused on a range of outcomes that had resulted from the activities of the PA security services, particularly the improved environment for economic activity.

However, not all endorsements of the PA's security forces' actions were quite so all-encompassing, though they did tend to focus on the same broad parameters to frame their narratives. For example, a middle-aged mother who was studying English with a local NGO tied her perspective to personal experiences of hardship under the siege and during the period of lawlessness that preceded the surge. Unlike the previous two examples, this interviewee was particularly focused on Israel's culpability for creating the harsh conditions during the Intifada. She noted that the situation had improved for her in a day-to-day sense: 'girls are protected by the police. They are good for family safety – they will beat men for harassing families'.[7]

In a similar vein, a shop owner in central Nablus, whom this author interviewed frequently throughout December 2009 and again in late 2011, was initially strongly supportive of the PA. His comments were framed directly by prioritising his family's interests. He expressed support for the PA's security agenda through the positive impact it had had, directly and indirectly, on their welfare. Yet over the period from 2009 to late 2011, his opinion changed and he became less willing to articulate support for the PA's narrative, through referencing new allegations of corruption against the PA and the futility of its institution-building programme.

Like the English-language student, the shop owner framed his interpretation of the security situation in direct relation to his family's experiences. For example, during the Intifada, he had stayed away from the city centre whenever there was a high risk of fighting because of responsibilities to his family. After the surge, he and his wife felt much safer in the city.[8] By late 2011, however, his attitude was remarkably different. He explained that he was angry with the PA leadership because new accusations had emerged about corruption. He expressed some hostility towards the PA as being ultimately responsible for the worsening economic climate in the West Bank. Evidently, the combination of alleged corruption at the highest level and the worsening conditions for ordinary businesses like his own was enough for him to feel a kind of detachment from the PA's agenda that he had not expressed previously.

Obviously, there are some important distinctions between the perspectives of the different interviewees. Clearly the first two interviewees (the former police officer and the high-ranking member of the Nablus Chamber of Commerce) held a much more positive view of the PA than the other two interviewees. However, both were speaking from standpoints that were closely aligned to the PA's official position because both shared important interests – usually a concern for security and stability – in common with the PA. On the other hand, the two other interviewees oriented their concerns with more direct reference to their familial responsibilities and the welfare of the general public.

On the other hand, the alternative, rejectionist account tended to situate interpretations of the PA's security agenda within a much broader historical context. This narrative highlighted the PA's dependence on the support of foreign governments and the integration of the PA's security agenda with foreign militaries, and implied that the security services had prioritised the concerns of those international actors over the interests of the general population. These interviewees tended to suggest a more profound meaning to both the crackdown on Hamas and the notion of an underlying reciprocal relationship between the PA, Israel and other external parties (particularly the US and its allies).

An example of this was expressed by Abdul Sattar Qassem, a nationally known political figure and university professor who was also a harsh critic of the PA. In Qassem's view, the role of the surge essentially constituted a distraction, which was manipulated by Israel and its allies in order to weaken Palestinian resistance to the occupation. According to him, the schism between Hamas and Fatah had always been a possible outcome of Israel's undeclared colonial policy of divide and rule.[9] Moreover, the contrasting treatment of Gaza versus the West Bank after the schism demonstrated Israel's ability to use Palestinian dependency to manipulate the population of the oPts through practices of punishment and reward. He stated that: 'Israel has created a system of dependence for Palestinians wherein we [the Palestinians] are provided with enough to live, but not enough to co-ordinate resistance. The PA is [and the PLO was] complicit in this throughout Oslo'.[10]

Another prominent member of Nablus' intelligentsia viewed the schism and the PA's surge through a lens that focused on the Israeli occupation as the ultimate power in determining the fate of the Palestinians. In this context, the PA was, at best, postponing an inevitable Israeli assault. In fact, he stated that an assault on Nablus and other cities in the West Bank comparable to the 2008–9 bombardment of Gaza was almost inevitable at some point in the future. As he put it, 'there is no doubt, what happened in Gaza will happen here. It is only a matter of time'.[11] Another common element in the narratives of the rejectionists was that they accepted that, at a basic level, the conditions in Nablus had improved and that the PA was able to restore some semblance of order and provision of services. Of course, this perspective was not held universally and it is worth noting that in some particular respects, the difference between the narratives of those rejecting the PA's rhetoric and those consenting to it was not that great. Over time, these doubts extended even further and the belief in the PA suffered.

Broadly speaking, the inhabitants of the West Bank were well aware of the limitations of the Fayyad government and did not accept the PA's legitimacy per se. The shift towards authoritarianism by the PA's security forces following the schism with Hamas was generally accepted because of the relative stability following a profoundly traumatic period. Yet, as discussed above, this acceptance did not last and in fact the outbreak of protests in 2011–12 can be seen as a direct challenge to the Fayyad government's authority and an inspiration for Abbas' opportunism. But before we go on to examine those events, it is necessary to slot in the remaining missing pieces of the security-authoritarianism-legitimacy jigsaw puzzle and discuss first foreign involvement in the development and execution of the security agenda of 2007 onwards. By doing so, it is possible to glean an enlightening insight into the environment within which the authoritarianism of the security forces was allowed to prosper and be encouraged.

'Security first'

The role of external third parties was essential to the 'surge' and the reorganisation and improvement of the security forces in the West Bank. If taken *prima facie*, the nature of the involvement of foreign governments appeared to simply overlap with and support the PA's statebuilding programme. Both the Palestinians and the PA's foreign supporters – especially among the donor communities – built on the promise that if the necessary steps of improving the security environment were undertaken, Palestinian progression towards further economic development and eventually liberation would be assured. According to this narrative, the role of these external third parties was to assist the PA along this path by providing funds, matériel and guidance to its security forces.

However, rather than simply accepting this, a more critical view has been posited. This critical perspective suggests that foreign involvement in the Palestinian security sector – and for Palestinian statebuilding in general – can be better interpreted as a form of counterinsurgency. This viewpoint suggests that the major donor governments that backed the PA never intended to allow for genuine Palestinian autonomy. The primary goal of this relationship was to bolster the PA security forces in order to prevent another rebellion against Israeli rule. This would be, essentially, a means to keep order and replicate a model that had worked fairly well for decades in various other authoritarian client states.[12] As Mandy Turner argues, 'if Western donor-led peacebuilding is understood as a form of counterinsurgency whose goal is to secure a population ... we see that peacebuilding has not failed – in fact, quite the contrary, it has largely succeeded' (Turner 2015, 74).

Palestine had occupied a special place as a testing ground for counterinsurgency strategies even from the time of the British Mandate. According to Laleh Khalili (2010, 414), this was as a result of 'its geostrategic significance ... and the position of Palestine's colonizers in global hierarchies of power'. Moreover:

> Palestine's centrality stems from the fact that with the Mandate, Palestinians were subjugated by perhaps the most powerful empire of its time, and today they are subjects of domination by Israel, the most important ally and client of the United States, the international hyperpower of our time.
>
> (Khalili 2010, 414)

This suggests that the Palestinian case study is revealing not only because it has served as an important site for experimentation and performance of counterinsurgency methodologies for such a long time, but also because it has drawn in the involvement of various great powers.[13] This conclusion is certainly supported by the data introduced in the previous chapter that British and US security services were heavily involved in the planning and implementation of the 'surge'. But it is also worth noting that both Khalili and Turner cite a critical role for the military-industrial (and academic) complex of these great power actors too (see also Bhungalia 2012).

As Khalili notes, 'independent think tanks such as the RAND Corporation, civilian universities, and military pedagogic institutions ... have been conduits for the transfer of counterinsurgency knowledge across borders. RAND has an entire library of writings on counterinsurgency, much of it by counterinsurgents. Their comparative works draw freely from various cases, including Israel/Palestine' (Khalili 2010, 419). Further, Turner's article cites a 2008 RAND Corporation report by John Mackinlay and Alison Al-Baddawy (2008). This report, Turner (2015, 75) explains, provides a useful example as to how organisations that are close to the US government see the significance of Palestine in relation to global counterinsurgency concerns. While the RAND report's discussion on Palestine notes that the PLO-led resistance to Israel was never likely to be successful in the practical sense of overthrowing Israel's rule, the broader ideational impact of the struggle was highly significant in its own right. As they put it for observers and supporters of Palestine, '"arriving" became less important than the morale-boosting experience of the "journey"' (Mackinlay and Al-Baddawy 2008, 18). Mackinlay and Al-Baddawy present the rise of the PLO in such a way that it might be read as a

The 'State of Palestine' 117

Hollywood-esque 'origin story' for contemporary regional conflicts: 'the PLO campaign is relevant because it was both a laboratory for and a forerunner of a much more virulent form of insurgent energy. Although the Palestinian insurgency began 30 years ago, the West learned nothing from it' (2008, 20). Moreover, Mackinlay and Al-Baddawy situate Palestine at the very heart of the apparent global struggle against militant Islamism and set up the challenge to 'the West' that it must learn from this struggle in order to defeat its current enemies:

> A successful counterstrategy needed first a long-term political plan that could remove or disarm the Palestinian sense of grievance and at the same time be acceptable to the Israelis and to the Arab states. This has proven impossible to achieve. At a more operational level, it also needed a cooperative campaign involving many different states and international agencies to diminish the virtual ascendancy of the insurgent, and to promote the actors that might have been trying to restore individual security to the populations at the front lines of the conflict.
>
> (Mackinlay and Al-Baddawy 2008, 20)

It is possible to read the involvement of Western governments and intelligence agencies in this light, not to mention Palestinian elites. If, in the past, it had been 'impossible to achieve' a general settlement of the Palestinians through these means, this did not necessarily mean that it always would be. But for now it was more important to focus on the 'operational' goals. These could be summarised as the pacification of the Palestinians and avoiding a potential third rebellion. Both RAND and several other Western-based think tanks went on to provide an intellectual explanation for the boosting of Palestine's security forces by Western military and intelligence agencies.

The sobriquet 'security first' described the viewpoint that was generally accepted within policy-making circles in the US. This was that security was the necessary (but not sufficient in its own right) first step towards resolving the Palestinian crisis. A 2007 RAND report stated that:

> Security trumps all else. Without it – as demonstrated by several decades of experience in Arab-Israeli peacemaking, including every agreement between Israel and one or more of its neighbors since 1949 – nothing else is likely to succeed in Israeli-Palestinian relations. Security considerations, therefore, must come first.
>
> (Anthony et al. 2007)[14]

A similar (2010) report for the Center for a New American Security stated that:

Security may be ten per cent of the problem, or it may be ninety percent, but whichever it is, it's the first ten per cent or the first ninety percent. Without security, nothing else we do will last.

(Sheehan 1988, quoted in Exum et al. 2010)

Further, other examples of Western plans for a security first approach include suggestions for replacing Israel's occupation with the presence of a foreign military force, for example, the North Atlantic Treaty Organizaton (NATO). This would be during a transitional period when Palestinian security forces could be trained and equipped as a replacement for the occupation as the guarantor of Israeli security (Gaub 2010). While the PA's rhetoric did not speak to the same issues of Israeli security quite so directly, in the first document to outline the direction of the PA's post-2007 agenda, the PRDP describes the necessity of improvements in the security situation in a way that is similar to those outlined by the US-based think tanks: as an essential first step for Palestinian society in order to enable progress both in terms of economic development and towards the ending of the occupation:

If a combination of political progress and an improved security environment accelerates the lifting of the occupation regime beyond current expectations, the level of public investment and private sector activity could increase significantly.

(Palestinian Authority 2007)

Reform and improvement of the security services was also the PA's highest priority. In fact, in the PDRP, the PA pledged to spend $257 million on *Security Sector Reform and Transformation*, although it offered very little detail regarding what this actually meant in practical terms. This sum is by far the largest area of PA spending identified in the PRDP and equates to nearly four times the quantity allocated to the next-largest area of spending (*Efficient and Effective Government* at $72 million). In 2011, Abbas essentially embraced the role laid out for him as a 'domestic' elite in the counterinsurgency literature by endorsing a plan for NATO to take over from the Israeli military in operating the apparatus of the occupation (*Haaretz* 2010). Essentially, Abbas' move demonstrated that even Palestine's President had effectively relegated the argument against occupation to a question of who was the more preferable occupier: NATO or Israel?

The role of the foreign involvement in the security sector reform during the Fayyad era can be understood at two levels. At the surface level, it appeared that in the aftermath of the schism, the EU and the US re-organised their involvement into a more coordinated effort to support the PA-led reform of the Palestinian security services. At a deeper level, the (primarily) US and UK connection with certain Palestinian security services was developed over a much longer period and comprised a much more insidious relationship. The following two sections look at both of these: first by examining the events and processes that occurred at the surface level and then, in the following section, peering behind the curtain to examine the covert relationship.

Foreign involvement in security sector reform

Officially, the US military programme – the United States Security Coordinator (USSC) – was established in 2005, but had been initially distracted from its goal of security sector reform by the necessity of helping to manage Israel's 'disengagement' from Gaza, and was then thwarted by the international boycott of the PA after Hamas' 2006 election victory (Dayton 2009). After the expulsion of Hamas, however, the USSC – by now under the command of US Army General Keith Dayton – officially took a more formal role in charge of an international force. This force was tasked with the training of Palestinian recruits from the Presidential Guard (answerable directly to Abbas) and the National Security Force (the largest security force and roughly analogous to a Palestinian army). This training took place at two main sites: the Jordan International Police Training Center (JIPTC), near Amman, and a PA training centre near Jericho. The training ostensibly focused on teaching the security forces 'gendarmerie-style' (Zanotti 2010) methods of counterterrorism and counterinsurgency. Recruits who were trained by the USSC were also encouraged to become desensitised to concerns relating to Israel's occupation of Palestine and to focus instead on their loyalty to the institution of the PA (Zanotti 2010, 18). A similar, though less expansive, programme was set up for the PA civilian police, which was financially supported by the EU as well as Norway and Canada. It was based in Ramallah and was particularly involved 'with reform and train-and-equip efforts with the Palestinian Civil Police (PCP) and in the criminal justice sector through the EU Police Coordinating Office for Palestinian Police Support (EUPOL COPPS)' (Zanotti 2010, 8).

The performance of these various services has been widely commended. In particular, both the US government and the Israelis were particularly happy with the way in which the newly trained troops handled the follow-up to the 'surge' in Nablus – the imposition of order in Jenin and then Hebron – and according to a US congressional report, 'JIPTC-trained personnel involved in the operation were even more disciplined and competent than their non-JIPTC-trained counterparts' (Zanotti 2010, 22). According to the Crisis Group (2010, 8), these actions also won public approval: 'from Jenin to Hebron, Palestinians praise[d] their security forces for "confronting criminals and thugs" and enabling "ordinary families to walk outside after dark"'.

In terms of the reforms themselves, this process produced a slimmed-down security force with a command structure that was relatively more coherent than that which had existed under Arafat. The following table presents the outcome of those processes. For the security services, the three main products of these reforms comprised further re-organisation, greater

Table 6.2 Structure of Palestinian security services c. 2009[26]

National	Interior	Intelligence
Preventative Security (4,000, including paid informants) – focuses on internal intelligence and political opposition. Was accused by Human Rights Watch and other NGOs of torture and murder during the schism with Hamas.	**Civilian Police** (approx. 8,000) – officers responsible for day-to-day policing and crime prevention, including traffic control. Aided by the EU-COPPS programme based in Ramallah.	**General Intelligence** (approx. 4,000) – 'theoretically focuses on intelligence collection outside the West Bank, conducts counter-espionage and liaises with intelligence agencies of other countries, but in practice, it largely overlaps with Preventive Security' (Crisis Group 2010, 2). It was also accused of human rights abuses against Hamas members.
National Security (approx. 7,000 personnel) – a 'gendarmerie-style' police force.	**Presidential Guard** (approx. 2,500) – bodyguard unit for PA officials and PA infrastructure with some policing and intelligence powers.	**Military Intelligence** (approx. 2,000) – responsible for internal PA investigations and countering threats from within the security structures.

regulation of payroll and employment in order to reduce the room for corruption and a clearer and more efficient command structure that divided the responsibilities of the different forces more logically. These reforms created six different operational branches of the security forces, covering three broad areas of jurisdiction. For the purposes of comparison, Table 6.2 presents the framework of the security forces post-PRDP (c. 2009) in a similar format to that of Table 6.1 above.

Each of these forces was sub-categorised to some extent and there were also areas of shared jurisdiction – for instance, between the Preventative Security's intelligence network and the General Intelligence organisation, or between the National Security Forces' prevention of crime programmes and the Civilian Police – yet each force remains a separate entity inasmuch as each has its own command structures and operational regulations (Crisis Group 2010). Beyond this organisational re-structuring, from 2007, the Fayyad government enforced further changes in the nature and operational behaviour of the security services – again in line with the requirements imposed by Israel and the other external parties.[15] This included high-profile changes in its leadership aimed at tackling the kind of nepotistic appointment processes that were left over from Arafat's era,[16] cutting the artificially large salaries budget and improvements to internal efficiency. However, the most significant change was that the PA fully accepted the role of external actors in training and infrastructural capacity building.[17]

Foreign agenda

The reformed Palestinian security services were not beyond controversy, though. This was partly because of the ambiguous relationship between Dayton, the Israelis and the leadership of the PA. Tensions were brought to public attention when Dayton gave a speech to a pro-Israeli think tank, the Washington Institute, in 2009. In the speech, Dayton appeared to be undermining the PA's claims of ownership over the security reforms, if not the entire statebuilding process. He also strongly emphasised the extent to which security sector coordination was a collaborative process with Israel and that the PA was its junior partner: 'we don't provide anything to the Palestinians unless it has been thoroughly coordinated with the state of Israel and they agree to it' (Dayton 2009).

Particularly controversial was the fact that Dayton seemed to present the PA security forces as collaborators with Israel while they were deployed within the West Bank to manage protests during the violent conflict in Gaza in late 2008. Though the protests were in fact relatively quiet, the environment was extremely tense and the PA went to significant lengths to try and manage public perceptions (Dayton 2009). Yet Dayton's comments exposed the reality that coordination had taken place, thus playing into Hamas' stereotype that the PA was effectively working as a patsy to America and Israel:

> So typically the Palestinian commander would call the Israeli commander in the area and say, 'We've got a demonstration going from point A to point B. That's very close to your checkpoint here at Bet El. We would appreciate it for two hours if you would leave the checkpoint so that we can get the demonstrators through, bring them back, you can come back'.
> And that's exactly what they did – amazing.
>
> (Dayton 2009)

The Fayyad government's response was to complain formally to the USSC and to distance itself from Dayton, reducing the level and frequency of informal meetings (see Perry 2011).

Yet behind the scenes, something far more insidious had been going on for some time. The role played by foreign intelligence agencies in shaping and bolstering the PA's security forces was not as it first appeared. As stated in the previous chapter, the role of UK and US intelligence agencies in both the planning and execution of the PA's assault on Hamas was significant. However, the level of complicity between the CIA and the two relevant Palestinian security forces – the Preventative Security and the General Intelligence – was much more integrated. According to some reports, the US government considered them 'an advanced arm of the war on terror' (Thrall 2010). Foreign involvement with Arafat's security forces had begun in the 1990s. In particular, this had centred on a relationship between covert forces such as the CIA and the British SIS and the two security forces that were particularly close to the President (the Preventative Security and the General Intelligence). The Clinton administration's greater interest in the 'peace process' in the late 1990s brought with it the direct involvement of CIA Director George Tenet, who sought to broker stronger ties between the Palestinian and Israeli security forces (Cobain 2009). (It is worth noting, of course, that it was Tenet who went on to author the Road Map, demonstrating the CIA's continued involvement with the issue under the Bush administration.) This was hardly an effective arrangement, though, and the lack of coordination between the covert forces and the other parts of donor governments led to significant duplication of efforts and much confusion (Sciolino 2000).

Officially, the US government took more of a back seat during the Intifada. But in reality, the CIA and Dayton remained deeply involved. Significantly, beginning in the early 2000s, the agency built a close relationship with two of Fatah's most powerful lieutenants, Mohammad Dahlan and Jabril Rajub (see Mahle 2005; Sikimic 2014). However, apart from making links and negotiating operational links between Israel and the Palestinians (sometimes to the objection and rancour of Rajub in particular), according to Melissa Boyle Mahle, American policy was largely aimless and 'ineffectual' (Sikimic 2014) throughout the late 1990s and 2000s – creating the 'outward appearance of doing something to move the "peace process" forward' (Mahle 2005), but in reality achieving little. Yet, with the rise of Hamas, the CIA's involvement transformed into something more substantial. According to media sources, Dahlan and his forces received special training and support in the effort to challenge Hamas' stronghold in Gaza (Mahle 2005).

Despite the blockade on working with the PA during the inclusion of Hamas as part of the unity government (2006–7), the USSC and the CIA maintained cooperative links with the General Intelligence and the Presidential Guard. This was legitimised by the fact that they were answerable directly to Abbas and not the government (Sikimic 2014). But despite their closeness to Abbas, the Americans were dismayed by his decision to work with Hamas. With British assistance (discussed in the previous chapter), they began formulating a plan to deal with the Islamists. This was 'Plan B' and on the ground it was led by Dayton, who engaged in further secret planning to produce more documents that fleshed out the alternative.

This alternative comprised a whole range of measures for capacity building in the PA. The document contained a particularly relevant appendix that detailed the security services and hinted at the drive against Hamas, but also outlined a much broader general approach. Most tellingly, this document was later re-written to make it appear as if the plan was a product of the PA President (Dayton 2009). The document, which was entitled 'An Action Plan for the Palestinian Presidency – 2007', was produced by the US State Department and argued that Hamas would surely benefit if Abbas were not kept as a strong centre of gravity within Palestinian governance. Thus, it outlined some suggestions for how Abbas could appear more convincing:

> Abbas, therefore, needs to present a concrete, meaningful, performance-based action plan that would render him more credible ahead of his discussions with the Israelis and the US ... [such a plan] should be considered as necessary components in the process of building a Palestinian State.
> (Rose 2008)

It is clear, then, that despite the fact that external third party involvement had been promoted as a means to ultimately end the occupation in line with the PA's rhetoric, evidence of what actually occurred points to the fact that this involvement had actually been directed at maintaining order and reinforcing trusted security institutions within the PA. With this in mind, Sayigh makes the link between the accelerating authoritarianism in the West Bank and the involvement of foreign covert forces explicit:

> In the West Bank, the intelligence agencies are emerging as autonomous power centres that acknowledge no higher, constitutional authority, even that of factions within Fatah with which they are closely allied. Both Abbas and Fayyad face an uncertain future ... they could be turned into little more than the civilian face for yet another Arab polity run by the mukhabarat (secret police), in this case with a strong, even pervasive behind-the-scenes role for Israel and the CIA.
> (US Department of State 2007)

There are three important outcomes of this process to consider. First was the expansion of the security forces' power, without the equivalent development of mechanisms of accountability, which helped to contribute to the acceleration of authoritarianism in Palestine (see Chapter 5). The second was the reinforcing of established US allies – the 'Fatah Old Guard' (Sayigh 2007, 16) – which inadvertently stymied reform. Third was the damage caused to the public image of the PA. In this case, in spite of various efforts to recast the covert agenda as Palestinian-led, the PA's legitimacy suffered from the perception that the government was too close to the US, particularly in the area of security coordination. This was largely a product of the fact that for many Palestinians, the role of the USSC – in its official capacity of training and supporting a Palestinian security force fit for a new state – was not always very easy to distinguish from its relationship with growing authoritarianism in the PA security forces and a moribund peace process (Sayigh 2007).

A storm in a teacup

As shown above (Table 6.2), polling data reflected public dissatisfaction with the Fayyad government throughout the period 2007–10. But as the following

124 The 'State of Palestine'

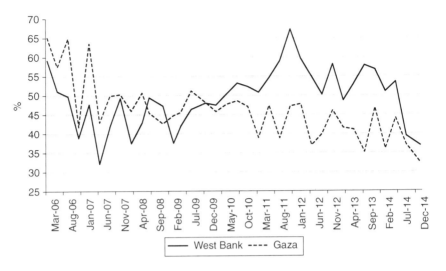

Figure 6.3 President Abbas' approval rating (West Bank and Gaza)[24]

graph shows, Abbas' personal reputation was also on the line. His approval rating failed to break the 50 per cent mark until mid-2010, and on four occasions between mid-2006 and 2009, it dropped below 40 per cent among West Bankers – the only Palestinians that he actually governed. As we can see, since December 2009, his popularity in Gaza has remained lower than in the West Bank and though there was a significant peak in his popularity among West Bankers at the time of his major speech at the UN in 2011, this did not last (for purposes of comparison, note that this was not replicated to the same extent among Gazans).

Abbas' fortunes declined further as the 'Arab Spring' spread from Tunisia to Egypt. The embattlement of his long-time ally Hosni Mubarak – described as the PA's most 'powerful patron' (Sayigh 2009) – and the rise of the Muslim Brotherhood, the organisation from which Hamas claims its lineage, were deeply troubling for Abbas for a number of reasons. It was, after all, Mubarak's regime that had kept Hamas contained within the Gaza Strip by blocking its access to the Sinai Peninsula, and had acted as a mediator between Israel and the Islamists (a role that kept Abbas at arm's length from an unwinnable situation; see Lynch 2011). But Mubarak's fall was also a blow in a broader sense. This was because he was seen as a figurehead for the 'moderate camp' among Arab leaders. He was an ever-present participant at peace talks and a stalwart supporter of Fatah's negotiation strategy. The fact that the Obama administration dithered and then apparently abandoned their ally in the face of the protests did not build confidence among the PLO hierarchy. According to the Crisis Group (2011, 1), 'several Palestinian leaders bemoaned what they considered Washington's hasty abandonment of Mubarak, some going so far as to suspect an American conspiracy to weaken the Arab world'. The ascendency of the Islamists in Egypt in the wake of Mubarak's fall appeared to offer the worst-case scenario for Abbas. In the end, the Brotherhood actually achieved little for Hamas, and throughout their period in office, Egypt maintained its closure of the Gaza Strip.[18] In fact, the Brotherhood's time in government – under the leadership of Mohammad Morsi – was short-lived and beset by internal fracturing. Barely a year after coming to power, Egypt's first democratically elected government was overthrown by a military coup, having faced overwhelming opposition from within the regime and from the general public for more or less the entire year.

But it was in this context that the Palestinian President needed to find a way to boost his legitimacy and the prospect of a Palestinian statehood bid presented an ideal opportunity. By taking the issue of recognising Palestine to a vote in New York, Abbas could potentially achieve three things: (a) give a grandstanding speech at the UN General Assembly, effectively lifting himself above the fray of domestic politics; (b) make a demand for a change that was both simultaneously and universally accepted – both internationally and among Palestinians – but that was (at that stage) likely to be entirely symbolic; and (c) take the opportunity to win plaudits at home by embarrassing the US and Israel, but without the risk of evoking the full ire of either.

Moreover, there were three factors that helped make this opportunity appear even more enticing. First was the evident frostiness of relations between the Israeli Prime Minister and the US President. They had apparently fallen out over the Obama administration's efforts to impose a ten-month partial freeze of Israeli settlement building during 2009–10, but it was also well-known that Netanyahu would have much preferred to have worked with a Republican administration. Provoking a further diplomatic spat was a good chance to highlight the wedge between the allies. Second was the fact that, by going to the UN, Abbas saw the possibility of outflanking his opponents on the domestic front. This would mean not only Hamas, which – now a *de facto* government in Gaza and forced into managing a miserable situation under the siege – had lost something of its allure as a resistance movement, but also Fayyad, who in late 2010 had begun to appear more like a rival.

Finally, by claiming ownership of a 'revolutionary process' that apparently challenged the US and the occupation head-on in an international forum, Abbas tried to present himself on the right side of the Arab Spring. In his 2011 speech to the UN General Assembly, he referenced these events directly: 'at a time when the Arab peoples affirm their quest for democracy – the Arab Spring – the time is now for the Palestinian Spring, the time for independence' (Abbas 2011). According to polling data, he was highly successful. According to the PSR's September 2011 poll, '83% support and 16% oppose going to the UN to obtain membership for a Palestinian state' (Palestinian Center for Policy and Survey Research 2011), though a majority also anticipated a US veto and reprisals from Israel.

This was Abbas' moment. He launched his attempt at a fait accompli: a single move that could simultaneously regain popular legitimacy, outmanoeuvre the Americans and Israelis by putting them in an awkward and compromising position, and steal the thunder from Fayyad's statebuilding plan.[19] In response, Fayyad backed away from the UN gambit. He publicly separated himself from the PLO's efforts, stating his view that 'conditions are not ripe for resumption of a political process capable of delivering an end to the Israeli occupation' (Milne and MacAskill 2015). This was not a complete *volte face* for the Prime Minister. In reality, he preferred a more nuanced approach that would have been less likely to corner the Americans and compel the predictable veto.[20]

By this time, however, the rift between Abbas and Fayyad was already wide. As interviews with former ministers in the Fayyad government revealed, the suspicion among the technocrats in the government was that Abbas was deeply concerned by Fayyad's broad appeal among the general public, but he was also sensitive to the pressure from Fatah allies who had lost out under Fayyad.[21] There were, however, bigger issues that actually gave the President the opportunity to dispense with Fayyad. The most important of these was the outbreak of large-scale protests in the West Bank in 2011 and a crippling fiscal crisis which, at a surface level, appeared to undermine the Prime Minister's economic credentials, but also highlighted two deeper issues: (a) the lack of genuine commitment of donor states to Palestinian development and progress towards independence – or, in other words, the 'emptiness of [donors'] claims regarding freedom and autonomy' (Turner and Kühn 2015, 144); and (b) the lack of progress that had actually been made in terms of the economic development of statebuilding.

Notes

1. For a useful overview, see Leech and Gaskarth (2015).
2. As some have pointed out, it may be better to think of this as being 're-recognised', as the PLO declared Palestinian statehood once before in 1988.
3. Parts of this section have also been published in my article 'After "Security First": An Analysis of Security Transition and "Statebuilding" in the West Bank 2007–11' (2014a).
4. All interviews were made anonymous for the safety of the interviewees, except in the case of Professor Abdl Sattar Qassem, who rejected the offer of anonymity and also referred to similar statements that had been published elsewhere.
5. Interview by the author, Nablus, 22 November 2009.
6. Interviews by the author, Nablus, 18 November 2009 and 9 December 2009.
7. Interview by the author, Nablus, 14 December 2009.
8. Interviews by the author, Nablus, throughout June 2010.
9. This conclusion has been suggested by other analysts, in particular with reference to the 'Village Leagues'; see Milton-Edwards and Farrell (2010).
10. Qassem at an informal lecture at Project Hope offices on 21 October 2009.
11. Interview by the author, Nablus, 15 December, 2009.
12. For example, Egypt under Mubarak; see Brownlee (2012).

13 It is interesting to note that a report by Kate Utting for the Royal United Service Institute – a think tank close to the British military – discusses the period 1945–8, where the British military was ejected from Mandatory Palestine by the insurgency of Jewish groups that would go on to form the State of Israel, in the context of learning lessons for contemporary conflicts. The existence of this report suggests that, for analysts like Uttering at least, it is not only the Palestinian insurgencies against great-power rule in this region that are worth studying; see Uttering (2009).
14 Demonstrating RAND's closeness to the US establishment, it is worth noting that one of the authors of this particular document, Robert Hunter, is a former US Ambassador to NATO.
15 Although a major aspect of this reform was instigated in 2005, both through the Law of Services and as a direct result of a presidential order, 'Abbas ordered the retirement of many high-ranking and long-serving members of the PSF, replacing them with younger, more reform-minded officers'; see Crisis Group (2010).
16 These changes were instigated at the lower levels of the security forces. During an interview with a senior official in the PA Ministry of Interior (2010), prior to the municipal elections in 2006, the PA had, in an effort to shore up support for Fatah particularly in the Gaza Strip, used recruitment to the security forces as a bribe to encourage support. One of Fayyad's first acts in government was to terminate the employment of any recruits taken on during this period who had not yet completed their training. However, in an interview with an analyst for an international think tank (2010), this author was told that there was significant suspicion that Fayyad had been forced to act more sympathetically towards the personal interests (financial or otherwise) of senior officers in the security services in order encourage them to assert a greater degree of loyalty to the PA rather than to Fatah. Data from research interviews, June and July 2010.
17 In line with the critical view of such reforms being undertaken as a part of a broader counterinsurgency push, it is interesting to note that the USSC project was also a source of big business to the private enterprises that comprised part of the US's military industrial complex. Indeed, according to Zanotti (2010, 19): 'The U.S.-based company DynCorp International is the primary contractor in charge of training, strategic planning, and equipment delivery ... $72.6 million worth of non-lethal equipment assistance from the State Department have been apportioned for PG and NSF troops ... The equipment furnished by DynCorp includes uniforms, field gear (tents, tarps, canteens, etc), vehicles, surveillance equipment (scopes and binoculars), first aid/medical gear, riot control gear, computers and other standard items'.
18 It is worth noting that the events of the 'Arab Spring' were also disruptive to Hamas' traditional alliances. With the outbreak of civil war in Syria, Hamas abandoned its long-standing alliance with the Assad regime and decamped to Qatar. It also separated itself decisively from Assad in 2012 and declared its support for the Syrian people; see Milton-Edwards (2013).
19 Cables from the South African Intelligence Agency in February 2015 revealed that Abbas was subject to considerable pressure from the US at the time of the statehood bid; see Milne and MacAskill (2015).
20 As I noted in an earlier article, 'Recognising Palestine: Six Critiques of the PLO's Internationalisation Strategy' (Leech 2014c): 'Fayyad, favoured approaching the UN Security Council with an interim proposal. This would ask them to enforce a resolution that did not demand statehood overtly, but instead asked for "ending the occupation". This could then have been followed later with an upgrade to statehood. The virtue of such an approach would have been that it would have effectively asked the US to do something that it might have been more likely to do. That is: agree to end the occupation – a goal that at least in its public statements it has been generally supportive of – rather than recognise a statehood bid by [the]

PLO that was not part of a broader framework. Though because the difference between these two efforts depends on the mere wording of each resolution, it may seem that neither was more likely to prove effective at bringing the key states into the consensus'.
21 Research interviews with two former officials in the Fayyad government, Ramallah, September and October 2014.
22 Data from the PSR. Graph complied by the author. The full question was: 'After the separation between Gaza and the West Bank, Hamas and the government of Ismail Haniyeh remained in power in Gaza and considered itself the legitimate government while President Abu Mazin formed a new government headed by Salam Fayyad followed by a new government headed by Fayyad and it too considered itself legitimate. What about you: which of the two governments do you consider legitimate – the government of Haniyeh or the government of Abu Mazin and Fayyad?' Note: in compiling the data for all charts, where there were multiple positive/negative responses, these were grouped, e.g. 'Good' and 'Very Good' were grouped together.
23 Data from the PSR. Graph complied by the author. Questions were: (a) 'Would you say that these days your security and safety, and that of your family, is assured or not assured?'; and (b) 'Tell us how do you evaluate the performance of the government headed by Salam Fayyad? Is it good or bad?' Despite the apparent directness of the question, in the case of Fayyad's approval rating, an additional option was included in the polling question. This allowed respondents to offer indifference. Thus, it would not be fair to compare the approval rating of Fayyad's government directly to that of Abbas' approval rating as President, as no such additional option was included in his case.
24 Data from the PSR. Graph complied by the author. The question was: 'Are you satisfied or not satisfied with the performance of Mahmud Abbas since his election as President of the PA?'
25 Data from the PSR.
26 Data for table taken from Crisis Group (2010). Note: civil defence (fire and natural disaster) programmes are sometimes still considered part of the security services structure as they official answer to the Ministry of Defence, but since they do not conduct practical policing or carry the same weight of influence in a political sense as they did under the Arafat regime, they are not included in this table.

7 'Economic peace'

In late November 2008, Israel's Prime Minister, Benjamin Netanyahu, addressed the United Jewish Communities General Assembly and outlined his view of what would become known as 'economic peace'. According to Haartez, Netanyahu said:

> We must weave an economic peace alongside a political process ... That means that we have to strengthen the moderate parts of the Palestinian economy by handing [over] rapid growth in those areas, rapid economic growth that gives a stake for peace for the ordinary Palestinians.
>
> (Ahren 2008)

In reality, Netanyahu's plan offered little that wasn't already widely understood as a main – and openly stated – objective of both Israeli and international efforts in Palestine. However, for the Prime Minister, the significance of 'economic peace' was more relevant in his domestic context. This was the challenge that Netanyahu faced in reconciling his right-wing domestic support base – which was strongly opposed to concessions to the Palestinians – and pressure from the US to, at least, play the role of peacemaker. In this regard, 'economic peace' was developed as a more conservative alternative to the 'disengagement plan' – which Ariel Sharon and Ehud Olmert had pursued – though it did not stray far from the basic logic of 'asymmetric containment' in the sense that it retained the basic relationship of Israeli dominance over a fragmented and encircled Palestine (see Khatib 2008).

For Netanyahu, in fact, 'economic peace' became the first element in a three-pronged approach intended to maintain the status quo by subtly shifting the tone and topic of discussion. The additional elements were: (a) to move the conversation on from the issue of accepting a 'two-state solution' – something that Netanyahu would do, albeit reluctantly and with numerous caveats, in a speech in 2009 – to the question of a new demand that the Palestinians accept Israel as a 'Jewish State';[1] and (b) to dilute American pressure on Netanyahu's administration by playing on the already fractious political environment in the US.[2]

But for other relevant actors, Netanyahu's 'economic peace' speech represented little more than the Prime Minister's acknowledgement, with its own spin of course, of a process that was already under way. And the reaction was more or less what was to be expected. International third parties, particularly Tony Blair, the Special Envoy of the International Quartet (an ad hoc group of interested parties), and the US administration (Cook 2013) – embraced it (Horovitz 2008). The PA, however, objected to the term 'economic peace' because it did not endorse Palestinian statehood, and the Palestinian population responded with suspicion, particularly in the wake of continued Israeli military action in the Gaza Strip. For instance, in an interview with the *Journal of Palestine Studies*, the then head of the Palestinian Monetary Fund (and later Deputy Prime Minister), Mohammad Mustafa, outlined the PA's objections to 'economic peace':

> We absolutely and categorically reject Netanyahu's project. There can be no economic peace without political peace and without the establishment of an independent and sovereign Palestinian state … Anyone serious about a better economy must first treat the political issues, starting from their very roots.
>
> (Karim, Tamari and Farraj 2010, 42)

In practice, however, there was little difference between 'economic peace' and the agenda of the PA. Both were predicated on a worldview that held that market forces could offer an alternative to political deadlock and could – potentially – act as a moderating influence on the appeal of political Islam (Feldman 2009).[3] This meant that all sides could claim credit for the apparent successes. As noted above, with respect to the dramatic spike in Palestinian economic growth between 2008 and 2010, these successes were evidently not insignificant, so much so that even the otherwise sober Palestinian Economic Policy Research Institute referred to the period as a 'boom' in one of its reports – though the report was far less sanguine regarding the distribution of economic growth among the Palestinian population or its sustainability (Larudee 2012).

Though this apparent improvement in conditions was rapid, it was also superficial and a product of increases in foreign aid as well as limited reduction in Israeli restrictions on movement. As a report by the United Nations Conference on Trade and Development (UNCTAD) (2010, 2) explained:

> Growth in the West Bank was driven mainly by unprecedented aid inflows. However, the restrictions on the movement of Palestinian goods and labour, and the destruction of much of the productive base, substantially reduced the economic benefits of this massive aid and limited it to the short term … The performance of the economy also reflects a very modest relaxation in the Israeli mobility restrictions within/to/from

the West Bank. However, not only does the relative improvement largely exclude Gaza and most parts of the West Bank, it remains reversible.

Clearly, then, the basic restrictive framework that had impeded the development of the Palestinian economy in previous years had not been removed. Instead, what may have seemed at first glance to be a hopeful sign of progress – perhaps towards 'economic peace', if that phrase can be taken at face value – was in fact merely evidence that the occupation's chokehold on the Palestinian economy was temporarily loosened while at the same time international donors funnelled in enormous quantities of aid.

The main goal of this chapter is to explain the background to this situation by examining the broader political and economic conditions encompassing Palestine's economy. This chapter presents this argument in two main sections. First, it looks at the broader nature of Israeli–Palestinian economic relations during the period in question, focusing on the basic logic of Israeli, Palestinian and international policy during this period. Second, it presents a snapshot of the major issues curtailing development in the Palestinian economy over the past few years. For the most part, this focuses on the structural impediments to economic development, which are tied to Israel's occupation and to the legal framework encompassing Israeli–Palestinian economic relations. It also notes the issue of inefficacies within the system resulting from corruption and the significant dependence on foreign aid. The next chapter follows up this discussion by looking at the particulars of the PA's economic programme during the statebuilding project and notes that, though there were at least two aspects of the plan that were – taken on their own merits – laudable, for the most part, the plan failed to address real issues of concern.

The main restrictions on Palestinian economic development

But what were these restrictions that so impeded the prospects of sustainable economic growth? Discussions in previous chapters have introduced the so-called 'Paris Protocol', a product of the Oslo process, which serves as the main legal framework for Palestine's economic relations, and have explained that – despite including some positive elements – it had a severely debilitating effect overall. This section expands on this; it looks at the protocol in more depth, but also looks at other significant factors that restrict Palestine's economic prospects. These include Palestine's dependence on foreign aid, the dominance of Israel's economy and the roots of the PA's fiscal instability.

The Paris Protocol

Although the general intentions of the Paris Protocol were to enable greater Palestinian control over its own economic destiny – albeit within limits – and in many ways the broad, immediate effect of its implementation was an improvement in basic conditions for many Palestinians, there were significant restrictions imposed on Palestinian autonomy. Finally, while the Protocol, as with all of the Oslo agreements, was meant to act as an interim step on the path to broader liberation, this transition was never realised.

As well as exceeding the transitory time limit that had been set for the establishment of a Palestinian state (that was originally intended to come into existence in the late 1990s), the Protocol has been violated numerous times, especially by Israel. Most of these violations can be categorised in terms of ignoring, limiting or selectively interpreting many of the Palestinian rights outlined in the agreement. The obvious power imbalance has resulted in a number of differences between the letter (and the spirit) of the original agreement and the practical way in which it has been implemented. According to Khalidi and Taghdisi-Rad (2009), the overall impact of the Protocol should be seen in a critical light, particularly because the way in which Israel implemented the agreement has subjected the smaller, weaker Palestinian economy to a rigorous liberalisation agenda, for which it was poorly suited.

Fiscal instability

As stated above, the PA suffered a serious fiscal crisis in 2011–12. This was triggered by delays in the provision of foreign aid, but was rooted in the longer-term diminishment of government revenues and increased spending by the PA. Austerity measures undertaken by the PA in an effort to control the crisis contributed to popular unrest in 2012 (see Leech 2014a). However, reports from various international agencies still make a strong case for urgent action to achieve fiscal stability.

One major source of this instability can be discussed under the rubric of 'fiscal leakage', which describes the loss of government revenue through inefficiencies. In Palestine, fiscal leakage 'exceeded $310 million in 2011, equivalent to 3.6 per cent of total gross domestic product (GDP) and 18 per cent of the tax revenue of the Palestinian National Authority. Around 40 per cent of the fiscal leakage is related to direct and indirect imports from Israel, and the remaining 60 per cent is in the form of evasion of customs duties' (Elkhafif, Misyef and Elagraa 2014, III). Such inefficiencies were the product of three factors: (a) an obstructive trade relationship that depended on indirect imports through Israel; (b) weak Palestinian control over exports; and (c) 'inconsistencies in the working mechanism for collection of purchase taxes and evasion of customs duties' (Elkhafif, Misyef and Elagraa 2014, III).

The most effective way of summarising the impact of these factors is to focus specifically on the practical reality of the tax collection process under the Protocol, as this encompasses examples of how each of the three main factors play out. The primary concern regarding fiscal leakage is with respect to the collection of indirect taxes (taxes drawn from transactions, such as levies on trade or purchase tax). The total cost of this loss is incalculable. However, it can be categorised in terms of its impact on 'diminished investment, production and employment, and in turn, a shrunken tax base and smaller direct tax revenues for the Palestinian National Authority treasury' (Elkhafif, Misyef and Elagraa 2014, 10). In addition, Israeli measures also undermine the PA's right to collect direct taxes, drawn primarily from profits and salaries.[4]

Direct taxation

According to Article V of the Paris Protocol: 'Israel and the Palestinian National Authority will each determine and regulate independently its own tax policy in matters of direct taxation, including income tax on individuals and corporations, property taxes, municipal taxes and fees'. It goes on to specify that Israel should transfer 75 per cent of the income taxes collected from Palestinian workers in Israel and 100 per cent of the taxes collected from Palestinian workers in Israeli settlements. Israel also deducts social security taxes and health insurance from Palestinian workers in Israel, despite the fact that the workers do not receive benefits in return. The total cost of these deductions is difficult to measure, though UNCTAD estimates the value in millions, even billions of dollars. Moreover, Israel has used the withholding of taxes collected on behalf of the PA as a punitive measure, most recently in January 2015 in response to the PLO's efforts to access the ICC. Israel had also taken similar steps before, only to release funds when the consequential fiscal difficulties looked likely to endanger the PA (BBC 2014).

Indirect taxation

There are two main ways in which the indirect taxation regime imposed by the Protocol comprise structural inefficacies and thus contribute to fiscal leakage. These are through: (a) restricting the PA's freedoms in terms of policy making and thus limiting its capacity to adapt to changing conditions; and (b) allowing for Israel unilateralism in policy terms without accounting for the – often detrimental – impact of such decision making on the Palestinian economy.

A clear example of the first issue is evident through the structure of VAT collection under the Protocol. Israel began VAT in the West Bank and Gaza Strip in 1976 and amended it in 1985.[5] The Paris Protocol in 1994 gave this system legitimacy and further entrenched it. According to the Protocol, the PA collects VAT on all goods and services produced in Palestine and those that are imported. The PA can set VAT no less than 2 per cent lower than Israel (effectively limiting it to a 15 per cent baseline). A clearance system is in place to allow the transfer of all (direct and indirect) revenues collected by the Government of Israel on behalf of the PA. This means that the Protocol allowed the PA a small margin for amendments to this tax.[6]

In addition, for products imported to Palestine via the Israeli crossings but from outside Israel, taxes collected should be transferred to the PA – within six days – as long as the end use is in Palestine. This is detailed in Article

III of the Protocol, which requires that the PA follow the same customs and tariff structure as Israel. In effect, this system formalises that which was introduced in the oPts in 1967. This structure prevents the PA from using its discretion over customs and tariff rules that might otherwise represent a useful toolset for protecting the local productive economy and encouraging growth (though it exercises limited rights to impose tariffs on imports from Jordan and Egypt). For Palestine, customs revenues account for 25 per cent of total public revenue. Decreases in revenue from sources like customs duties can harm economic growth in Palestine by reducing the PA's capacity to invest in the public sector. Yet, according to UNCTAD, 'the majority of customs and tax rates are set and modified over time according to the needs and evolution of the economic situation in Israel without considering Palestinian needs, thus exclusively serving the interests of the Israeli economy' (Elkhafif, Misyef and Elagraa 2014, 18). In other words, if and when Israel reduces the amount that is gleaned from customs taxes and tariffs (which it might do for legitimate domestic reasons), this can have a direct impact on the funding available to the Palestinian public services (health, education, etc.). Such a reduction in public expenditure is likely to result in an extra burden for the private sector and the uncertainty surrounding it is also likely to reduce the appeal for foreign investments (El-Jafari and Doaud 2011).

The second issue – the impact of Israeli unilateral decision making without regard for its impact on the Palestinian economy – is evident in the examples regarding the implementation of purchase tax in particular.[7] The way in which the purchase tax regime functions is problematic for the Palestinian economy because it does not protect Palestinian industries from their larger, more developed Israeli counterparts. According to Elkhafif, Misyef and Elagraa (2014, 19):

> Levying this tax has effectively weakened the competitiveness of similar Palestinian goods. Although it is imposed on both Palestinian and Israeli goods and imports to both markets, Israeli goods do not suffer from trade complications, high transportation costs or the lack of appropriate infrastructure. Further, Israeli goods, unlike their Palestinian counterparts, can benefit from economies of scale.

In an effort to counteract this effect, between 1999 and 2005, the PA's Ministry of Finance elected not to collect purchase taxes on most products except for alcohol and cigarettes. This therefore constituted another form of fiscal leakage. Overall, Israel amends its trade and taxation policies frequently and often in such a way that ignores the requirements to coordinate trade policy between Israel and the PA that is set out in the Protocol. Israel's broader interests align with neoliberal policies and it has continued to implement these in spite of its agreements with the PA. According to UNCTAD, Israel 'has absolved itself of all commitments regarding coordination and consultation through the Joint Economic Committee, even though Articles II and III of the

Protocol stipulate that any changes in import taxation policies are to be made known beforehand and in consultation between the two parties' (Elkhafif, Misyef and Elagraa 2014, 20).

Lack of a Palestinian currency

Following from the Paris Protocol, the Israeli shekel, the US dollar and the Jordanian dinar were granted status as the main currencies in the Palestinian territories. This granted Israel – whose banks continued to operate in the Palestinian territories – significant power and effectively entrenched another mechanism of control over the Palestinian economy. Approximately 10 per cent of all Israeli shekels are used in the Palestinian market, which may be worth around $300 million per annum to Israel's economy.

The fact that the Palestinian market is dominated by the Israeli currency has four main outcomes. As Shaban (2013) explains:

- It creates demand for the shekel on international currency markets that would not otherwise be there (in fact, there is little demand for the shekel at all outside Israel and Palestine).
- Because most international aid is supplied in currencies that must be exchanged into shekels – in Israeli banks – for use in the Palestinian market, the demand on the shekel is artificially inflated by Palestinian dependence on foreign aid. Moreover, those banks will also gain a profit from performing those exchanges.
- Further, 'Palestinians are also deprived of benefiting from the issuance profits, and their economy is subjected to the fluctuations of the Israeli market'.

In addition, Israeli banks sometimes fail to replace damaged shekel bills from Palestinian banks on a one-for-one basis, effectively taking large quantities of money out of the Palestinian economy.[8]

Opportunities lost to the occupation

In addition to the impact of the Paris Protocol on the PA's finances, the material infrastructure of the occupation is also extremely debilitating to the Palestinian economy in other respects. In particular, this can be broken down into three categories of issues: (a) restrictions on movement and communications; (b) access to natural resources; and (c) impact on the labour market.

Restrictions on movement and communications

As discussed in previous chapters, Israeli restrictions on movement within the oPts have led to a range of important consequences, including the highly fractured nature of Palestinian society. In the West Bank this is manifest through the complex overlay of: (a) territorial divisions created by the 'Oslo II' agreements of 1995; (b) the construction of Israel's 'separation barrier'; and (c) the archipelago of Israeli settlements and their related infrastructure.[9]

In terms of impediments to development, Israel's restrictions on movement are highly debilitating. This issue is primarily a result of the inability to calculate the nature of potential impediments to transporting people or goods. In December 2013, there were 256 surprise checkpoints as compared with approximately 340 in March 2012. Between January and September 2011, there was an average of 495 surprise checkpoints. This is a dramatic increase from the average of 65 surprise checkpoints between September 2008 and March 2009 (B'Tselem 2015). Ostensibly, the number and scale of checkpoints in the West Bank are tied to the broader political and security climate (though this rationale neither accounts for the possibility of random checkpoints nor the fact that Israel forces and settlers in the West Bank can themselves be seen as a 'security threat').[10] Moreover, checkpoints have, to some extent, been politicised in their own right by the Israeli government, which occasionally reduces the number of checkpoints as a gesture of 'goodwill' (for an example, see *Haaretz* 2009).

While it might seem obvious that the prevalence of checkpoints may be inconvenient, humiliating and even damaging to the economy by delaying or discouraging travel that would otherwise be important to normal business, the true cost of checkpoints is much broader. This is because checkpoints effectively insert an element of risk into normal business that would not otherwise be present. As Neve Gordon and Dani Flic (2009, 552) explain, the reason why the impact of these checkpoints can have such a detrimental impact on the Palestinian economy is largely because of the inherent uncertainty they create:

> [Checkpoints] rupture the connection between time and space, making it virtually impossible to calculate the relationship between the two, a relationship which most people living in the West take for granted. Thus, the restrictions on movement as well as the destruction of the infrastructure of existence create a profound sense of disorientation; the possibility of calculating the future is accordingly undermined, and one tends to lose all sense of control. It is as if one is left at the mercy of fate, charity, and faith.

Even at times when the risk factor is minimised and crossing times are relatively predictable, the additional cost in terms of time, opportunity and potential business of checkpoints remains very real. One way to demonstrate this is to look at the standard methods Israel uses to examine the goods transported across entry points to Palestine. This is known as the 'back-to-back' system. As explained by a PA spokesperson, Abdel Hafiz Nofal, in 2011:

'Economic peace' 137

> The back-to-back truck-loading system, which applies to all West Bank exports, does not allow trucks to cross into Israel. Instead, goods are offloaded from a Palestinian truck and inspected before being moved to an Israeli truck for final delivery within Israel or overseas ... PA customs and border officials are prohibited at Allenby Bridge and at crossing points between the West Bank and Israel ...
>
> Palestinian goods moving to or from Jordan must cross Allenby Bridge, where cargo is removed from Palestinian trucks, inspected, and then loaded onto Jordanian trucks. The process takes 4–8 hours or longer, and Allenby's scanners cannot handle large cargo, reports the World Bank.
>
> (*IRIN* 2011)

Taken together with the other restrictions on movement (settler-only roads, road blocks, sieges and closures), the impact has been dramatic. For the West Bank, the following points should be noted: (a) restrictions make it harder for Palestinians to commute to work; (b) restrictions make the transportation of goods more difficult; (c) transportation costs are increased, leading to lower profits; (d) internal trade is made more costly, inefficient and less certain; and (e) Palestinian importers and exporters have limited access to international markets due to Israeli restrictions on crossing points. The economy of the West Bank has effectively become split into small localities with very limited access to international markets and virtually no access to natural resources (B'Tselem 2011a).

More recent efforts, led by the Quartet, have been directed at making some checkpoints – in particular, those between the West Bank and Israel – less invasive. Examples of this include the USAID-funded upgrade of 'crossing points' between Jenin and Nazareth at Jalama (discussed in Chapter 4). One long-term impact of these developments is that the Palestinian economy has been skewed away from productive industries and towards ever-greater reliance on the services sector. As Figure 7.1 shows, services comprise the largest area of economic activity in Palestine.

Services are also the largest sector for employment.[11] While there is, of course, nothing inherently wrong with a large service sector for the Palestinian economy,[12] the point here is that, by comparison, the other sectors of potential economic activity – such as construction and manufacturing – where Palestine has considerable economic potential are evidently underdeveloped. Another, less obvious side to this issue is the impact on other forms of communications. For example, how Palestine's networked communications services (Internet and mobile phone access) are underdeveloped relative to comparable states. For Palestinians, networked communications remain severely limited by Israeli restrictions. These prevent the construction of cell towers, importing equipment for the advancement of Ethernet and fibre optics. According to Niksic, Eddin and Cali (2014, 37):

138 'Economic peace'

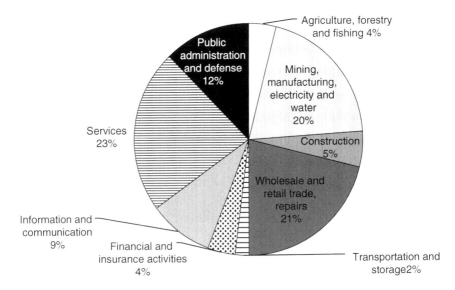

Figure 7.1 Breakdown of West Bank GDP by sector (economic activity), 2013[19]

To provide optimal signal coverage throughout the West Bank, the two Palestinian mobile operators would need to erect a total of 330 towers in Area C. Over the last 10 years, one operator has applied for licenses from the Israeli Authorities to erect 60 such towers. So far, only one final approval for a single site has been granted.

Data from 2012 shows that Internet penetration is at 57.7 per cent in Palestine, which is comparable with other Middle Eastern states. However, despite widespread usage of smartphones, Palestine is denied access to 3G networks because Israel refused to grant the PA access to sufficient bandwidth (Hess-Skinner 2015). Many Palestinians are therefore forced to use Israeli networks to connect. It is estimated that this may cost the Palestinian economy around $100 million each year (Niksic, Eddin and Cali 2014). Again, if these issues were resolved, the potential resulting contribution to the Palestinian economy would be around $48 million, or 0.5 per cent of Palestinian GDP (Niksic, Eddin and Cali 2014).

Access to natural resources

Area C comprises about 61 per cent of the West Bank territory. According to the details in Oslo II (1995), Area C should have been transferred to Palestinian control by 1997, yet it remains under complete Israeli control. Area C is not only the home for most natural resources in the West Bank – it is also the key to creating a contiguous Palestinian state within the West Bank.

Israel's unilateral control of Area C impedes economic development there and is extremely detrimental to the Palestinian economy overall. According to Niksic, Eddin and Cali (2014, 51):

> The alleviation of today's restrictions on Palestinian investment, movement and access in Area C could bring about significant expansion of many sectors of the Palestinian economy ... Relatively conservative estimates show that the direct gains, in terms of potential value added in these sectors, would amount to at least USD 2.2 billion, equivalent to some 23 percent of 2011 Palestinian gross domestic product.

The three main aspects of this are agriculture, access to the Dead Sea and potential for mining and construction. The fact that these issues are apparently irresolvable at this point contributes significantly to the skewing of Palestine's economic output towards such a disproportionate dependence on the services sector. In the mid-1990s, agriculture contributed 14 per cent of the West Bank's GDP; however, by 2011, this had fallen to 5.1 per cent. Yet there are currently twice as many Palestinians employed in agricultural labour than there were in the mid-1990s. This represents significant inefficiency in the agricultural labour market (Niksic, Eddin and Cali 2014).

This trend is directly linked to the restrictions imposed on Palestinian agriculture and investment in related infrastructure by Israel, but also speaks to the fact that there are few alternative avenues of economic development in the rural West Bank. Israel's restrictions 'impede access to large swathes of fertile land and essential water sources as well as constrain the development of the infrastructure needed for modern market-oriented agriculture' (B'Tselem 2014). A critical factor contributing to this situation is a lack of access to water. The division of the water supply was established as part of the Oslo process. This established that, for water from the mountain aquifer (comprising approximately one-third of underground reserves), 80 per cent would supply Israel, while only 20 per cent would be under Palestinian control. However, Palestinian access to water is in fact even more limited than these restrictions mandate. Due to technical constraints, the Palestinians obtain only about 73 per cent of their supply granted to them under the Oslo process. Various donor-funded projects have sought to improve access to water (B'Tselem 2014), though Palestinians are regularly forced to purchase water supplies from Israeli companies.[13]

The second issue, relating to denial of access to the Dead Sea, also prevents the development of a potentially highly significant contribution to the West Bank economy. If this were to take place, it would be through two main avenues of economic activity: exploiting the vast mineral wealth and developing the tourism industry. The World Bank report notes that both Israel and Jordan benefit greatly from their exploitation of Dead Sea minerals and suggests that if the requisite investment and logistical improvements were made, Palestine could have a chemical extraction industry on a similar scale to that of Jordan's (adding around 9 per cent to Palestine's GDP). Tourism at the Dead Sea would also be a significant boost for the Palestinian economy. Currently tourism contributes only 3 per cent of Palestine's GDP and constitutes only 2 per cent of the labour market, though data suggests that this has increased from a deep trough in the early 2000s. Based on comparisons with the Israeli industry, at full potential tourism for the Palestinians could lead to an increase of nearly 3,000 jobs. It could also lead to 'annual revenues of some USD 290 million and value added of about USD126 million, equivalent to 1 percent of 2011 Palestinian GDP' (Niksic, Eddin and Cali 2014, 65).

The third issue relates to mining and construction. As it stands, stone mining and quarrying contributes about 15,000 jobs to Palestine's labour market and about 2 per cent of the Palestinian economy. Stone is Palestine's most important export at about 17 per cent of total exports. Palestinian stone enjoys an international reputation. There is also considerable potential for further expansion of this industry, yet it faces significant restrictions. Israel's Civil Administration controls the issuing of permits in Area C. In fact, according to the World Bank, no new permits have been issued to Palestinian companies to open quarries in Area C since 1994. Companies that continue to operate risk significant penalties (of up to $30,000) and unscheduled closures:

> The opportunity cost of restricted Palestinian access to ... marble and stone in Area C is significant. Accurate and comprehensive data are however unavailable ... [yet] a conservative estimate of potential value added of USD 241 million per year can be made, though equivalent to 2 percent of 2011 GDP.
>
> (Niksic, Eddin and Cali 2014, 25)

Israeli restrictions also severely impede the demand side of the construction industry. Demand for housing is still extremely high and, as a result, it is estimated that Palestinian property prices have increased by approximately 24 per cent since 1996. In spite of these restrictions, the PA, with backing from Qatari investors, has planned and begun construction of a new city north of Ramallah called Rawabi. This is intended to create 6,000 new homes. However, the development continues to be impeded by Israeli restrictions (Kershner 2014).

Impact on the labour market

The three main issues of concern relating to the Palestinian labour market are: (a) the high level of unemployment; (b) the extremely low participation of women in the labour force; and (c) the low level of wages. Figure 7.2 shows that, compared to the average rate for other developing countries in the region, Palestine has a higher rate of unemployment. The unemployment rate in Palestine has grown significantly from a low of around 11 per cent in 1998, at which time Palestine's was only just higher than Israel's (9 per cent) and was

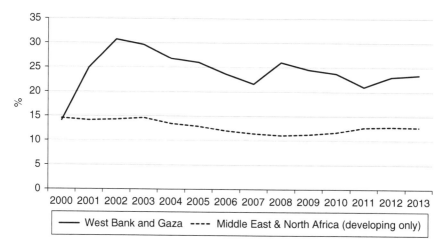

Figure 7.2 Unemployment as a percentage of labour force, Palestine vs. average of developing states in the region[20]

comparable with Iran and Yemen. It was far below Iraq (19 per cent), Libya (19 per cent) and Algeria (23 per cent).[14]

Palestine has a lower rate of female participation in the labour force than the regional average (29 per cent). The situation is particularly bad for educated women, 'as women's unemployment rate increases with their educational attainment, in contrast with men' (Al-Kafri and Omeira 2012). This situation is likely to be the product of a range of factors, including:

- the political and military constraints of the occupation which restricts women's access to work opportunities;
- weak demand for women's labour;
- the fact that women face more hurdles in accessing credit compared to men;
- overwhelming competition for Palestinian women-owned enterprises (particularly in the agricultural sector) created by the deep penetration of Israel's goods into Palestinian markets;
- a significant mismatch between skills learned in formal education and the necessary skills for accessing the labour market;
- patriarchal structures in Palestinian society; and
- the legal regime, which excludes many economic activities that are dominated by women.[15]

Clearly, some of these factors are applicable to both men and women, though the severity of the labour market crisis leaves little room for any form for improvement in either women's or men's access to jobs. Data from

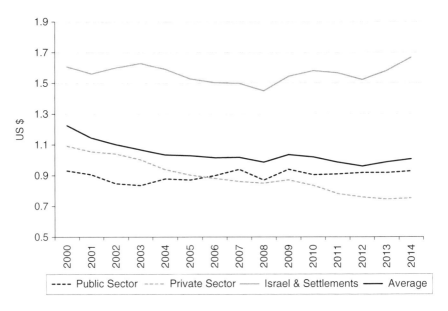

Figure 7.3 Average daily wage in the West Bank by sector (real terms)[21]

interviewees seemed to confirm these findings: 'there are few offers available for men and women ... because of traditions ... most of the jobs will go to men ... At a certain level if you compete [as a women] you might win, but when the unemployment is extremely high ... then [the jobs] will go to men'.[16] One factor that might account for some of the discrepancy is that many women are employed in the informal sector and, as such, accounting for their participation in the labour market is less strict. This issue is particularly evident in the agricultural sector and – particularly relevant to Nablus – in so-called micro-industries such as textiles. In these contexts, women tend to work in a family setting and the labour is neither fully recognised nor regulated.[17]

The final major issue in relation to the Palestinian labour market is the issue of low wages, in particular, as this issue relates to the moribund state of the private sector. As shown by Figure 7.3, the average daily pay in Palestine had decreased in real terms during the period 2000–12. Moreover, while public sector wages have remained relatively consistent throughout the period – though there was a slight peak between 2005 and 2007 – private sector wages have fallen quite significantly to only around 68 shekels in 2014. Daily pay in Israel and the settlements has increased by nearly 21 shekels from its lowest in 2007 to 2014.

Again, even though pay conditions are poor across the board, women are again worse off. According to the International Labour Organization – a branch of the UN – there is a significant pay gap between genders in Palestine.

This gap is much larger in some sectors than others. On average across all sectors, women's median daily wage is 84 per cent that of men's. For women employed in the manufacturing sector, the median daily pay is 57 per cent that of men's. For the most part, this discrepancy is not a product of the fact that men and women are paid different amounts for the same work; it is the result of the fact that occupations that are more frequently filled by women are paid less well than jobs usually undertaken by men. This phenomenon is present in both the public and private sectors (Al-Kafri and Omeira 2012). The most profound example is in construction, where not only are men paid the highest daily rate of all sectors, but there are also so few women employed that there is no data to record an average wage for women.[18]

It is also worth noting that although the PA introduced a minimum wage law in 2013 at a rate of 1,450 shekels ($375) per month, evidence suggests that it has been completely ineffective. This was despite the fact that the minimum wage was below the relative poverty line of 2,293 shekels ($593) and the deep poverty line was 1,832 shekels ($474). As the PCBS points out, 'in the West Bank about 22.9% of wage employees in the private sector received less than minimum monthly wage' (PCBS 2015).

Dependence on foreign aid

As discussed in previous chapters, the PA was heavily dependent on international donors and in many respects was forced to pay an extremely high political price for this. In raw economic terms, donor funds not only provided much of the initial capital the PA needed to fund its institution building, but also covered a large deficit in the PA's annual finances. At the beginning of the statebuilding process, 87 international donor states pledged some $7.7 billion ($7.4 billion according to some early reports) in support of the PRDP when it was launched in Paris. It was made clear that this pledge was tied to the political progress on negotiations made at the Annapolis Peace Conference in 2007 and was predicated on the functionalist assumption that a 'virtuous cycle of economic growth arising from parallel actions by the PA and Israel' (World Bank 2008a, 2) could be realised (LaFranchi 2007). This was only the tip of the iceberg, however, as Tartir and Wildeman (2014, 433) note:

> One calculation put total aid given at around USD 24.6 billion between 1993 and 2012. Aid inflows increased from an annual average of USD 656 million between 1993 and 2003, to over USD 1.9 billion since 2004; and international aid increased by 17 times overall between 1993 and 2009.

This level of spending obviously bought international donors significant power in the West Bank, but beyond this obvious point, there were two important additional implications that are worth noting. Despite its apparent scale, the level of foreign aid that was supplied often fell short of what was required in order to maintain the PA's basic operations. Moreover, the mechanisms through which aid money was dispersed within Palestine were – despite appearances – fiercely political. This problem was understood by the donor institutions themselves and, according to one report produced by the World Bank (2008b, 9):

> Since Paris, the PA has been unable to plan expenditures beyond a two-month horizon due to difficulties in securing support for the recurrent budget, and delays in translating development project pledges to actual commitments ... thus necessitating regular PA efforts to secure monthly assistance packages from a variety of donors, many of whom have pledged funds in Paris but have yet to transfer resources.

In spite of these concerns, international donors were fully prepared to use their financial support for the PA as a means to exercise influence over domestic Palestinian politics. Analysis of the policies actually pursued by the PA shows that the primary concerns of donors were in fact: (a) the good governance and anti-corruption measures; and (b) reforms of public infrastructure development that would seek to mitigate the impact of fiscal leakage to the PA. Of course, neither of these goals in their own right was foolish. The real sources of the problems with these policies resulted from the way in which they were to be tackled. In answer to both issues – corruption and fiscal leakage – the donor-led response effectively ignored the reality of the occupation. And in so doing, they promoted policies that only added to the burden faced by some of the most vulnerable Palestinians.

Rather than detailing the progress of 'economic peace', then, the data presented in this chapter outlines a process of continued fragmentation and containment of the Palestinian economy through the structures of Israel's domination. As this chapter has shown, the Palestinian economy today remains fundamentally weak, regardless of the statebuilding agenda and – particularly with respect to the prevalence of foreign aid – there are aspects that are weaker now than they were prior to 2007. The next chapter looks at the particulars of the PA's economic agenda in detail and goes into more depth as to why this failure was more or less inevitable.

Notes

1 For a fascinating and detailed insight into the background of Netanyahu's thinking in relation to this issue, see *MADAR* (2013) and also Shalhat (2015).
2 This would come to the fore most prominently in early 2015, when Netanyahu – at the height of a domestic election campaign – accepted an invitation from the speaker of the US House of Representatives, a Republican and an ally, to speak to a joint session of Congress. Even in the context of a strongly pro-Israel media environment, this proved controversial on two counts: first, the White House considered the Prime Minister's visit a breach of protocol; and, second, Netanyahu used the occasion to publicly berate the President over a his policy of pursuing an agreement

between the US, Iran and a number of other states of Iran's nuclear programme. See Mearsheimer and Walt (2012), Baker (2015) and *New York Times* (2015).

3 According to Nathan Thrall (2014), this last goal – of challenging one of Hamas' main points of appeal – was in fact relatively successful: 'The real barrier to a West Bank uprising has not been, as Hamas has claimed, Abbas's collaboration with Israel. It has been social and political fragmentation, and the widespread Palestinian acquiescence that national liberation should come second to the largely apolitical and technocratic projects of statebuilding and economic development. These are far greater obstacles for Hamas'.

4 Because of the weaknesses – especially in terms of productivity – of the Palestinian economy, direct taxation is not as reliable a source of regular income to the Palestinian treasury as it might be in a more advanced economy. In general terms, this is not unusual for developing economies, though many of the weaknesses in the Palestinian economy are specific.

5 'VAT is defined as an indirect tax levied on each transaction, whether it involves a good or a service. It is a tax imposed on the increase in the value of the transaction, meaning that it is levied on the difference between the buying price and the selling price (profit) at all stages of the transferral of goods or services from one seller or manufacturer to another until it reaches the end user' (Elkhafif, Misyef and Elagraa 2014, 22).

6 For the PA, VAT resulting from purchasing products from the Israeli market should be calculated based on a 'clearance bill mechanism', a document that proves purchase or sale of goods between the two markets. This bill is both: (a) a condition for clearance revenue between the two sides; and (b) the only official document that goes with the movement of goods and services across the two markets. The VAT on locally produced goods requires clearance between both sides and tax collection is undertaken according to the end use of the good or service. VAT is an important source of income to the PA and revenue cleared through these measures constitutes an increasingly large portion of that. According to UNCTAD (based on official statistics from the PA treasury), 'clearance revenues reached $1.5 billion in 2011, some 20 per cent above the year before, due to the 19 per cent increase in the amount of clearance from VAT and the 16 per cent increase in import taxes. Clearance revenue from fuels constitutes one third, customs duties, another third, and VAT, the remaining third' (Elkhafif, Misyef and Elagraa 2014, 22–3).

7 Purchase tax differs from VAT in that it is usually levied as part of the production cost or sales price (and therefore is effectively included in the price of a product rather than being added at the end). Purchase tax is also selectively applied to particular goods/services while VAT is usually more or less universally applied to all transactions. It also differs from customs that focus on imported products only. Instead, purchase tax may be imposed in order to achieve particular economic or political goals. For instance, higher rates of purchase tax can be used to discourage the use of products considered damaging to the society or its environment (e.g. cigarettes and alcohol), or to products considered non-essential but with a high profit margin (e.g. cosmetics), or to help protect local industries by making competing imported goods less competitive. It is imposed in high rates on goods that have negative effects on the environment and health. It is also imposed on complementary goods and goods with high profit margins, such as cars, car parts, cigarettes, alcohol, fuels and cosmetics. Purchase taxes have been levied in the oPts since 1967 (following Israeli military orders 31, 643 and 740, the Israeli purchase tax law of 1952, law No. 1/1962 and other Israeli laws). See Elkhafif, Misyef and Elagraa (2014).

8 According to Shaban (2013), 'the situation in Gaza is a clear example in this regard. Since the imposition of the Israeli blockade in 2007, after Hamas took over the Gaza Strip – which Israel has declared "a hostile territory" – Israeli banks stopped dealing directly with banks in Gaza. This has caused a chronic shortage of shekel

'Economic peace'

bills in the Gaza market, which in turn has led to a significant difference in the currency exchange rates between the Gaza market and the markets of the West Bank and Israel. This resulted in the creation of a parallel black market that took advantage of the difference in the exchange rates'.
9 In Jerusalem and Gaza, the nature of restrictions on movement is different, but its consequences contribute to far worse overall economic and social conditions in those enclaves.
10 Violence carried out by Israeli settlers is frequently directed towards Palestinians, though in some cases Israeli settlers have been considered a security threat by the State of Israel itself. For statistics on violence between Israeli settlers and Palestinians, see data from UN OCHA at: www.ochaopt.org.
11 According to data from the PCBS, services comprised about 30 per cent of employment for males in the labour force and nearly 60 per cent for females in the labour force in 2013.
12 Indeed, according to some analyses, growth in the services sector can be seen as the key to overall economic development; see UNCTAD (2012).
13 See Niksic, Eddin and Cali (2014).
14 All data from the World Bank's databank, available at: http://databank.worldbank.org/data/home.aspx.
15 For example, self-employed workers, seasonal workers, unpaid family workers, domestic workers and those involved in unpaid domestic care and reproductive work at home. See Botmeh (2013).
16 Interview with representatives from an NGO focused on women's access to business.
17 Based on interviews with trade union representatives in Nablus, 19 November 2009. Another related concern is child labour. According to the PCBS, in 2010 there were 65,000 children between 5 and 14 (about 6 per cent) who were working either paid or unpaid. More males are employed than females and the agricultural sector is the biggest employer of children (47.6 per cent of children aged 10–17). See PCBS (2011) and ILO (2012a).
18 Note that the available data does not differentiate between construction in settlements, Israel and the oPts.
19 All data from the PCBS. Graph complied by the author.
20 All data from the World Bank. Graph compiled by the author.
21 All data from the PCBS. Graph compiled by the author. Note: the real wage is approximate as it is based on the nominal wage from the West Bank divided by Consumer Price Index for all of Palestine.

8 Disaster, capitalism and Palestine

When Salam Fayyad left office in June 2013, he left a mixed record on the economy. During the first two years of the technocratic government (mid-2007 to 2009), the rate of economic activity in the West Bank and the Gaza Strip rocketed by nearly 30 per cent (see Figure 8.1).[1] However, the record also included a severe fiscal crisis beginning in 2011, falling average wages across the board (except for Palestinians working in Israel and the settlements) and a stymied, near-debilitated private sector.

The previous chapter presented the case that the basic structures that contained and limited the Palestinian economy (which were – for the most part – a product of Israel's occupation) remained unaffected throughout the period. In terms of the PA's economic programme, then, this clearly meant that it was ineffective. Though the PA's economic agenda cannot be blamed for creating such debilitating economic conditions, despite promising economic development and movement towards greater independence from Israel, the PA evidently did not achieve much in the way of sustainable development. Moreover, in some cases, the PA's actions – particularly in relation to imposing a raft of neoliberal policies under the heading 'good governance' – actually made conditions more difficult for some Palestinians.

The PA's economic agenda during this period can perhaps be best viewed as comparable to a failed conjuring act. It involved an audacious attempt at misdirection – through developing a pretence that the PA had greater influence over the Palestinian economic climate than it did – but ultimately, rather than regaling its audience with a bold and thrilling payoff, the climax of this stunt was a flop. Moreover, given the conditions under which the PA was operating and the tools with which it attempted to create change, disappointment was inevitable.

Simply put, the goals that the PA outlined would have been nearly impossible to achieve under even the most favourable of circumstances. The task was made all the more difficult by virtue of the fact that the policy framework adopted by the PA – a strongly neoliberal model of development – was one that was very poorly suited for the purposes of pursuing national liberation. In something of an echo of the PA's relationship with foreign governments

148 *Disaster, capitalism and Palestine*

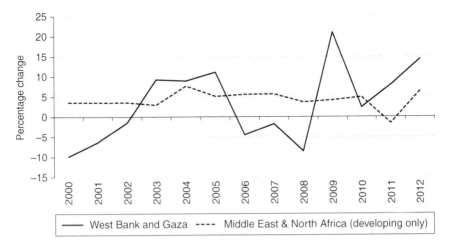

Figure 8.1 Percentage change in GDP growth rates 2000–12, West Bank and Gaza Strip vs. regional average (developing countries)[44]

vis-à-vis the security sector, the PA played out the role of a local sheriff to the global and regional power structure.

This chapter presents the case for this conclusion in five main sections. The first presents an overview of the PA's economic agenda. The second looks at the key policies designed to reform and grow the Palestinian economy. In particular, this section discusses the policies of 'good governance' and the PA's shift towards industrial zones. The third looks at how and where these policies either (a) fell short or (b) actually made conditions worse for some of the most vulnerable West Bank communities. The fourth focuses specifically on the elements of the PA's agenda that can be considered its 'resistance' strategy and specifically the PA's 'boycott campaign'. Finally, the chapter discusses the development of the fiscal crisis under the PA, which ultimately led to the end of the Fayyad government.

Disaster capitalism

As discussed in previous chapters, the primary justification for the PA's undemocratic character – after the 2006 election was effectively annulled – was that this would enable Palestine to advance economically and that development would act as leverage on Israel and its allies to establish a Palestinian state (though, as we have seen, this was always unlikely to occur given the fact that the PA's efforts never seriously challenged the severe limitations on the economy imposed by the occupation's material structure). According to the PA's documents, 'development' meant three things: improvements in the social environment, economic growth and combating corruption (Palestinian Authority 2007). The PA also launched a campaign of boycotts against Israeli settlements, which was designed to supplement this appeal for legitimacy. The PA tied its approach to development to a broader notion of progress towards peace. However, this definition falls far short of genuine political change.[2]

The PA priorities were broad and directed both towards economic growth and improvements in public welfare. The latter included improvements in law and order, the economy and combating corruption. The PA also claimed it would focus on development in rural areas and would also pursue a range of other measures designed to demonstrate its claim over Area 'C' as integral to the future Palestinian state. In practice though, the policies that it had pursued in the West Bank were designed specifically to re-orient the economy and effectively integrate Palestinian labour policies with the security requirements of Israel's occupation apparatus. The PA's pursuit of a 'good governance' framework, developed with the support of the British government's DFID, created conditions that were equivalent to economic deregulation. This allowed already powerful elites to extend their control over the market even further than they had done previously under the PA.[3]

As was the case under the PA's security agenda, Nablus was on the frontline. In such a way that brings to mind Naomi Klein's concept of 'disaster capitalism', it was precisely because Nablus had suffered so badly during the Second Intifada that it could be considered a testing ground for the neoliberal economic policy (Klein 2008). The events of the Intifada had wrecked the economy and undermined several of the city's powerful dynasties. Nablus could be seen as a blank canvas and ripe for reform. More specifically, the PA's plans for Nablus were based on the conviction that its economic structure had to change from an old system of informality, clientelism and outdated industry, and embrace a new order of 'good governance' and free markets. Indeed, there was no going back. In the eyes of a former PA official, Nablus would have to change, as it could not withstand the rising tide of globalisation – in particular, cheaper labour costs in Turkey and the Far East – that undermined the traditional distribution routes for Nabulsi textiles to reach European and American markets.[4]

However, even at the end of Fayyad's term of office, many of the PA's intended changes remained incomplete. The PA's budget was still heavily dependent on the support of international donors and the PA was unable to plan effectively or adapt quickly enough for changing circumstances. Moreover, its inability to secure enough donor funds to cover its expenditure (its deficit was estimated at $1.1 billion going into 2012) led to the fiscal crisis in 2011 and, ultimately, to the end of the Fayyad government.

Good governance, anti-corruption and neoliberalism

In 2004, Mohammad Dahlan, then a major figure within Fatah, told *The Guardian* that some $5 billion of aid monies donated to the PA 'have gone down the drain, and we don't know to where' (Urquhart 2004). Corruption was (and remains) a very real concern for both donors and the PA, and its impact was extremely harmful to general Palestinian welfare. The perceived corruption of the PA was one of the defining features of the 2006 legislative elections, and the inability of the PA's institutions to police themselves was recorded by international observers.[5] Previous chapters have already discussed how the PA's 'bully praetorian republic' rested on the distribution of rents as the primary means of maintaining support both from elites and the general public. Yet in the aftermath of the Intifada, the split between the PA and Hamas, and the advent of the statebuilding programme, donors took a new interest in dealing with this issue. This was manifest in a new focus on the principles of 'good governance'.

In its simplest terms, good governance was meant to be an answer to inefficiency and fraud within the PA and as a means to rebuild the public's confidence. However, in reality, the impact of this agenda went far beyond merely addressing corruption alone. Its main outcomes can be broken down into three different categories: (a) the efforts to address corruption directly (which were largely positive); (b) anti-rent-seeking efforts, which were one-sided, poorly implemented and devoid of context; and (c) efforts to impose market solutions on Palestinian decision making.

The first of these categories, the policies that were directly anti-corruption efforts, were largely positive. In particular, under Fayyad, the PA introduced a code of conduct for Palestinian factions (2011) and a well-resourced Anti-Corruption Commission (2011), which has successfully undertaken several high-profile investigations into the internal workings of the PA (*Maan News* 2012). The Fayyad government also created greater transparency by ensuring that public sector pay would only go through registered bank accounts. The outcomes of this in terms of public perception were also noticeable, if not dramatic. As Figure 8.2 demonstrates, perceptions of corruption have remained consistently high since 2006, though under Fayyad, it dropped from above 80 per cent to around 70 per cent.[6]

However, the second aspect of the 'good governance' agenda was not so benign. This was because according to its neoliberal terms of reference, the anti-corruption rhetoric made no distinction between actual corruption and other forms of rent-seeking practices that may – in some circumstances – be helpful/necessary for Palestinian economic development.

As Mushtaq Khan points out, there is neither an absolute nor an obvious distinction between corruption and rent-seeking behaviour. Moreover, in some circumstances, some rent-seeking behaviour can be beneficial to economic development, especially in contexts – like Palestine – where the private sector faces significant and often complex constraints. As Khan argues, with regard to the occupation, rents and rent-seeking were virtually impossible to eradicate in the context of Palestine because of the nature and impact of Israel's occupation policies.[7] Some forms of rent had developed as a necessary means by which the Palestinian economy adapted to the constraints imposed

Disaster, capitalism and Palestine 151

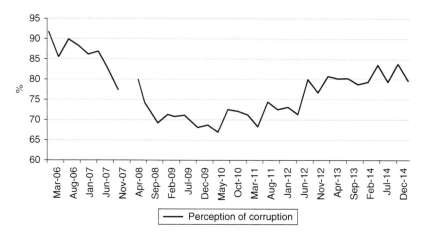

Figure 8.2 Perceptions of corruption in the PA among West Bank Palestinians (%)[45]

on it by Israel's occupation, particularly during the intense period of closure in the early 2000s:

> The [PA] did not control a contiguous territory, it had almost no fiscal autonomy, and it did not control its own borders, including internal borders between enclaves. These arrangements made executive centralization and corruption not just possible but almost inevitable ... Palestinian traders had to set up elaborate systems of influence and often of bribery involving Israeli customs and other officials simply to be able to trade on a day-to-day basis.
>
> (Khan 2004, 17)[8]

Yet, in this context, 'good governance' was manifest in the donors' insistence on transparency in the PA's use of their money. While it is obviously sensible to expect that the recipients of donor aid should avoid and/or curtail corrupt activities, it would never be reasonable for donors to demand such without taking into account the political context, at least to some extent. Yet that was exactly what the donors did. Moreover, their efforts essentially ignored the fact that the behaviour of donors themselves effectively supported rent-seeking relationships by fostering close relations with established elites and encouraging a clientalistic relationship with Palestinian civil society (Nasr 2004). As Linda Tabar and Sari Hanafi have found, rent-seeking among donor sponsored NGOs was a recognised problem:

> rent-seeking in the NGO sector increasingly requires the adoption of discourses defined by donors and this in turn determines which elites can participate in this rentseeking ... some of the Palestinian NGOs declared

> to us that they produce fake receipts for expenditures to the tune of the entire budget in the initial proposal.
>
> (Tabar and Hanafi 2004, 20)

Moreover, rent-seeking behaviour has had a direct impact on the distribution of power and privilege within Palestinian society:

> Corruption is encouraged by the phenomenon of aid recipients paying themselves high salaries. The high salaries are themselves an aspect of the process through which the new elite has emerged ... donors, especially USAID, insist on high employee wages. For example, the salary of a director of a PNGO that accepted funds from USAID rose from $1,800 to $3,500 a month, because USAID set the director's salary. Such high salaries inevitably create incentives for rent-seeking activities as the new elite competes to capture these positions.
>
> (Tabar and Hanafi 2004, 20)

The fact that the good governance framework was based on an ideological commitment to the centrality of the market-led decision making was also deeply problematic. This was based on the neoliberal notion that market solutions are necessarily the best, or fairest, means of orienting economic affairs. This assumption is obviously problematic in the context of Palestine, given what has already been discussed regarding the nature of the PA as a 'bully praetorian republic' and the fact that a product of this has been the emergence of monopoly elites.

Even taking into account the genuine corruption that was evident, it was also the case that the development of the monopoly class was in fact applauded and praised by international sponsors (Nakhleh 2011). Even when market-centric policies have been pursued, it cannot be assumed that a genuinely competitive environment would be produced in the medium or long term.[9] In Palestine, a particularly relevant example of how this process operated was through the PA's reform of the banking system. According to a former minister, one of the key steps that the PA had taken in order to improve conditions for Palestinian entrepreneurship was the requirement that banks operating in the West Bank would make more funding available domestically in the form of small loans and loan guarantees.[10]

However, where this had been brought into operation, the effect was not to encourage growth in small and medium-sized businesses, but rather to fuel consumer spending on imported goods. This problem was articulated by the manager of the Al-Rafah Microfinance Bank in Nablus:

> People come without investments and no savings. They pay for cars and things for their houses. For one to two years everything is for the banks, there is no production. Everything is on services. [There is] major inflation

potential, this is likely to lead to an explosion ... in 20 years of experience I have never made [as many] loans like [in] the last two years.[11]

Of course, where loans were used mostly for short-term consumable purchases, such as a new car, they may have had some positive impact on the Palestinian economy.[12] However, this benefit would be extremely limited. Beyond that, what is certainly true in the short term is that the larger companies that were responsible for importing these consumer goods would expand their consumer base into lower income brackets which now had access to easier credit.

Moreover, it is evident that private sector growth is clearly not a natural product of a market-led environment in Palestine. As discussed in the previous chapter, while there had been something of a 'boom' (particularly in the service sector) in the first two years of the Fayyad government, it was easily reversible and has not been matched by more productive sectors such as industry. This problem was summarised by UNCTAD (2011):

> While manufacturing output declined by 6 per cent in 2010, hotels and restaurants, construction, public administration and agriculture grew, at rates of 46, 36, 6 and 22 per cent respectively. However, the growth rate for agriculture came after continuous decline for a decade, whereby the level of value added in the sector in 2009 was 47 per cent of the level a decade earlier.

The decline of manufacturing is significant for two reasons: (a) there is an immediate loss in potential output, which translates to lower than optimal GDP growth; and (b) there are longer-term implications in the form of 'technological regression' (UNCTAD 2011).[13]

Neoliberalism and industrial policy

The PA's industrial policy was ostensibly designed to re-structure the sector in order to bypass the various restrictions on movement (discussed in the previous chapter). However, in reality, it effectively enabled the embedding of the occupation infrastructure further into the West Bank with the blessing of both the PA and international donors.

The industrial zones programme is outlined in the PA's planning document 'Homestretch to Freedom'. It states that 'a national campaign has been launched to put an end to the sale of Israeli settlement products, and industrial estates are being constructed and rehabilitated' (Palestinian Authority 2010, 3). The creation and restoration of large-scale industrial zones in the West Bank was directly tied to the principle of resistance to Israeli rule and the pursuit of Palestinian statehood. However, it is clear from the data presented below that these industrial zones constituted one of the main means through which the PA was integrating the framework of a future state with the existing apparatus of Israel's occupation. Furthermore, these industrial zones follow from a model already adopted in both Jordan and Egypt during the 1990s, and based on these examples, it is reasonable to suggest that their potential positive impact on the Palestinian economy could only ever be extremely limited.[14]

By 2010, there were four industrial zones included in this project in the West Bank, each of them supported by the PA, Israel and third-party governments. Two others existed in Gaza (although only one of them was completed) and South Korean and Indian sponsors were considering a further prospective industrial zone. The zones in the West Bank included in this project were: (a) the al-Jalama zone, near Jenin, with the sponsorship of Germany and Turkey; (b) the Bethlehem zone, supported by France; (c) the Jericho Agricultural Park (or 'Valley of Peace' project) in the Jordan Valley, built with Japanese support; and (d) the Tarqoumiyya Industrial Estate, near Hebron, sponsored by the World Bank and Turkey (Bahour 2010; United Nations Development Programme (UNDP) 2013).[15] One immediate negative impact of these industrial zones was land expropriation. In 2000, this took the form of the compulsory purchase of 933 dunums (230.5 acres) and though the project was suspended during the Intifada, it re-started again in 2007. This proved to be deeply unpopular with local residents and has been met with resistance:

> Some farmers, however, are refusing to give up their source of livelihood for the creation of an industrial zone that will end their way of life and destroy their natural and economic resources. Around 20 farmers recently filed a lawsuit against the PA (Sansour and Tartir 2014).

The PA's defence of these developments has focused on claims that their main impact would be felt in terms of increased employment (UNDP 2013). However, data from comparable examples suggests that these industrial zones were only ever likely to offer low-level manual labour employment for the Palestinians and ensure that Palestinian labourers would be subject to intense and intrusive security screenings as a matter of course. Rather than advancing progress towards Palestinian independence, these zones would maintain public dependence on foreign support. This would be as a result of shifting the focus of foreign financing from direct donor aid, which is then dispersed through the public sector, to a market-oriented strategy wherein Palestinians 'sell their labor for the benefit of those commercial entities established in the industrial zones, which will depend on Israeli goodwill to succeed' (Bahour 2010).

Perhaps the most troubling aspect of the industrial zones plan is that through the security measures that would be applied with regard to Palestinian labourers working in these zones, Israel's occupation apparatus would be entrenched to an even deeper level. It is telling that these plans were organised by Israel during the height of the Second Intifada and that they were deliberately designed to be different from those industrial states planned in the 1990s.

The primary differences were that Israel would retain control over security matters, while Palestinians would staff the zones, and they would be housed on Palestinian lands. As already discussed in the previous chapter, Israel's occupation policy has already begun to shift more towards the use of private enterprise in order to create the appearance of impartiality. It is worth noting that one site that was the prototype for this privatisation was the checkpoint at al-Jalama, which was integrated into an industrial zone complex. During late 2009, this author passed through this checkpoint, as an extract from my research diary describes:

> The process was long, intimidating and very slow but they did not question us ... In total we waited for just short of two hours at this last stage [while an] armed guard wandered around on the network of steel platforms above our heads. He was wearing a yellow baseball cap – which bore the logo of whatever security firm it was [Modi'in Ezrachi], and a sort of macho/military uniform in grey. Of course the most obvious thing about him was the M16 rifle that hung from a strap over one arm ... We watched for hours as a steady dribble of Palestinians passed through from the left leaving the West Bank, and from the right coming in. Almost everything was done in Hebrew; although I heard the guards often ask for identity cards in Arabic.[16]

Moreover, Khalidi and Samour have suggested that one product of intense training undertaken by the Palestinian security forces – under the direction of the US military – would be to enable them to serve as the first line of a security screening process for Palestinian labourers working in those industrial zones (Khalidi and Samour 2011, 15). As one interviewee suggested:

> The new industrial zones will use Israeli transport companies, they will employ Israeli or foreign drivers or 'clean' Palestinians ... but the whole function of the zones is to link Palestinian labour to the Israeli economy permanently.[17]

There are numerous other concerns relating to the actual value that such zones would have for the Palestinian economy overall. Indeed, evidence from Jordan's QIZs – a comparable case study – suggests that the positive impact that they have had on Jordan's economy has been limited. While *prima facie* Jordan's industrial zones have been economically fruitful – in terms of increasing Jordan's GDP and improving its balance of trade – overall, the project, which was established as part of the Israel–Jordan 'peace process' in the early 1990s, can only be considered a limited success.

This is for three reasons: (a) the QIZs are relatively isolated from the rest of the economy, in that they are connected by some energy and transport infrastructure links, but these are limited and, beyond that, the QIZs have few forward and backward links; (b) in some cases, the terms of the treaty, which ensure that products manufactured in the QIZs utilise a particular percentage of material produced in Israel (this figure varies according to the type of product produced and has also been altered during the period of existence of the QIZs), have undermined pre-existing Jordanian industry, which cannot compete; and (c) the limited rights for labour employed in these zones had made jobs there particularly undesirable for Jordanian workers and, as a result, a high percentage of foreign workers are employed and the multiplier effect of these wages is therefore fractional (as a high proportion leaves the country in terms of remittances).[18] Thus, even in Jordan, which has many advantages of statehood that even a recognised Palestinian state would lack, there are significant problems relating to this approach. It is possible to extrapolate from this that both Israel and the PA would have cause for strong concern over security issues arising from popular unrest even after these zones were established and operational.

Therefore, notwithstanding the serious need to modernise Palestine's economy, the industrial zone strategy constituted a rapid and radical shift to a system which would grant few workers' rights and, in all likelihood, would operate under a strict surveillance framework and be integrated with the occupation. The rapidity of this change and the apparent lack of any serious social safety net would also mean that it is very likely that those who suffered badly under the status quo would also be badly affected in the short term.[19]

Neoliberal reforms and vulnerable communities

The PA's neoliberal agenda also failed to take into account the special circumstances faced by vulnerable communities in the West Bank. Independent studies demonstrated that poverty and other forms of hardship were serious problems for the general Palestinian population in refugee camps and Areas 'B' and 'C'. The PA's reforms failed to challenge the underlying causes of these problems, and in some cases their policies made them worse. For example, as data in the previous chapter has shown, economic growth in the West Bank has occurred while, at the same time, both employment level and real wages have declined. Moreover, rising inflation particularly affected the most vulnerable communities. For example, as Figure 8.3 demonstrates, unemployment among refugees (especially for those residing in refugee camps) remains higher than among the rest of the Palestinian population.

Refugees remained particularly vulnerable to poverty throughout the period of the statebuilding programme and, according to UNRWA, in 2011, refugees were 'not benefiting from recent economic growth in the West Bank: access to most sectors of the economy – in particular to work in Israel and the Settlements – have significantly decreased for refugees while significantly increasing among non-refugees' (UNRWA 2011). Poverty was a profound problem throughout the West Bank and a report by Save the Children in 2009 identified two areas in the West Bank where it considered communities to be

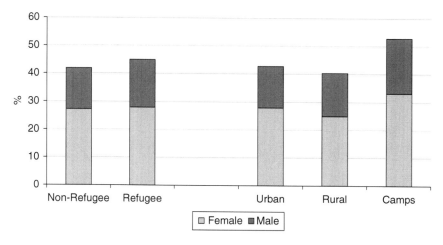

Figure 8.3 Unemployment rates among refugees vs. non-refugees and according to location of residence, West Bank, 2014 (%)[46]

at particularly high risk. These were the communities located in Area 'C'[20] and in the 'seam zone', between the so-called 'Green Line' and the Separation Wall.[21]

Save the Children identified a range of particular causes for concern that affected the livelihoods of Palestinians in those areas, most of which could be attributed to the direct impact of Israel's occupation policies.[22] These concerns are obviously of critical importance for the welfare of the general Palestinian population. In many cases they represented an existential crisis for the affected communities and also demonstrated one of the serious flaws in the PA's strategy of avoiding confrontation with Israel over the occupation apparatus. However, the report also identified two factors that could be seen as directly challenging the value of the PA's policy agenda: (a) the concern of growing poverty within vulnerable communities in Area 'C'; and (b) the impact this was having on encouraging migration to urban areas. Obviously, both of these concerns are connected to each other and they are also both tied to the PA's agenda. According to Save the Children, in 2009, 'the primary reason why respondents wanted to move was because of lack of access to basic services' (Save the Children 2009, 32).

However, since then, specific PA policies designed to stem the flow of fiscal leakage made matters worse. Typically this took the form of installing prepay systems. They were first introduced for controlling the electricity supply and then later for water. The implementation of this metering system made it much more difficult for West Bankers with low/uncertain incomes to meet their most basic needs. Moreover, this is particularly troubling as they echo similar steps taken by oppressive regimes in the past; as Khalidi and Samour (2011, 13–14) explain, in 2011, the PA had begun

> implementing plans to install up to 300,000 prepaid electricity meters across Palestinian households to end ... a 'culture of entitlement'. Rural areas and refugee camps will also be included, echoing the installation of meters in the South African township of Soweto (a key locus in the anti-apartheid struggle).

This conclusion was borne out in several interviews undertaken in the village of Qaryut. In a focus group with the village council in 2009, the (then prospective) change to the electricity supply was the highest priority of discussion. At the time, Qaryut bought its electricity supply directly from the Israeli Electricity Company and was connected to the nearby settlement of Shilo. Revenue from reselling the electricity supply was the main source of income for the village administration.[23] However, according to the members of the village council, not only would this shift mean the loss of any independent income for the village, it would also mean an increase in costs and the loss of the kind of flexibility that was essential for life under such difficult conditions:

> The main problems of the Northern Company [the company that would serve the Nablus region and the rest of the north of the West Bank] was [that] it would make electricity much more costly overall. New connections might cost much more. [At present] If I need to recharge my electricity then I just need to phone [another council member] and he can do it – or if I have problems I can get someone to help me. This won't be available when the company has [its] headquarters in Nablus.[24]

In addition, there are two further concerns relating to this shift in policy: (a) that this decision was done without consultation with local populations; and (b) that it would make it easier for Israel to exercise control over the electricity supply in the future. This would be the case because, under the new system, there would only be four points of connection for the West Bank to Israel and these would be separate from the connections supplying settlements.[25]

However, in discussions with villagers in the Nablus region, the opinions of interviewees were not always negative towards all aspects of the PA's development programme. For example, in Qaryut, the village council spoke positively regarding the use of donor funds to build new facilities in the village, while in Yanoun, the mayor described the impact of a redeveloped water network in appreciative terms[26] – though they noted that this progress was reversible as Israel and its settlers had frequently attacked and/or threatened to destroy even those structures paid for through donor funds (Bauwens 2012). Overall, the reform programme of the PA was seen as inadequate to meet the urgent needs of communities in Area 'C' and, as such, it was failing to challenge the basic paradigm of Israeli dominance. Where it had made progress, there were no guarantees that this could be sustained.[27]

The PA's 'resistance' strategy

The PA also initiated a programme that was intended to challenge the continued presence of settlers and settlements in the West Bank. According to the PA's planning document 'Homestretch to Freedom', 'a national campaign has been launched to put an end to the sale of Israeli settlement products, and industrial estates are being constructed and rehabilitated' (Palestinian Authority 2010, 3). This boycott strategy was outlined by Dr Hasan Abu-Libdeh, the then Minister of the National Economy, in a speech given at the Peres Centre, Tel Aviv in 2010:

> This campaign is focused on helping Palestinian consumers to be cognizant of their rights, and to distinguish between illegal settlement products and legal Israeli products imported via the existing Paris economic protocol. Consumers today are being given the tools to make conscientious decisions to replace settlement products in their homes with other international and Israeli products, while giving priority to Palestinian ones in support of economic nation building.

The PA's boycott was carefully planned in order to demonstrate that it was different to the more prominent Boycott Divestment and Sanctions (BDS) movement, which advocated a blanket boycott of Israeli goods.[28] The PA law banned the purchase of goods from settlements in June 2010 and established a public-private organisation to coordinate the programme, the al-Karameh National Empowerment Fund, and undertook a nationwide campaign to raise awareness of the boycott with the use of various resources, including a glossy catalogue of settlement products (*Maan News* 2010a). Though the PA boycott remained within the terms of the Paris Protocol, Israel's initial response was to withhold the transfer of 17 per cent of the PA's tax revenue (which it collects on behalf of the PA).

The PA boycott initially appeared to hold a number of advantages over the BDS campaign. Most obvious was the fact that the PA boycott was much easier to implement because it still allowed Palestinians to purchase products originating from within Israel, which – as discussed elsewhere – are prevalent throughout the West Bank. The BDS campaign suffered from the fact that it was perceived as an elite project dominated by a generally foreign-educated, Ramallah-based bourgeoisie. In addition, the PA boycott, initially at least, appeared to have managed to present itself as a grassroots movement. This was largely a result of the fact that it mobilised youth support. Its advocates went from door to door asking people to pledge not to buy settlement goods. If they faced opposition, they had the resources available to make a persuasive argument, and if the household pledged to join the campaign and proved to be free from settlement goods, the advocates would affix a small sticker to the door – a symbol of solidarity. In late 2010, these stickers were visible all over the Old City of Nablus and elsewhere.

However, it did not take long before the flaws in the PA's boycott of settlements emerged. In November 2011, Issa Smeirat, a student researching for his master's degree at Al-Quds University in Abu Dis, concluded that many members of the Palestinian business class were heavily invested in Israel and in Israeli settlements in the West Bank. According to a further investigation in the *Haaretz* newspaper:

> Private Palestinian investment in Israel, as of 2010, amounted to $2.5 billion in a conservative estimate, and according to a more optimistic estimate this investment possibly even amounts to $5.8 billion. For purposes of comparison, private Palestinian investment within the West Bank, as of 2011, was only $1.5 billion.
>
> (Hass 2011)

Moreover, critics of the PA's boycott argued that the BDS campaign was sounder. This was because BDS was based on the principle that both settlements and Israel's policies towards the oPts were illegitimate because they both existed outside the remit of international law.[29] Yet according to some perspectives, the PA's boycott did not represent any serious competition to the BDS. In some respects, the PA's boycott had been of benefit to BDS because, as a result of its promotion through the media both at home and abroad, the notion of boycotting Israel had entered mainstream thinking. However, in itself, the PA's boycott was seen rather as an attempt to address its current (and profound) lack of a popular mandate. In other words, the PA was a 'heavy burden on Palestinian shoulders'[30] and was 'desperately seeking legitimacy'.[31]

There was also some qualified support for the PA's boycott of settlement goods. This was largely because it had captured the popular imagination and in both boycotts, the cost of the occupation for Israel was being increased by an attempt both to stifle revenue to Israel from the Palestinian market and associating the Palestinian cause with non-violent protest and examples of other boycotts, such as that employed against apartheid South Africa, which seemed to demonstrate that boycotting could be both a just and effective method. But again the positive impact of this was overshadowed by the much more damaging effects of the existing agreement between Israel and the PLO. According to a Palestinian-American businessman based in Ramallah:

> The [PA] boycott – is an excellent move and it is very well run – it makes people feel they are part of some kind of resistance ... the problem is that it doesn't challenge the Paris Protocol – why should we stick to this agreement? ... Israel does not keep to [the] Paris [agreements]'.[32]

Table 8.1 Percentage of the Palestinian workforce employed in Israel and the settlements 2007–13[48]

	2007	2008	2009	2010	2011	2012	2013
Percentage of workforce	8.9	10.1	10.2	10.5	10	9.7	11.2

Table 8.2 Data from June 2010 opinion poll on public attitudes to PA boycott policies (%)[49]

Oppose sale of settlement goods	72.1
Support sale of settlement goods	25.6
Support preventing work in settlements	34.1
Oppose preventing work in settlements	64.2

This support for the BDS boycott rested on the approval of the fact that through it, Palestinians could take a principled stand against all Israeli products. Such examples provided both stable focal points for the campaign that would remain constantly relevant to students and the community, and be illustrations to others (Palestinians and internationally) to show that Palestinian agency could be used discriminately, non-violently and effectively. Regardless of the PA's policy on boycotting settlement goods only, the general public, civil society and political parties, acting independently of the PA, could be making greater efforts to endorse and promote a boycott of Israeli goods wherever possible:

> Civilians can still boycott. Political parties and civil society should be driving towards increasing boycott of all Israeli products – if Fatah [acting as a political party independent of the PA] called for BDS wouldn't it make a huge difference?[33]

There was another side to this effort, though, that proved less successful. This was an effort to ban Palestinian labourers from working in the settlements. However, this part of the campaign proved largely ineffective. As the data presented in Table 8.1 demonstrates, the percentage of the Palestinian workforce employed in Israel and the settlements actually increased under the Fayyad government.[34]

It appeared, then, that public opinion regarding the settlements was self-contradictory. The public opposed the sale of settlement products, but would not condemn other Palestinians for manufacturing them. As Table 8.2 shows, while the boycott on the sale of settlement products enjoyed popular support, a majority of West Bankers opposed the PA's ban on Palestinians working in the settlements.

Of course, the very existence of a Palestinian labour force in settlements was always a contentious issue (*Maan News* 2010b). Yet given the difficulties of obtaining work permits within Israel itself and the lack of equivalently paid employment opportunities within the Palestinian economy, it could be argued that Palestinian workers in settlements have few alternatives (though this argument is not beyond dispute). Persuasively, Who Profits? (2013) suggests that Palestinian labour in Israeli settlements is morally equivalent to sweatshop labour:

> A business that operates illegitimately cannot demand legitimacy on behalf of the workers and at their expense. The case of sweatshops is a useful example for illegitimate corporate activity that cannot be justified by providing work for those in need. As is the case with settlement companies, sweatshop operators manufacture their products in low-wage societies, seeking lower production costs.

Yet, while this domestic public ambivalence regarding the PA's boycott policy remained, in the international sphere, the notion of a boycott gained some significant ground. Again, neither the PA nor the BDS campaign could claim total credit for this success (though BDS was evidently a much more powerful force within civil society in both North America and Europe). Instead, change came about – particularly in the context of European–Israeli relations – because of efforts within certain governments to adhere to a stricter interpretation of the EU-Israel Association Agreement (2000).

Some efforts were made in 2008 to eliminate this practice, though a more effective challenge was launched in December 2012 when the European Commission – the EU's executive body – directed that 'all agreements between the State of Israel and the EU must unequivocally and explicitly indicate their inapplicability to the territories occupied by Israel in 1967'. This was followed up in June the next year by further guidelines that set out the territorial limitations under which the Commission would grant EU support to Israeli entities.[35] Moreover, according to Dimitris Bouris, many EU officials advocated 'that the EU should use its economic leverage towards Israel more often' in order to promote its goals of peace through statebuilding (Bouris 2013).

The BDS campaign enjoyed even more widespread impact. Encouragement from BDS activists was instrumental in encouraging numerous high-profile musicians, artists and public figures to cancel events in Israel. The movement also enjoyed high-profile support from within academic institutions and labour unions in Europe and North America, as well as various examples of consumer boycotts and other forms of activism.[36] Yet, it is worth noting that the movement deliberately adopted a broad interpretation of activism that, for example, included boycotts regardless of whether they are limited to settlements or address all relations with Israel. Predictably perhaps, Israel's response to these developments was dominated by the more reactionary arguments. Some of the more nuanced cases against boycotts lost out to the shriller ones. Moreover, some of the more right-wing politicians attempted to use the issue – particularly with reference to the EU's actions – to stir up

Disaster, capitalism and Palestine 163

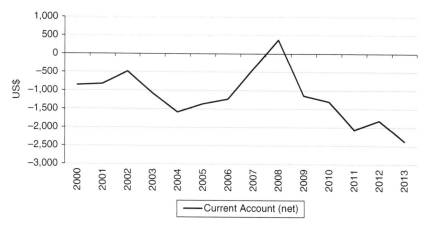

Figure 8.4 PA current account 2000–12 (US$)[47]

resentment,[37] while on the domestic front, Israel's Knesset banned the advocacy of boycott among its citizens (Lis 2011).

Fiscal crisis and austerity

The relationship between the PA and external actors such as the EU was clearly quite complex, particularly in terms of how and why their support was manifest. Though clearly motivated by both neoliberal principles and an enduring focus on imposing a – clearly Israel-centric – interpretation of 'security' on the Palestinians, donors were not immune from making obvious, avoidable and near-catastrophic blunders. The clearest example of this in relation to the statebuilding project was the advent of the Palestinian fiscal crisis in 2011–12. Having endorsed and then actively supported numerous reforms of the PA throughout the period since 2007 – many of which dramatically increased the PA's dependence on foreign aid – beginning in 2010, many of the donors simply failed to fulfil their financial commitments to the PA within the required timeframe.[38] Ever since its inception, the PA's finances had become a constant problem. As Figure 8.4 shows, only once since 2000 did the PA's current account break even.

While it is certainly not unusual for states to constantly run a current account deficit, what is unusually troubling about the PA's situation is that: (a) it was so heavily dependent on foreign aid; and (b) despite the aid, the deficit was evidently growing. In 2012, the Portland Trust (2012) highlighted both the centrality of foreign aid to this equation and the fact that growth had been lower than predicted. Indeed, while the PA required $1.5 billion from international donors, actual contributions totalled about $983 million. Thus, the PA sought to deal with the problem through the accumulation of debt 'by borrowing from the local banking sector, increasing net domestic bank borrowing by $140m ... and accumulating arrears of $0.5bn to the private sector and the public pension fund' (Portland Trust 2012). Moreover, while some claims circulated in the press that much of this deficit cutback was the result of cuts in funding by Arab states, this was officially denied by the PA (Assadi 2010; *Maan News* 2010b).

The issue was compounded when, in May 2011, Israel withheld tax revenue owed to the PA as a punitive step in the wake of a Hamas–Fatah unity arrangement (Jabrin 2011). Yet, despite the role of neoliberal reforms at the very epicentre of the problem, international donors were clear that the required response to the crisis was austerity. The World Bank, for instance, simply stated that 'it is important that the PA accelerates reform efforts to increase domestic revenues', going on to explain that the answer to this lay in 'strengthening revenue administration', 'broadening the tax base' and 'containing expenditure' (World Bank 2012). Of course, in the light of the previous chapter's discussion of the structural constraints limiting the PA's access to most of its revenue streams and the fact that the PA was subject to Israel's will in terms of accessing revenue collected from its existing tax base, the first two suggestions by the World Bank were obviously absurd. However, the third suggestion, of containing expenditure, was fully embraced by the PA.

Perhaps in an effort to dilute the appearance of neoliberal influence on his policy agenda – and unusually for him – Fayyad outlined the necessity for austerity with reference to Islamic tradition:

> We must take inspiration from the Prophet's life in order to overcome this ordeal, this crushing financial crisis that we face. We must also seek social justice and a more equitable distribution of the burdens of the occupation, its oppression, practices and designs.
>
> (Al-Naami 2011)

The brunt of the PA's agenda was to come in the form of proposed tax increases. This included doubling the upper limit on income tax to 30 per cent, extending the tax requirements to sections of the population that had previously been exempt, and taxing pensions and other transactions. In addition, more than 25,000 government employees would be required to take early retirement. Moreover, these acts were to be in addition to measures designed to curtail fiscal leakage (discussed above) and were forcefully rejected by the general population.[39]

Popular protests and the end of Fayyad's premiership

The public rejection of austerity in Palestine coincided with the advent of popular protests across the region, and there was some dispute among donors over whether or not they counted as part of a 'Palestinian Spring' (Wildeman and Tartir 2014). For the PA, there was less time and space available for such deliberations. While Abbas in particular had initially sought to capitalise on the notion of the 'Arab Spring' by first appropriating the statebuilding project and then folding in the narrative of a mass popular movement, events took a different course.

As this author has noted elsewhere, throughout 2011–12, there were a total of 59 incidents of popular demonstration across the West Bank. While the PA orchestrated one of these demonstrations (a set-piece celebration of the Tunisian Revolution), the majority – 42 in total – were either against the PA or involved some form of conflict with the security forces.[40] Of these, 21 incidents of protest were directed against the PA over the high cost of living (see Leech 2014b). The most antagonistic protests took place in January 2012. Ostensibly these protests were triggered by a prospective meeting between Abbas and Shaul Mofaz, the Israeli Vice Prime Minister, though this was against the backdrop of the fiscal crisis and in the context of the PA's lack of legitimacy. Similar protests continued through February and the Fayyad government was forced to scale back its austerity agenda.[41]

This did not quell the discontent, however, as incidents of protest peaked in the summer and autumn of 2012, with seven in June and eight in September. While those protests that occurred later in the year tended to be less violent and were, almost uniformly, directed at the rising cost of living, tensions between the general population and the Fayyad government, as well as between Fayyad and Abbas, continued into early 2013. Ultimately, the Prime Minister's position was untenable and his resignation was accepted in mid-April.

By the end of his term, Fayyad was politically surrounded. Both the main bodies of Fatah and Hamas wanted him out, and Abbas, despite pressure from Fayyad's American allies, eventually fired him. Rami Hamdallah, a British-educated former President of An-Najah National University with a reputation for political independence despite nominal membership of Fatah, was appointed as Fayyad's replacement (though Hamas, which was not consulted, did not recognise his premiership until the formation of a unity government in 2014). In an effort to assert his leadership on the PA, Hamdallah resigned only a fortnight into the job. He was to be re-appointed as head of a new government in September.

Broadly speaking, Hamdallah continued the main economic programmes of the Fayyad era, including support for industrial zones and the pre-pay meters. However, the slackening of the PA's approach to public sector employment began at the end of the Fayyad government and continued under Hamdallah; as one interviewee explained, 'the PA has returned to the idea that public sector jobs are a kind of social safety net'.[42] Moreover, the new Prime Minister enjoyed improving approval ratings, from a low of 30 per cent in June to 46 per cent in September 2013. However, according to one interviewee, his government was significantly weaker than Fayyad's, especially when it came to reining in Abbas or controlling the security forces.[43]

As for Fayyad, as noted previously, he launched his own NGO, 'Future for Palestine', from a neat collection of offices in downtown Ramallah. The former Prime Minister – now unshackled from the burdens of office – joined the 'Atlantic Council', a prestigious American think tank, and – in an article for the widely read journal *Foreign Affairs* – explained his perspective that the structural dominance of Israel had denied the Palestinians a state:

> Oslo has obviously failed to deliver Palestinian statehood … This has contributed to a progressively receding sense of possibility about Palestinian statehood, with the ensuing sense of gloom undoubtedly reinforced by a completely unbearable state of the human condition in the occupied Palestinian territory.
>
> (Fayyad 2014)

In retrospect, even for a talented and resilient Prime Minister with important allies in the West, the end goal of building a state under such conditions was never seriously possible. Rather, 'the game', so to speak, was – and always had been – rigged.

Fayyad had tried something new and his government's approach was tactically astute in international forums, through the process of cooperation with international donors and the adept balancing of political opponents and allies alike, to force the international community to follow through on their often-stated commitment to a 'two-state solution'. Moreover, notwithstanding the impact of other non-PA-related civil society activism and indirect factors, this approach achieved some success, which was particularly evident in the recalibration of European trade relations with Israel. Similarly, the Fayyad government's accomplishments in reducing corruption should not be overlooked. However, the domestic cost of this agenda was the incorporation of a neoliberal agenda that promised unrealistic benefits only to disappoint in most cases and make matters worse in some others.

The idea that the Palestinians would somehow miraculously be freed from nearly 50 years of occupation through the implementation of the PA's raft of so-called statebuilding policies was never realistic. After all, these were policies that: (a) incorporated many of Israel's most draconian 'security' measures in the industrial zones; (b) failed to challenge the dominance of already powerful elites; and (c) made conditions harsher for those who were already vulnerable. Fayyad's post-premiership declaration was that 'Oslo is Dead'. But in reality, it remains alive. Certainly, Oslo's promise of statehood and independence has been exposed as hollow, but the agreements themselves – as well as the political-economic and military superiority of Israel that they helped secure – maintain a very real and debilitating grip on Palestinian lands and Palestinian lives.

Notes

1 Data from the PBCS shows that while there was growth in Gaza at that time – mostly led by the so-called 'tunnel economy' – for the most part, this shift was attributable to economic activity in the West Bank. For more details on Gaza's tunnels and the economic impact, see Pelham (2012).
2 As defined in Chapter 2, the key tenets of this were: (a) a reduction in Israeli control over Palestinian political and economic agency; (b) an increase in the capacity of Palestinians to control their own political and economic agency; and (c) that these two processes are sustainable over a long period of time.
3 One particularly poignant example of how these links undermined the PA's own rhetoric of pursuing statehood was that, according to academic research (followed later by investigations by both Israeli and Palestinian journalists), several of these same elites had millions of dollars' worth of investments in the very settlements that the PA was attempting to boycott. See Bannoura (2011).
4 This could potentially be achieved by focusing on multilateral collaboration, which could lead to cheaper labour and transport costs – particularly where it would mean obviating Israel's negative influence over exporting and importing to the oPts – and where possible to exploiting the 'niche' marketing advantages of using the 'holy land' name in branding according to a former official in the PA, interviewed in Ramallah, 21 June 2009.
5 The total sum lost to the corruption in the PA is difficult to assess, though in 2006, an investigation by the then PA Attorney General, Ahmed al-Meghami, suggested that under Arafat, PA officials might have caused the loss of at least $700 million of public monies through embezzlement and mismanagement.
6 The slight bump in early 2010 was likely to be tied to a sex scandal involving a senior aide to Abbas and the fact that Abbas' presidential term officially expired at that point. The PCPSR report from March 2010 stated: 'Findings show that 72% have heard about reports of scandals and charges of corruption in the Palestinian Authority or saw a video tape mentioned in those reports and more than two thirds of them (69%) believe those reports and charges to be accurate while 24% do not'. For more details on the scandal itself, see Kershner (2010).
7 A study by AMAN (2011), the Palestinian partner of Transparency International, found that 41 per cent of Palestinians polled admitted to utilising 'wasta' – the use of connections and influence to expedite transactions – when involved with the public sector services.
8 Khan also points out that rents are far from unusual in more advanced market economies and, in fact, rents and rent-seeking equates to a multi-billion dollar industry in the US in the form of lobbying. In the West in particular, this is seen as an integral part of modern capitalist-democracy and thus any demand that developing economies cannot progress while rents and rent-seeking form part of their economy is unrealistic.
9 Of course, it is also possible to learn from other examples in more developed economies that the swift imposition of a neoliberal power structure often uses discourses of the virtue of the free market as a façade to cover up the fact that dominant capitalists can extend their influence more through using political influence and their superior capital supplies to undermine competition. See, *inter alia*, Nitzan and Bichler (2000, 2002); Klein (2008); Crouch (2011).
10 Research interview with a member of the PA, Ramallah, 21 June 2009.
11 Interview with manager of Al-Rafah Microfinance Bank, 14 July 2010.
12 For example, it may improve members of that family's access to shops or jobs further from home, and would also add a little extra to the PA's revenue (via purchase taxes).

13 'Technological regression' refers to the decline in the ability of an industrial sector to produce technologically advanced products because of a loss of skills or inadequate equipment.
14 This conclusion is further supported by evidence in recently leaked documents from the PA that the land used for an industrial zone planned for Jenin would 'come under the full control of the foreign power funding the project' (Silver 2012).
15 There were already other industrial zones in the West Bank, for instance, a large estate between the Balata and Askar refugee camps east of Nablus. According to a high-ranking member of the Nablus Chamber of Commerce, this industrial zone was a possible site for renewal. He stated that plans included 2000 new workshops, for, among others, blacksmiths, carpenters and other specialist trades. This was presented as highly beneficial to both the populations of Area 'C' – through creating employment opportunities – and the city environment – by separating industrial space from residential areas. However, according to another Nabulsi interviewee who was sceptical as to the prospect of rehabilitating this industrial zone, the issue had been raised on numerous occasions as a possibility by PA officials, industrialists and in the media, yet little had actually happened and, in his opinion, if it was to occur, it would be unlikely to have a particularly positive impact on the city: research interviews, 2009–10. This author visited this industrial estate in July 2010. Based on these observations, there were some factories using its space and facilities, but overall it was functioning at a very low capacity.
16 Extracts from field notes, 26 November 2009.
17 Research interview with a senior analyst in a major Palestinian think tank in Ramallah, 12 July 2010.
18 The Jordanian government's decision to further exclude workers in the QIZ in 2008 and 2011 from the minimum wage limit has only served to worsen working conditions. Harsh working conditions have led to low Jordanian engagement in the QIZs, where there are only about 8,000 Jordanians (mass mobilisations in 2010 and 2011) due to violations of labour rights, wages and working conditions of migrant workers in the apparel sector. To address the decent work deficits in the garment sector, the Better Work Jordan Programme is seeking to broker a collective bargaining agreement at the sectoral level between the General Trade Union of Workers in Textile Garment and Clothing Industries and the Jordan Garments, Accessories, & Textiles Exporters' Association.
19 The need for increased training opportunities for small enterprises in the Nablus region and beyond was identified in 2003 by a Bisan report. See Makhool (2003).
20 'According to the UN Office for the Coordination of Humanitarian Affairs (OCHA), there are 418 villages with at least part of their built-up area located in Area C, including 161 villages with a majority of their built-up area in Area C and 130 villages completely inside Area C. OCHA estimates that 44,100 Palestinians live in the 130 villages completely inside Area C. Given the number of mixed A/B/C villages, the actual population is certainly much higher (Save the Children 2009, 19).
21 The seam zone 'refers to those areas of the West Bank that are situated between the Green Line (the 1949 Armistice Line) and the Separation Wall. While there is an overlap between population figures for the seam zone and Area C, the population living in the seam zone areas is particularly vulnerable to Israeli policies and practices. In a study of the humanitarian impact of the Wall and its associated permit regime in the northern West Bank, OCHA estimates based on community sources indicate that over 9,000 Palestinians were living in the seam zone areas declared "closed" by Israeli military order in the Jenin, Tulkarm, Qalqiliya and Salfit districts. While not a comprehensive estimate this figure points to a sizeable population that is both extremely marginalized and vulnerable' (Save the Children 2009, 19). The report by Save the Children also identified 'The Gaza Buffer Zone'

and East Jerusalem as areas of high concern. However, as they fall outside the scope of this study, they are not discussed here.
22 Examples include restrictions on movement, inability to access property, land confiscation and property demolition.
23 Electricity was bought at 0.5 NIS per KWh and sold on to the villagers at 0.7 NIS per KWh. While the system was under the control of the village council, this also allowed for some flexibility in the payment of bills, as under the system set up by the Paris Protocol (1995), these arrears would then be extracted from the PA by Israel through withholding tax revenue (which Israel was tasked with collecting on the PA's behalf). This had been considered a major problem for the PA and was one of the key priorities identified by international donor agencies as a potential means of increasing revenue. See World Bank (2015a).
24 Research focus group, Qaryut, 14 July 2010.
25 Ibid.
26 Research interview, Yanoun, 11 July 2010.
27 For more detail on the issue of water meters, see Hamdan (2012).
28 See Barghouti (2011).
29 According to this reading, the Oslo process actually undermined international standards that were critical to Palestinian legal claims against Israel: for example, UN Security Council Resolutions 194 and 242, and the 4th Geneva Convention. See Barghouti (2011).
30 Research interview with BDS representative, Ramallah, 18 July 2010.
31 Ibid.
32 Research interview with a Ramallah-based business consultant, Ramallah, 5 July 2010.
33 Ibid.
34 It is likely that this was partly a product of the fact that the wages in the settlements and Israel remained considerably higher than in both the Palestinian public and private sectors, albeit that those labourers also endured very poor working conditions.
35 'Statement by the Delegation of the European Union to the State of Israel on the European Commission Notice' (2013) For a useful overview of British trade with the Israeli settlements, see Gelder and Kroes (2009).
36 Further details on various different actions that BDS claims as 'victories' are available on its website: wwwwww.bdsmovement.net/victories.
37 For example, Naftali Bennett, leader of hawkish Bayit Yehudi party and a minister at the time, called the EU's actions 'Economic Terrorism', while Avigdor Lieberman, the then Foreign Minister, propagated farcical claims that labelling settlement products differently from produce from Israeli proper was motivated by anti-Semitism. See Hadid (2015).
38 As MAS (2011) has argued, it is important to note that 'the primary reason for the fiscal crisis is growth in wage expenditure unmatched by revenue growth' and, moreover, the security sector wage bill has grown considerably as a result of the security policies enacted by the PA under the direction of foreign actors. Thus, it is reasonable to surmise that international interference contributed significantly to this problem.
39 Data from interview with a Palestinian economist, December 2012. Similar data was made available in the Arabic and English-language press.
40 Ten others protests were directed against other actors (not the PA) and six were in favour of a unity deal between Hamas and Fatah.
41 The meeting itself was highly symbolic and the PA's response was brutal. See Leech and Quzmar (2012) and Mustafa (2015).
42 Interview with a senior Palestinian economist, Jerusalem, April 2015.
43 Interview with a former Minister for Information in the Fayyad government, Ramallah, October 2014.

44 Data from World Bank. Graph compiled by the author.
45 All data from the PSR. Graph compiled by the author. Note: there is no data available for March/April 2008.
46 All data from the PCBS. Graph compiled by the author.
47 All data from the PCBS. Graph compiled by the author.
48 Data from the PCBS. Graph compiled by the author. Moreover, where there have been successes in terms of highlighting the illegality of settlement-based industry – for example, a significant controversy surrounding the Sodastream factory based in the Mishor Adumim industrial zone (near Ma'ale Adumim) in 2013/14 – the PA's boycott was largely absent from the discussion. Many news sources cited the BDS movement instead. For examples, see Black and Sherwood (2014); Leibovitz and Butnick (2014); Wainer (2014).
49 According to the same poll, West Bankers were also less than sanguine about the likely impact that the boycott would have on the PLO's bargaining position in negotiations with Israel. Indeed, while 21.7 per cent of those polled thought that the policy would make no difference, some 44.1 per cent believed that the boycott would do more harm than good.

9 Conclusions

This final chapter draws together the key findings of the book as a whole and seeks to summarise them in an accessible way. Its main argument is that the PA's statebuilding plan was, in essence, a contradiction in terms. This was because the programme presented itself as a process by which a Palestinian state would be built by Palestinians themselves. By springing into life, this 'State of Palestine' would signify the end of a long-running conflict and the liberation of an entire population from the misery of foreign occupation. In reality, though, what happened was that the only real institutional development that took place was confined to the security forces, and it was driven by major Western powers in coordination with Israel. The remainder of 'the state', which comprised an admittedly inefficient social support system, was cut back. Thus, rather than achieving liberation and peace, what came out of statebuilding was a lopsided police state that was even less capable of providing even basic services to its own population.

This chapter is structured in the following way. First, it discusses how and why the statebuilding project was a failure, both in the context of the broader Israel–Palestine conflict and also in terms of the more comprehensive framework for political change outlined in the course of this book. Second, it highlights the two main themes of the PA's policy agenda under the statebuilding project. These were the creeping advance of authoritarianism in Palestine and the absence of significant economic development. In both cases the discussion identifies key contradictions between the stated aims of supporters of the statebuilding project (including the PA and international donors) and the actual outcomes of the political and economic processes that were undertaken. In particular, this analysis shows how, while both the PA and international donors promoted the rhetoric of democracy, the overall outcome of the process was the enhancement and entrenchment of authoritarianism. A similar contradiction is evident between the ostensible goal of sustained economic and social development in Palestine and the actual outcomes of the process, which actually weakened the existing (albeit inefficient) *de facto* social support network without offering any effective alternative. The statebuilding project can be seen as a mechanism designed to bypass the public will.

The final section steps back to consider these findings in the context of, first, a wider overview of the conflict and, second, a broader theoretical approach to social and political change. It concludes that the notions of achieving political change in Palestine and statehood for Palestine are far from the same thing. Moreover, while there are evidently extreme risks inherent in pursuing more comprehensive political change, no one should have been seduced by the chimera of the statebuilding programme.

Defining failure

At the time of writing, some four years after the statebuilding programme's original deadline, Palestine remained far from 'statehood' in the terms of any reasonable appraisal. Not only does the occupation persist in the West Bank, but also the political rift between Hamas and Fatah is such that Palestine is split between two *de facto* governments. In the West Bank, conditions are in some ways as serious as they have been for a long time. Democracy remains suspended, while there has been little respite from economic crisis since the end of the 2010 aid-driven 'boom'.

In Gaza, on the other hand, the situation was far worse. Since 2007, the Gaza Strip subsisted under a harsh blockade imposed by Israel and Egypt. The siege has been profoundly debilitating to economic and social life in the Gaza Strip. However, the negative effects were amplified significantly by several rounds of conflict between Israel and Palestinian military organisations. In particular, Israel and Hamas engaged in major hostilities in 2008–9 ('Operation Cast Lead'), 2012 ('Operation Pillar of Defence) and 2014 ('Operation Protective Edge'). Data from B'Tselem indicated that 1,767 Palestinians and 66 Israelis, and one foreign national, were killed in the 2014 campaign, which was the worst of the three.[1] According to Oxfam in 2015, rebuilding Gaza might take up to 100 years under the existing siege conditions (Blair 2015).

While there were some voices of discontent within the Western intelligentsia about the persistence of this siege (Carter and Robinson 2014), what is perhaps the most important lesson that is directly related to the topic of this book is that for the most part, there has been little effective criticism of Israel's policies even from those governments that have apparently championed a 'two-state solution'.[2] In spite of winning an endorsement of its status as a state by the vast majority of the UN General Assembly, Palestine remains occupied by Israeli forces. In the West Bank, a few largely cosmetic changes – such as the rebranding of checkpoints and the apparent reduction in the number of armed incursions by Israeli forces since the Second Intifada – have not disguised the fact that Palestine remains occupied and subject to ongoing colonisation. The dramatic increase in settlement activity, the apparent permanence of the Separation Wall and the continued partition of East Jerusalem are overt examples of this. But the more subtle issues (only some of which have been discussed in this book), including those relating to trade, currency and political autonomy, continue to provide evidence of Palestine's prolonged lack of sovereignty.

Beyond merely looking for sovereignty, however, this book has sought to redefine the terms of this discussion. In Chapter 2, this book laid out a broader standard of political change:

- a reduction in Israeli control over Palestinian political and economic activity;
- an increase in the capacity of Palestinians to control their own political and economic activity; and
- that these two processes are sustained over a long period of time.

Clearly, the evidence demonstrates that none of these criteria was met. First, there was no serious reduction in Israeli control over political and economic activity that was not reversible. While at face value the experience of living under occupation – particularly in cities such as Nablus – changed since the end of the Second Intifada, the structural and military constraints that were in place at the time were merely rolled back, not removed.[3] For Palestinians in rural areas, the violent interactions with Israeli settlers have increased.

Second, by any meaningful measure, there was a decrease in the capacity of Palestinians to control their own political and economic activity. The PA's statebuilding programme was written in coordination with foreign governments (particularly the UK government's DFID) and was heavily dependent on foreign aid. The culmination of this process was that Palestinian democracy was undermined. The security forces demonstrated a serious lack of respect for both the basic rights of ordinary Palestinians and the civilian leadership. Additionally, the role that international donor institutions played in (a) shaping the PA's economic policies, (b) undermining the PA's fiscal position by failing to adapt to the increasing demand for aid, leading up to the fiscal crisis of 2010–11, and (c) the punitive measures enacted by Israel through withholding Palestinian tax revenue are all examples that speak to the weakening of Palestinian control over their own political and economic activity.

Put simply, while all sides have presented themselves variously as staunch supporters of a 'two-state solution', the evidence clearly demonstrates that Israel's strategic superiority – maintained at the expense of Palestinian agency – was never seriously challenged. The only reasonable conclusion that can be drawn from this analysis is that statebuilding could never have been a serious attempt at achieving meaningful change to the lopsided power relationship between Israel and the Palestinians.

Cognitive dissonance

On virtually every front, the statebuilding programme either failed to achieve progress towards Palestinian independence or, in some cases, the processes of change that were either initiated or accelerated under the heading of statebuilding have worsened the situation. The statebuilding plan was founded as a kind of 'third way' after the failure of both the previously tried strategies: (a) violent uprising; and (b) direct negotiations. However, another way of putting this was that it was the only thing that the PA could do under the circumstances. Its apparent goals were to build institutions, demonstrate Palestinian commitment to peaceful development and to make a Palestinian state 'inevitable'. But as time would tell, this 'third way' turned out to be no way forward at all; instead, it was a chimera.

The institutions that were built rested on the quicksand of unreliable foreign aid and were subject to the will and interference of foreign governments. This led to an unserviceable debt, popular discontent and an apparently unstoppable demise of Palestinian democracy. The clearest example of this failure was in the transformation of the security forces. While there was a clear case to be made that the PA's security forces had always put their own interests first at the expense of the general population (and that that failure was compounded by the desperate events of the Second Intifada), their 'reform' under the statebuilding programme only served to consolidate their authoritarian structure. If the 2006 elections were a threshold event – which presented Palestinians with their first truly competitive election – the overturning of its result and the violent purge of Hamas from the West Bank in its aftermath effectively smothered the Palestinian democracy in its infancy. Western intelligence agencies played a significant role in these events despite calling repeatedly for greater democratic accountability in the PA.

While the most obvious conclusion to draw from this account is that the statebuilding project was a failure, there are also additional lessons from this analysis. The first of these is that the role of external actors involved in this project has been, to say the very least, duplicitous. While the UK and the US continued to champion progress and reform, the alliance that they maintained with the Fatah 'Old Guard' allowed the rot of petty authoritarianism to spread deeper through the PA's political and security infrastructure. There are various views as to how to view this apparent hypocrisy. As discussed previously, Mandy Turner suggests that it can be conceptualised as part of a 'counterinsurgency' strategy on the part of Western governments. Her suggestion relates this analysis of the West's true anti-democratic intent to their provision of enormous levels of foreign aid that was provided to the PA.

However, if we take into account a broader view of these data – particularly focusing on the scale and impact of foreign aid over the whole period of the statebuilding project – another view emerges, namely that the West's actions were a product of a kind of cognitive dissonance. This refers to the contradiction between (a) he role of Western governments in supporting the PA's statebuilding project financially throughout 2010, only to (b) dramatically cut their support in 2011. This led, ultimately, to popular discontent and the demise of the Fayyad government.

The Palestinian fiscal crisis of 2010–11 – which coincided with the 'Arab Spring' in the rest of the region – had effectively been caused by a breakdown in coordination of the various parties in arranging the timing of their payments. In other words, just at the time that the PA was required to meet its financial commitments (which had expanded vastly as a result of the statebuilding project), its principal backers let it down. This left the PA in a desperate state and unable to meet its commitments. It effectively undermined public confidence in the statebuilding project.

Therefore, though there is very clear evidence to support Mandy Turner's argument that the relationship between some Western governments and the PA can be characterised as 'counterinsurgency' in the context of the security forces, the evidence also suggests that not every aspect of the role played by Western governments in the process fits this interpretation exactly. If the goal of the foreign intervention was to undermine opposition to the PA – so as to bolster its status as a client regime – the fact that the West stood idle during an avoidable fiscal crisis, which precipitated social unrest, suggests that donor governments' poor planning undermined their 'counterinsurgency' goals in Palestine. Thus 'counterinsurgency' can be understood as the broad thrust of the West's role here, yet the clumsy nature of its implementation should also be recognised.

Neoliberalism and the 'peace process'

The role of donors in the fiscal crisis is not the only example of internal contradiction, however. Another example is inherent in the very basic philosophy underlying the statebuilding project itself. This was manifest in the neoliberal policies that were presented as part of the statebuilding process. Yet, in reality, these were state-shrinking measures which cut back the *de facto* social support network provided by the public sector. In some cases the outcome of these measures was deeply damaging to Palestinian society particularly in terms of reducing the basic services required by some of the most vulnerable sectors of society. In other words, just as the Palestinian state was being 'built', it was also being hollowed out.

A lucid example is drawn from the PA's efforts to tackle fiscal leakage. Of course, it was justifiable that fiscal leakage was identified as a problem that undermined the stability of Palestinian governance. However, the evidence plainly suggests that the primary causes of fiscal leakage emanated from the nature and structure of the PA's relationship to Israel. In particular, this was as a product of: (a) the Paris Protocol and its impact on the labour market and trade regime; (b) the structures of the occupation (including the denial of access for Palestinians to natural resources); and (c) the punitive measures enacted by Israel, such as the withholding of tax revenue. Yet the measures enacted by the PA to curtail fiscal leakage targeted services utilised by its own population. Specifically, these involved imposing harsher controls on access to amenities.

These efforts to curtail fiscal leakage can be seen in the context of a broader plan to scale back the public sector. Similarly, defenders of these austerity measures can (and did) argue persuasively that the system that existed prior to reform was inefficient. However, this argument is problematic because it ignores both the fact that in Palestine conditions were such that there was an essential need for some kind of social security system – even if it was wasteful and corrupt – and that the PA's agenda was doing nothing to replace the services that austerity measures were removing.

The PA cannot take all the blame for this, however. According to a fairly standard neoliberal interpretation, such as that which was put forward in numerous World Bank and IMF reports, the most important issue facing the Palestinian economy was the disproportionate size of the public sector in comparison to a small and stagnating private sector. According to this view, it was therefore necessary for the PA to rebalance that relationship. In practice, that meant the PA needed to put its own house in order by: (a) reducing fiscal leakage; (b) curtailing corruption entirely; (c) cutting the public sector wage bill and other related employee benefits; and (d) increasing the size of the tax base. In addition, the PA should have encouraged private sector growth by using the recovered revenue (as well as available foreign aid) as incentives for private businesses to invest.

As we have seen, both the PA's own documentation and that produced by the IMF and the World Bank sometimes present a relatively optimistic view of what could be achieved should this guidance be followed. Examples drawn from reports detailing the 2010 'boom' prove this point:

> The goal is clear: a Palestinian state that can deliver services and economic prosperity to its population. By many measures, the PA is delivering on much of this promise at this stage already.
>
> (IMF 2010)

Evidently this progress was not sustainable. This was largely a product of the fact that the 'boom' itself was a creation of donor aid and temporary relaxation of the occupation's restrictions. Additionally, this vision of neoliberal economic progress is intimately tied to the 'peace process'. In the context of the Oslo 'peace process' this was meant to manifest in the form of institutional collaboration between Israeli, Palestinian and other Arab institutions through which, it was hoped, there could develop enough common ground to form the basis of a successful resolution to the conflict (Bouillon 2004). However, while the contemporary proponents of neoliberal reforms acknowledge that the prospects for progress on this front have greatly decreased, successful negotiations remain a cornerstone of their vision:

> A resumption of negotiations and subsequent breakthrough could allow the Initiative for the Palestinian Economy (IPE) and other initiatives to move forward and provide a large investment stimulus that could boost real GDP growth substantially over time.
>
> (IMF 2014)

However, notwithstanding the numerous arguments that are highly critical of neoliberalism in more general theoretical terms (especially as a development strategy) it is important to note that for the most part, there are very good, clear reasons why the neoliberal strategy is ill-suited to this context. Again, it is of course not unreasonable to be in favour of negotiations or for reforms to an inefficient public sector per se. But what is problematic about this entire neoliberal line of argument is that it focuses on ensuring that the PA pressed ahead with austerity-centred reforms even though there was little prospect for progress on other fronts. In other words, if this neoliberal argument can be presented in very simple diagrammatic terms, it would be as follows:

Austerity-focused Palestinian reforms + Greater Palestinian control of its economy (most likely produced by successful negotiations)	=	Sustainable (economic and social) development in Palestine (based on a private sector growth)

The neoliberal logic is that sustainable development is a product of two factors: (a) reforms and (b) progress in removing the restrictions imposed by Israel that would enable Palestinian control over its own economy. However, as we have seen, there was no progress in reducing Israeli control over the Palestinian economy and yet the internal Palestinian reforms – most of which have been directed at reducing the role PA in providing a social safety net – were undertaken anyway. The overall outcome of this has been largely negative (though the improvements in the PA's anti-corruption mechanisms should not be overlooked). In a revised diagram, this would be:

Austerity-focused Palestinian reforms + No additional Palestinian control of its economy	=	Dramatically reduced role of the PA in social support + A moribund private sector + Greater dependence on foreign aid

While the statebulding project emphasised various measures to curtail the PA's social support services with a view to stimulating the private sector, the limitations on the Palestinian political and economic agency meant that for many – especially the most vulnerable – the outcome was worse than the status quo ante.

The bigger picture

As Salam Fayyad's tenure in office came to an end, his legacy – most notably his contribution to the Palestinian statebuilding project – was mourned publicly by one of his most prominent international cheerleaders, Thomas

Friedman of the *New York Times*.[4] In a column entitled 'Goodbye to All That', he wrote: 'Salam Fayyad was the 'Arab Spring' before there was an Arab Spring' (2013). Friedman's sober tone seems to capture something important about how many observers saw this period of Palestinian history. This was regarded as a missed opportunity.[5]

Though at face value Friedman's column appears to be a simple lament for a failed experiment, on closer analysis of this text in the context of the broader shifts in the region to which it alludes, there is perhaps more going on. Friedman seems to be making the case for a kind of romantic conservatism akin to that articulated by Edmund Burke in the immediate aftermath of the French Revolution. Like Burke, who also warned against the barbarity of violent excess, Friedman also warns against the violent excesses of radical change. Also like Burke, Friedman finds fault with those in established power who have abused or neglected their responsibilities to find peace:

> [Fayyad] was what the Arab Spring was supposed to lead to: a new generation of decent Arab leaders whose primary focus would be the human development of their own people, not the enrichment of their family, tribe, sect or party.
>
> (Friedman 2013)

This argument is telling because it highlights the essentially flawed logic that underlies this view of statebuilding. What Friedman seems to favour is the creation of a Palestinian state and end of the conflict, but without any real change in the basic structures of power.

Of course, one could argue that Friedman has a point. The enormous human, political and economic cost of the 'Arab Spring' in every country where significant protests took place in 2011 (with the qualified exception of Tunisia) is a lesson that warns against popular movements opposing entrenched oppressive regimes. However, this cautionary tale falls short of offering a serious lesson in the case of Palestine because it presents a false dichotomy between apparent stability under oppression and social disaster that comes about as a product of extremism and unrestrained human excess. Yet in Palestine, with or without statebuilding, life under the Israeli occupation is an ongoing social disaster. It is the norm.

What preceded the period of statebuilding was nothing like stability; rather, it was an era of sustained occupation, discrimination and dispossession for Palestinians *en masse*, the fragmentation of Palestinian society and the colonisation of Palestinian lands. While Friedman's logic warns against the potential dangers of rapid or radical change, he fails to take into account the inherent violence of the status quo. When he warns his readers of the potential for destruction, he ignores the fact that ordinary Palestinians comprise the constituency that is: (a) *most* familiar with the devastating cost of violence in the context of this conflict; (b) the *least* in control of their own destiny; and

(c) the *most* vulnerable to negative consequences of actions by more powerful agents.

While recognising the profound loss, and legitimate grievance, experienced by those Israelis (and other nationals) who have suffered as a result of the conflict, it is a demonstrable fact that Palestinians in the oPts have suffered greatly as a result of the everyday violence that is the status quo under occupation. This has been directly through Israel's military action and indirectly through a range of factors resulting from the occupation and the broader power imbalance in the relationship. In Nablus during the Second Intifada, this translated into a struggle for survival under a unremitting siege coupled with internal strife and lawlessness. Yet, when the siege came to an end, the Second Intifada was followed by an apparent return to some kind of rule of law, although this came at the price of even greater reductions in autonomy and the suppression of basic rights. All improvement during that time contained the latent threat of a return to chaos. According to Raja Khalidi (2012), this lesson has been internalised generally:

> In the wake of a second, militarized and failed intifada, most of those living under occupation and PA administration meekly have accepted, if not embraced, the limited focus of the PA on 'self-improvement' that has overwhelmingly defined the Palestinian reform and governance narrative for the past five to ten years.

Morbid symptoms of the current interregnum

As stated in the introduction, this book is written with a Western audience in mind; it is not intended to speak for Palestinians or to offer Palestinians any 'guidance' on how or what to do next. Instead, it was written to address what this author has identified as an alarming misunderstanding of the West's role in the conflict among most mainstream literature on the subject. It would not be consistent with this intention to suggest any measures or actions for Palestinians themselves to take in order to address the current situation; rather, it is perhaps better to address this book's final thoughts to the audience for which it is primarily intended.

The current dynamics that are at play in the context of the Israel–Palestine conflict are profoundly one-sided. The vast majority of top-down analysis that is presented on the subject within academic, journalistic and popular literature is profoundly misleading because these tend to offer the reader a perspective that is explicitly or implicitly infused with the assumption that achieving some form of superficial political re-organisation at the level of 'statehood' represents a 'solution' to the conflict.

Yet, as this book has sought to demonstrate, 'statehood' or statebuilding that occurs without more serious change taking place at a more profound level (which would be the re-organisation and redistribution of power more equally among the various parties involved) would be meaningless.

While all parties involved sought to maintain the myth that symbolic 'statehood' would be some kind of a panacea, they would not confront the basic material structures that denied Palestinians basic agency. The post-2007 statebuilding agenda – like the Oslo process before it – was not something that failed on a technicality; rather, it did so because it was fundamentally weak.

For the Western audience, this book's conclusion is evidently difficult, particularly in the context of devastating strife across an increasingly complex Middle East. Yet in spite of the obviously strong appeal of simple narratives in this context, this author implores the Western audience to reject the false dichotomies that simplify this conflict into violent radicalism versus stability under occupation. The alternative to violent revolution need not be (nor should be) the normalisation of less dramatic forms of 'everyday' violence. Instead, another way forward is possible; *that* would be a truly distinctive 'third way'. In the meantime, until the old order based on these flawed premises finally meets its ultimate demise, allowing new realities to emerge, we can expect little improvement overall. As Gramsci (1991, 275–6) reminds us:

> The crisis consists precisely in the fact that the old is dying and the new cannot be born; in this interregnum a great variety of morbid symptoms appear.

Notes

1 All data from B'Tselem. Casualties on the Palestinian side included: 431 minors (one minor participated in the hostilities); 200 women (under the age of 60); and 85 persons aged 60 and over. Of the Israeli casualties, 64 lost were soldiers and two were civilians killed by rocket fire. Total loses from the 2012 campaign comprised 167 Palestinians killed, including 87 civilians. Six Israelis – two soldiers and four civilians – were also killed. And during Operation Cast Lead (2008–9), 1,398 Palestinians were killed, including 764 civilians, while nine Israelis were killed, including three civilians.
2 For example, the British Prime Minister David Cameron – who had previously drawn an equivalence between the Gaza and a 'prison camp' – stated that 'as PM, putting yourself in the shoes of the Israeli people, who want peace but have to put up with these indiscriminate attacks – that reinforces to me the importance of standing by Israel and Israel's right to defend itself' (BBC 2010). Similarly, a spokesperson for the Pentagon defended sending additional arms shipments to Israel in the middle of the 2014 Gaza war by explaining that the US government was 'committed to the security of Israel, and it is vital to US national interests to assist Israel to develop and maintain a strong and ready self-defense capability' (Dathan 2015; Lewis and Sherwood 2014).
3 Evidence of this can be seen from the fact that Israeli forces have re-entered ostensibly PA controlled areas on several occasions and at will.
4 We can view Friedman's argument here as the articulation of how the mainstream – albeit ostensibly liberal – establishment looked back on the statebuilding project. Friedman is widely acknowledged as a mouthpiece of the US elites and had apparently advised President Obama on the role of the US in the region in May that year. See Fernández (2011) and Landler (2011).

5 However, to be fair to Friedman, his argument in this case does differ from the more common and patronising refrain that 'the Palestinians never miss an opportunity to miss an opportunity' – a misquote from Israeli journalist Abba Eban – which has been articulated frequently to blame the persistence of Israel's occupation on those who are occupied. For an example of this, see Harris (2011).

Bibliography

Abbas, Mahmoud. 2011. 'Full Transcript of Abbas Speech at UN General Assembly'. *Haaretz.com*, 23 September. www.haaretz.com/news/diplomacy-defense/full-transcript-of-abbas-speech-at-un-general-assembly-1.386385.
——2012. 'Abbas' Speech to the General Assembly'. Presented at the UN General Assembly, November. www.cfr.org/palestinian-authority/abbas-speech-un-general-assembly-november-2012/p29579.
——2014. 'The General Delegation of the PLO to the U.S./Statement by H.E. Mr. Mahmoud Abbas before United Nations General Assembly Sixty-Ninth Session'. Presented at the the General Delegation of the PLO to the US, 26 September. http://plodelegation.us/2014/09/statement-by-h-e-mr-mahmoud-abbas-before-united-nations-general-assembly-sixty-ninth-session.
Abunimah, Ali. 2011. '"Force, Might and Beatings": Indelible Images of the First Intifada'. *The Electronic Intifada*, 9 December. http://electronicintifada.net/blogs/ali-abunimah/force-might-and-beatings-indelible-images-first-intifada.
Agence France Press (AFP). 2006. 'Hamas Readies for Government, Israel Prepares Sanctions'. *Agence France Presse*, 17 February.
Agha, Hussein and Robert Malley. 2001. 'Camp David: The Tragedy of Errors'. *New York Review of Books*, 9 August. www.nybooks.com/articles/archives/2001/aug/09/camp-david-the-tragedy-of-errors.
Ahren, Raphael. 2008. 'Netanyahu: Economics, Not Politics, is the Key to Peace'. *Haaretz.com*, 20 November. www.haaretz.com/print-edition/news/netanyahu-economics-not-politics-is-the-key-to-peace-1.257617.
Al-Haq. 2008. 'Torturing Each Other: The Widespread Practices of Arbitrary Detention and Torture in the Palestinian Territory'. www.alhaq.org/attachments/article/188/Al-Haq%20-%20Torturing%20Each%20Other%20-%20Executive%20Summary%20%5BEnglish%5D.pdf.
——2010. 'Al-Haq Letter to Prime Minister Dr. Salam Fayyad Regarding Human Rights Concerns in the West Bank', 6 February. www.alhaq.org/advocacy/topics/palestinian-violations/281.
Al Jazeera. 2008. 'Annex I – Palestinian Performance on Security'. *Al Jazeera Transparency*. http://transparency.aljazeera.net/files/2298.PDF.
Al-Kafri, Saleh and Mansour Omeira. 2012. 'Women's Participation in the Palestinian Labour Force: 2010–2011'. International Labour Organization. www.ilo.org/wcmsp5/groups/public/---arabstates/---ro-beirut/documents/publication/wcms_218024.pdf.
Al-Naami, Saleh. 2011. 'Palestinians Protest against Fayyad's Austerity Measures'. *Al-Ahram*. http://weekly.ahram.org.eg/Archive/2012/1084/re3.htm.

Allen, Lori. 2008. 'Getting by the Occupation: How Violence Became Normal During the Second Palestinian Intifada'. *Cultural Anthropology* 23(3): 453–87.
AMAN. 2011. 'Corruption Report'. www.aman-palestine.org/en/reports-and-studies/1387.html.
Amnesty International. 2001. 'Israel and the Occupied Territories: Broken Lives – A Year of Intifada'. www.amnesty.org/en/library/asset/MDE15/083/2001/en/0ac91c49-d8e7-11dd-ad8c-f3d4445c118e/mde150832001en.html.
Anderson, Lisa. 1987. 'The State in the Middle East and North Africa'. *Comparative Politics*, 1–18.
Anderson, Perry. 2015. 'The House of Zion'. *New Left Review* II(96): 5–37.
Anthony, C. Ross, Glenn Robinson, Steven Simon, Kevin Jack Riley, Seth G. Jones, David Brannan, Anga Timilsina et al. 2007. *Building a Successful Palestinian State*. Washington DC: RAND Corporation. www.rand.org/pubs/monographs/MG146-1.html.
Applied Research Institute Jerusalem (ARIJ). 2008. 'Israeli Segregation Wall: An Israeli Political Agenda in the West Bank'. Monitoring Israeli Colonization Activities in the Palestinian Territories. The Applied Research Institute Jerusalem. www.arij.org/files/admin/2003/2003%20Israel's%20unilateral%20segregation%20plans%20in%20the%20OPT.pdf.
Assadi, Mohammed. 2010. 'Palestinians Say Arab States Cutting Aid'. *Reuters*, August. http://in.reuters.com/article/2010/08/19/idINIndia-50941320100819.
Associated Press. 2010. 'Palestinians End Torture of Hamas Prisoners'. *New York Times*, 3 January. www.nytimes.com/2010/01/04/world/middleeast/04hamas.html.
——2012. 'PA: Dozens of Hamas Charities Dismantled in West Bank'. *Haaretz.com*. www.haaretz.com/news/pa-dozens-of-hamas-charities-dismantled-in-west-bank-1.234427.
Ayubi, Nazih N. 1996. *Over-stating the Arab State: Politics and Society in the Middle East*. London: I.B. Tauris.
Azouley, Ariella and Adi Ophir. 2009. 'The Order of Violence' in Adi Ophir, Michal Givoni, and Sari Hanafi (eds), *The Power of Inclusive Exclusion: Anatomy of Israeli Rule in the Occupied Palestinian Territories*. Cambridge, MA: MIT Press, pp. 99–140.
Babst, Dean V. 1964. 'Elective Governments: A Force for Peace'. *Wisconsin Sociologist* 3(1): 9–14.
Bahour, Sam. 2010. 'Economic Prison Zones'. *Middle East Research and Information Project*, November. www.merip.org/mero/mero111910.
Baker, Peter. 2015. 'In Congress, Netanyahu Faults "Bad Deal" on Iran Nuclear Program'. *New York Times*, 3 March. www.nytimes.com/2015/03/04/world/middleeast/netanyahu-congress-iran-israel-speech.html.
Bannerman Associates. 2004. 'Implications of Sharon's Disengagement Initiative', 6 April. http://transparency.aljazeera.net/files/179.PDF.
Bannoura, Saed. 2011. 'Study Shows Palestinian Businessmen Invested $2.5 B in Israeli Settlements in 2010'. International Middle East Media Centre. www.imemc.org/article/62529.
Barghouti, Omar. 2011. *Boycott, Divestment, Sanctions*. Chicago: Haymarket Books.
Bauwens, Daan. 2012. 'EU Denounces Israel's Destruction of Aid Projects in West Bank'. *The Electronic Intifada*, 17 May. http://electronicintifada.net/content/eu-denounces-israels-destruction-aid-projects-west-bank/11301.
BBC. 2004. 'Al-Aqsa Backs Abbas Candidacy'. *BBC News*, 28 November. http://news.bbc.co.uk/1/hi/world/middle_east/4049819.stm.

——2010. 'David Cameron Describes Blockaded Gaza as a "Prison"'. *BBC News*, 27 July. www.bbc.co.uk/news/world-middle-east-10778110.

——2014. 'Israel Sets Palestinian Tax Sanction'. *BBC News*, 11 April. www.bbc.co.uk/news/world-middle-east-26982166.

BDS Steering Committee and National Committee for the Commemoration of the Nakba. 2008. 'Bethlehem Investment Conference: Development Or Normalization?' *Stop the Wall*. www.stopthewall.org/national-bds-steering-committee-bethlehem-investment-conference-development-or-normalization.

Ben-Ami, Shlomo. 2006. *Scars of War, Wounds of Peace: The Israeli-Arab Tragedy*. Oxford University Press.

Benn, Aluf. 2004. 'Analysis/Sharon's Threat on Arafat is a Matter of Timing'. *Haaretz.com*, 24 April. www.haaretz.com/news/analysis-sharon-s-threat-on-arafat-is-a-matter-of-timing-1.120548.

Bhungalia, Lisa. 2012. '"From the American People": Sketches of the US National Security State in Palestine'. www.jadaliyya.com/pages/index/7412/'from-the-american-people'_sketches-of-the-us-nati.

Bichler, S. and J. Nitzan. 2007. 'Israel's Roaring Economy'. *Global Research*, 6 July. www.globalresearch.ca/index.php?context=va&aid=6234.

Birzeit University. 2005. 'Palestine Human Development Report 2004'. Development Studies Programme. http://hdr.undp.org/sites/default/files/occupied_palestinian_territories_2004_en.pdf.

Bishara, Amahl. 2009. 'The Targeted and the Untargeted of Nablus'. *Middle East Research and Information Project*, no. 235. www.merip.org/mer/mer235/targeted-untargeted-nablus.

Black, Ian. 2011. 'Palestine Papers: Mohammed Dahlan'. *The Guardian*, 25 January. www.theguardian.com/world/2011/jan/25/palestine-papers-muhammad-dahlan.

——2014. 'French and Irish Parliaments Call for Recognition of Palestinian State'. *The Guardian*, 11 December. www.theguardian.com/world/2014/dec/11/france-ireland-europe-recognise-palestine-israel.

Black, Ian and Seumas Milne. 2011. 'Palestine Papers Reveal MI6 Drew Up Plan for Crackdown on Hamas'. *The Guardian*, 25 January. www.guardian.co.uk/world/2011/jan/25/palestine-papers-mi6-hamas-crackdown.

Black, Ian and Harriet Sherwood. 2014. 'Scarlett Johansson Row Has Boosted Israeli Settlement Boycott, Say Activists'. *The Guardian*, 6 February. www.theguardian.com/world/2014/feb/06/scarlett-johansson-israeli-settlement-boycott-activists.

Blair, David. 2015. 'Rebuilding Gaza Could Take 100 Years if Israel Keeps Blockade, Says Oxfam'. *Daily Telegraph*, 26 February. www.telegraph.co.uk/news/worldnews/middleeast/israel/11437649/Rebuilding-Gaza-could-take-100-years-if-Israel-keeps-blockade-says-Oxfam.html.

Blair, Tony. 2003. Speech Opening Parliament's Debate on the Iraq Crisis in the House of Commons, 18 March, www.theguardian.com/politics/2003/mar/18/foreignpolicy.iraq1.

Botmeh, Samia. 2013. 'Barriers to Female Labour Market Participation and Entrepreneurship in the Occupied Palestinian Territory'. Centre for Development Studies, Birzeit University. www.christianaid.org.uk/Images/Barriers-to-Female-Participation-in-Labour-Market-2013.pdf.

Bouillon, Markus E. 2004. *The Peace Business: Money and Power in the Palestine-Israel Conflict*. London: I.B. Tauris.

Bouris, Dimitris. 2013. *The European Union and Occupied Palestinian Territories: State-Building without a State*. New York: Routledge.

Boutros-Ghali, Boutros. 1992. *An Agenda for Peace*, vol. 11. New York: United Nations. http://unic.un.org/aroundworld/unics/common/documents/publications/agendaforpeace/agendaforpeace_dutch.pdf.

Braizat, Musa S. 1998. *The Jordanian-Palestinian Relationship: The Bankruptcy of the Confederal Idea*. London: I.B. Tauris.

Bregman, Ahron. 2002. *Israel's Wars: A History since 1947*, 2nd edn. New York: Routledge.

Brod, Daniel. 1990. *The Kibbutzim and Their Debt: Policy Considerations*. Washington DC: Institute for Advanced Strategic and Political Studies.

Bröning, Michael. 2011. *The Politics of Change in Palestine: State-Building and Nonviolent Resistance*. London: Pluto Press.

Brownlee, Jason. 2012. *Democracy Prevention: The Politics of the U.S.-Egyptian Alliance*. Cambridge University Press.

Brown, Nathan. 2003. *Palestinian Politics after the Oslo Accords: Resuming Arab Palestine*. Berkeley: University of California Press.

——2008. 'The Road Out of Gaza'. *Carnegie Endowment for International Peace*, 14 February. http://carnegieendowment.org/2008/02/14/road-out-of-gaza.

Bruno, Michael and Patrick Minford. 1986. 'Sharp Disinflation Strategy: Israel 1985'. *Economic Policy*, 379–407.

Brynen, Rex. 2000. *A Very Political Economy: Peacebuilding and Foreign Aid in the West Bank and Gaza*. Washington DC: United States Institute of Peace Press.

B'Tselem. 2011a. 'Effect of Restrictions on the Economy'.. www.btselem.org/freedom_of_movement/economy.

——2011b. 'Statistics on Punitive House Demolitions'. www.btselem.org/punitive_demolitions/statistics.

——2012. 'Fatalities since the Outbreak of the Second Intifada and Until Operation "Cast Lead"'. http://old.btselem.org/statistics/english/Casualties.asp?sD=29&sM=09&sY=2000&eD=26&eM=12&eY=2008&filterby=event&oferet_stat=before.

——2014. 'Discriminatory Water Supply'. www.btselem.org/water/discrimination_in_water_supply.

——2015a. 'Checkpoints, Physical Obstructions, and Forbidden Roads'. www.btselem.org/freedom_of_movement/checkpoints_and_forbidden_roads.

——2015b. 'Palestinians Killed During the Course of a Targeted Killing in the Occupied Territories, before Operation "Cast Lead"'. www.btselem.org/statistics/fatalities/before-cast-lead/by-date-of-event/wb-gaza/palestinians-killed-during-the-course-of-a-targeted-killing.

Buck, Tobias. 2010. 'Allegations of West Bank Torture Increase'. *Financial Times*, 21 November. www.ft.com/cms/s/0/c5ceda42-f58b-11df-99d6-00144feab49a.html#axzz3QoVkf4Yp.

Bush, George. 2001. 'Address to a Joint Session of Congress and the American People'. http://georgewbush-whitehouse.archives.gov/news/releases/2001/09/print/20010920-8.html.

——2003. 'Remarks by President George W. Bush at the 20th Anniversary of the National Endowment for Democracy'. www.ned.org/remarks-by-president-george-w-bush-at-the-20th-anniversary/.

Bush, George and Ariel Sharon. 2004. 'Exchange of Letters Sharon-Bush 14-Apr-2004', 14 April. www.mfa.gov.il/MFA/Peace+Process/Reference+Documents/Exchange+of+letters+Sharon-Bush+14-Apr-2004.htm.

Bibliography

Carter, Jimmy and Mary Robinson. 2014. 'Gaza Blockade Must End'. *The Guardian*, 5 August. www.theguardian.com/commentisfree/2014/aug/05/gaza-blockade-must-end-un-first-step-settlement.

Catignani, Sergio. 2008a. 'The Israel Defense Forces and the Al-Aqsa Intifada: When Tactical Virtuosity Meets Strategic Disappointment'. European University Institute, Max Weber Programme. http://cadmus.eui.eu/bitstream/handle/1814/8135/MWP-2008-04.pdf?sequence=1.

——2008b. *Israeli Counter-insurgency and the Intifadas: Dilemmas of a Conventional Army*. Abingdon: Taylor & Francis.

Chehab, Zaki. 2007. *Inside Hamas: The Untold Story of Militants, Martyrs and Spies*. London: I.B. Tauris.

CIA. 2009. 'Making High-Value Targeting Operations an Effective Counterinsurgency Tool'. *WikiLeaks*. https://wikileaks.org/cia-hvt-counterinsurgency/WikiLeaks_Secret_CIA_review_of_HVT_Operations.pdf.

Cleveland, William L. and Martin Bunton. 2009. *A History of the Modern Middle East*, 4th edn. Boulder, CO: Westview Press.

Cobain, Ian. 2009. 'CIA Working with Palestinian Security Agents'. *The Guardian*, 17 December. www.guardian.co.uk/world/2009/dec/17/cia-palestinian-security-agents.

Cobban, Helena. 1985. *The Palestinian Liberation Organisation: People, Power, and Politics*. Cambridge University Press.

Cook, Catherine, Adam Hanieh and Adah Kay. 2004. *Stolen Youth: The Politics of Israel's Detention of Palestinian Children*. London: Pluto Press.

Cook, Jonathan. 2013. 'Tony Blair's Tangled Web: The Quartet Representative and the Peace Process'. *Journal of Palestine Studies* 42(2): 43–60.

Coughlin, Con. 2005. 'Israel Protests at MI6 Mission to Halt Hamas Suicide Bombings'. *Daily Telegraph*, 21 August. www.telegraph.co.uk/news/worldnews/middleeast/israel/1496671/Israel-protests-at-MI6-mission-to-halt-Hamas-suicide-bombings.html.

Council on Foreign Relations (CFR). 2012. 'Al-Aqsa Martyrs Brigade'. www.cfr.org/israel/al-aqsa-martyrs-brigade/p9127.

Cox, R. W. 1983. 'Gramsci, Hegemony and International Relations: An Essay in Method'. *Millennium: Journal of International Studies* 12(2): 162–75. doi:10.1177/03058298830120020701.

Crisis Group. 2008. 'Palestine Divided'. www.crisisgroup.org/en/regions/middle-east-north-africa/israel-palestine/B025-palestine-divided.aspx.

——2009a. 'Gaza's Unfinished Business'. www.crisisgroup.org/en/regions/middle-east-north-africa/israel-palestine/85-gazas-unfinished-business.aspx.

——2009b. 'Palestine: Salvaging Fatah'. Middle East Report 91. www.crisisgroup.org/en/regions/middle-east-north-africa/israel-palestine/091-palestine-salvaging-fatah.aspx.

——2010. 'Squaring the Circle: Palestinian Security Reform under Occupation'. www.crisisgroup.org/en/regions/middle-east-north-africa/israel-palestine/98-squaring-the-circle-palestinian-security-reform-under-occupation.aspx.

——2011. 'Palestinian Reconciliation: Plus Ça Change …'. www.crisisgroup.org/en/regions/middle-east-north-africa/israel-palestine/110-palestinian-reconciliation-plus-ca-change.aspx.

Crooke, Alastair. 2011. 'Europe's Failure on Middle East Peace'. *The Guardian*, 30 January. www.theguardian.com/commentisfree/2011/jan/30/europe-failure-middle-east-peace.

Crouch, Colin. 2011. *The Strange Non-Death of Neoliberalism*. Cambridge: Polity Press.

Dahl, Robert A. 1991. *Democracy and its Critics*. New Haven: Yale University Press.

Dana, Tariq. 2014. 'The Palestinian Capitalists That Have Gone Too Far'. *Al-Shabaka*. http://al-shabaka.org/briefs/palestinian-capitalists-have-gone-too-far.

Dathan, Matt. 2015. 'David Cameron Says Israel was Right to Defend Itself over Gaza Attacks Last Year'. *The Independent*, 28 April. www.independent.co.uk/news/uk/politics/generalelection/david-cameron-says-israel-was-right-to-defend-itself-over-gaza-attacks-last-year-10210203.html.

Dayton, Keith. 2009. 'Speech to the Washington Institute for Near East Policy by Lt. Gen Keith Dayton'. Washington Institute for Near East Policy. www.washingtoninstitute.org/html/pdf/DaytonKeynote.pdf.

Doumani, Beshara. 1995. *Rediscovering Palestine: Merchants and Peasants in Jabal Nablus, 1700–1900*. Berkeley: University of California Press.

——2004. 'Scenes from Daily Life: The View from Nablus'. *Journal of Palestine Studies* 34(1): 37–50.

Doyle, Michael W. 2005. 'Three Pillars of the Liberal Peace'. *American Political Science Review* 99(3): 463–6. doi:10.1017/S0003055405051798.

The Economist. 2012. 'The Calm May Not Last for Ever', 30 June. www.economist.com/node/21557812.

Eldar, Akiva. 2005. 'Back to the One-State Solution?' *MIFTAH*, 25 March. www.miftah.org/display.cfm?DocId=6989&CategoryId=5.

El-Jafari, Mahmoud and Yousef Doaud. 2011. 'Rebuilding the Palestinian Tradable Goods Sector: Towards Economic Recovery and State Formation'. *UNCTAD*. http://unctad.org/en/PublicationsLibrary/gdsapp2010d1_en.pdf.

Elkhafif, Mahmoud, Misyef Misyef and Mutasim Elagraa. 2014. 'Palestinian Fiscal Revenue Leakage to Israel under the Paris Protocol on Economic Relations'. *UNCTAD*. http://unctad.org/en/PublicationsLibrary/gdsapp2013d1_en.pdf.

Entous, Adam and Alastair Macdonald. 2008. 'With Abbas's Clampdown, Reports of Torture Grow'. *Reuters*, 4 December. www.reuters.com/article/2008/12/04/us-palestinians-torture-exclusive-sb-idUSTRE4B31W120081204.

EU Commission. 2013. 'Statement by the Delegation of the European Union to the State of Israel on the European Commission Notice'. http://eeas.europa.eu/delegations/israel/press_corner/all_news/news/2013/20131607_02_en.htm.

European Union External Action. 2014. 'EU Border Assistance Mission at Rafah Crossing Point'. www.eubam-rafah.eu/files/20140710%20EUBAM%20Rafah_en%202.pdf.

Exum, Andrew, Scott Brady, Richard Weitz, Kyle Flynn, Robert Killebrew, James Dobbins and Marc Lynch. 2010. 'Security for Peace: Setting the Conditions for a Palestinian State'. www.cnas.org/node/4362.

Farraj, K., C. Mansour and S. Tamari. 2009. 'A Palestinian State in Two Years: Interview with Salam Fayyad, Palestinian Prime Minister'. *Journal of Palestine Studies* 39: 58–74.

Fayyad, Salam. 2014. 'Oslo is Dead'. *Foreign Affairs*, 2 October. www.foreignaffairs.com/articles/middle-east/2014-10-02/oslo-dead.

Feldman, Nizan. 2009. 'Economic Peace: Theory versus Reality'. *Strategic Assessment* 12(3): 19–28.

Fernández, Belén. 2011. *The Imperial Messenger: Thomas Friedman at Work*. New York: Verso.

Fielding, David. 2003a. 'Counting the Cost of the *Intifada*: Consumption, Saving and Political Instability in Israel'. *Public Choice* 116(3): 297–312. doi:10.1023/A:1024831518541.

——2003b. 'Modelling Political Instability and Economic Performance: Israeli Investment During the Intifada'. *Economica* 70(277): 159–86.

Fischer, S., P. Alonso-Gamo and U. Von Allmen. 2001. 'Economic Developments in the West Bank and Gaza since Oslo'. *Economic Journal* 111(472): 254–75.

Fischer, Stanley. 1993. *The Economics of Middle East Peace: Views from the Region*. Cambridge, MA: MIT Press.

Friedman, Thomas L. 1994. 'Agency Offering an Aid Blueprint for Palestinians'. *New York Times*, 3 May. www.nytimes.com/1994/05/03/world/agency-offering-an-aid-blueprint-for-palestinians.html.

——2013. 'Goodbye to All That'. *New York Times*, 23 April. www.nytimes.com/2013/04/24/opinion/friedman-goodbye-to-all-that.html.

Friedrich, Roland, Arnold Luethold and Firas Milhem (eds). 2008. *The Security Sector Legislation of the Palestinian National Authority*. Geneva Centre for the Democratic Control of Armed Forces (DCAF).

Fukuyama, Francis. 1989. 'The End of History?' *The National Interest* 16: 3–18.

——1993. *The End of History and the Last Man*. Harmondsworth: Penguin.

G4S Israel. 2014. 'Human Rights Review of G4S Israel Human Rights Report and Legal Opinion Summary of Independent Review'. www.g4s.com/~/media/Files/CSR%20Reports/G4S%20Israel%20Independent%20Review%20Findings%20-%20June%202014.ashx.

Gaub, Florence. 2010. 'NATO in Palestine'. Research Paper 57. www.academia.edu/6246986/NATO_in_Palestine.

Gelder, Jan Willem van and Hassel Kroes. 2009. *UK Economic Links with Israeli Settlements in Occupied Palestinian Territory*. Castricum: Profundo.

Ghanem, As'ad. 2010. *Palestinian Politics after Arafat: A Failed National Movement*. Bloomington: Indiana University Press.

Giacaman, George. 1998. 'In the Throes of Oslo: Palestinian Society, Civil Society and the Future' in George Giacaman and Dag Jorund Lonning, *After Oslo: New Realities, Old Problems*. London: Pluto Press, pp. 45–59.

Gordon, Neve. 2008. *Israel's Occupation*. Berkeley: University of California Press.

Gordon, Neve and Dani Flic. 2009. 'The Destruction of Risk Society and the Ascendancy of Hamas' in A. Ophir, M. Givoni, and S. Hanafi (eds), *The Power of Inclusive Exclusion: Anatomy of Israeli Rule in the Occupied Palestinian Territories*. New York: Zone Books, pp. 457–87.

Government of Israel. 2003. 'Israel's Response to the Road Map'. www.knesset.gov.il/process/docs/roadmap_response_eng.htm.

——2005. 'Israel's Disengagement: 2005'. www.mfa.gov.il/mfa/aboutisrael/maps/pages/israels%20disengagement%20plan-%202005.aspx.

——2009. 'Jalama/Gilboa Crossing Upgraded for Vehicular Traffic', 11 November. http://mfa.gov.il/MFA/PressRoom/2009/Pages/Gilboa_crossing_upgraded_11-Nov-2009.aspx.

Gramsci, Antonio. 1971. *Selections from the Prison Notebooks of Antonio Gramsci*, trans. Geoffrey N. Smith and Quintin Hoare. New York: International Publishing.

Gramsci, Antonio and David Forgacs. 1988. *The Gramsci Reader: Selected Writings, 1916–1935*. New York: NYU Press.

The Guardian. 2004. 'Bush Backs Sharon's "Disengagement" Plan', 14 April. www.theguardian.com/world/2004/apr/14/usa.israel.

Gunning, Jeroen. 2007. *Hamas in Politics: Democracy, Religion, Violence.* London: C. Hurst & Co.

Haaretz. 2009. 'IDF Removes Jericho Checkpoint in "Goodwill" Gesture to Abbas', 17 June. www.haaretz.com/news/idf-removes-jericho-checkpoint-in-goodwill-gesture-to-abbas-1.278278.

——2010. 'Abbas: Jewish NATO Soldiers Could Defend Future Palestinian State', 7 August. www.haaretz.com/israel-news/abbas-jewish-nato-soldiers-could-defend-future-palestinian-state-1.306616.

Hadid, Diaa. 2015. 'Israeli Foreign Minister Denounces E.U. Proposal to Label Settlement Products'. *New York Times*, 17 April. www.nytimes.com/2015/04/18/world/middleeast/avigdor-lieberman-denounces-eu-settlement-product-label-plan.html.

Halper, J. 1999. 'Dismantling the Matrix of Control''. *News from Within* 15(9): 38–40.

——2000. 'The 94 Percent Solution: A Matrix of Control'. *Middle East Report* 30(3): 14–19.

——2001. 'The Key to Peace: Dismantling the Matrix of Control'. *Israeli Committee against House Demolitions.* http://icahd.org/get-the-facts/matrix-control.

Hamdan, Ayat. 2012. 'Inequality in the Palestinian Context: Privatizing "Poverty"'. Bisan Centre for Research and Development. www.worldwewant2015.org/file/287411/download/311601.

Hanieh, Adam. 2008a. 'Palestine in the Middle East: Opposing Neoliberalism and US Power Part 1'. *MRZine*, 19 July. http://mrzine.monthlyreview.org/2008/hanieh190708a.html.

——2008b. 'Palestine in the Middle East: Opposing Neoliberalism and US Power Part 2'. *MRZine*, 19 July. http://mrzine.monthlyreview.org/2008/hanieh190708b.html.

——2011. 'The Internationalisation of Gulf Capital and Palestinian Class Formation'. *Capital & Class* 35(1): 81–106. doi:10.1177/0309816810392006.

——2013. *Lineages of Revolt : Issues of Contemporary Capitalism in the Middle East.* Chicago: Haymarket Books.

Harris, David. 2011. 'The Palestinians: Once Again Missing an Opportunity?' *Jerusalem Post*, 19 July. www.jpost.com/page.aspx?pageid=13&articleid=366976.

Hass, Amira. 2002. 'Israel's Closure Policy: An Ineffective Strategy of Containment and Repression'. *Journal of Palestine Studies* 31(3): 5–20.

——2010. 'Otherwise Occupied/Access Denied'. *Haaretz.com*, 10 April. www.haaretz.com/weekend/week-s-end/otherwise-occupied-access-denied-1.284725.

——2011. 'Study: Palestinians Invest Twice as Much in Israel as They Do in West Bank'. *Haaretz.com*, 22 November. www.haaretz.com/print-edition/features/study-palestinians-invest-twice-as-much-in-israel-as-they-do-in-west-bank-1.396979.

——2012. 'The VIPs' Hush Money'. *Haaretz.com*, 18 January. www.haaretz.com/print-edition/opinion/the-vips-hush-money-1.407887.

Henry, Clement Moore and Robert Springborg. 2010. *Globalization and the Politics of Development in the Middle East.* Cambridge University Press.

Hess-Skinner, Laya. 2015. 'Smartphone Politics in the West Bank'. *Muftah*, 14 January. http://muftah.org/smartphone-politics-west-bank.

Hilal, Jamil and Mushtaq Husain Khan. 2004. 'Stateformation under the PNA: Potential Outcomes and Their Viability' in Mushtaq Husain Khan, Inge

Bibliography

Amundsen and George Giacaman (eds), *State Formation in Palestine: Viability and Governance During a Social Transformation*. New York: Routledge, pp. 64–120.

Hogan, Michael. 2008. 'The Proof is in the Paper Trail'. *Vanity Fair*, April. www.vanityfair.com/news/2008/04/gaza_documents200804.

Horovitz, David. 2008. 'Blair: Netanyahu Can Be a Peacemaker'. *Jerusalem Post*, 5 August. www.jpost.com/Israel/Blair-Netanyahu-can-be-a-peacemaker.

Hroub, Khaled. 2006. *Hamas: A Beginner's Guide*. London: Pluto Press.

Human Rights Watch. 2008. 'Internal Fight Palestinian Abuses in Gaza and the West Bank'. www.hrw.org/reports/2008/07/29/internal-fight.

Hunter, F. Robert. 1991. *The Palestinian Uprising: A War by Other Means*. London: I.B. Tauris.

Hussein, Cherine. 2015. *The Re-emergence of the Single State Solution in Palestine/Israel: Countering an Illusion*. New York: Routledge.

Ignatieff, Michael. 2002. 'Nation-Building Lite'. *New York Times*, 28 July. www.nytimes.com/2002/07/28/magazine/nation-building-lite.html.

ILO. 2012a. 'Child Labour and Protection in the Occupied Palestinian Territory'. www.ilo.org/wcmsp5/groups/public/---arabstates/---ro-beirut/documents/publication/wcms_236940.pdf.

—— 2012b. 'Decent Work Country Programme, Jordan 2012–2015'. www.ilo.org/public/english/bureau/program/dwcp/download/jordan.pdf.

IMF. 2010. 'Towards a Palestinian State: Reforms for Fiscal Strengthening: Economic Monitoring Report to the Ad Hoc Liaison Committee'. http://siteresources.worldbank.org/INTWESTBANKGAZA/Resources/WorldBankReportAHLCApril2010Final.pdf.

—— 2014. 'West Bank and Gaza: Report on Macroeconomic Developments and Outlook'. www.imf.org/external/country/WBG/RR/2014/063014.pdf.

IRIN. 2011. 'Analysis: West Bank Dogged by High Cost of Trade'. *IRIN News*, 1 September. www.irinnews.org/report/93625/analysis-west-bank-dogged-by-high-cost-of-trade.

Ishac, Diwan and Shaban Radwan. 1999. 'Development under Adversity: The Palestinian Economy in Transition'. http://documents.worldbank.org/curated/en/1999/03/437950/development-under-adversity-palestinian-economy-transition.

Issacharoff, Avi. 2008. 'PA Takes Back the Keys to a Key City'. *Haaretz.com*, 3 January. www.haaretz.com/print-edition/news/pa-takes-back-the-keys-to-a-key-city-1.236433.

Issacharoff, Avi and Associated Press. 2007. 'Livni: Rescue of IDF Major Proves Strength of PA Security Forces'. *Haaretz.com*, 27 August. www.haaretz.com/news/livni-rescue-of-idf-major-proves-strength-of-pa-security-forces-1.228264.

Issacharoff, Avi and Amos Harel. 2007. 'Fatah to Israel: Let Us Get Arms to Fight Hamas'. *Haaretz.com*, 7 June. www.haaretz.com/print-edition/news/fatah-to-israel-let-us-get-arms-to-fight-hamas-1.222473.

Isseroff, Ami. 2002. 'The Tenet Plan'. *MidEast Web*. www.mideastweb.org/tenet.htm.

Jabrin, Sharwan. 2011. 'Israel's Illegal Freeze of Palestinian Tax Revenue'. www.alhaq.org/advocacy/targets/european-union/506.

Jad, Islah. 2007. 'The NGO-ization of Arab Women's Movements' in Andrea Cornwall, Elizabeth Harrison and Ann Whitehead (eds), *Feminisms in Development: Contradictions, Contestations and Challenges*. London: Zed Books, pp. 177–92.

—— 2009. 'The Demobilization of Women's Movements: The Case of Palestine' in Srilatha Batliwala (ed.), *Changing Their World*. Toronto: Association for Women's Rights in Development (AWID), pp. 1–16. www.awid.org/sites/default/files/atoms/files/changing_their_world_-_demobilization_of_womens_movements_-_palestine.pdf.

Jamal, Amal. 2005. *The Palestinian National Movement: Politics of Contention, 1967–2003.* Bloomington: Indiana University Press.

Jensen, Michael Irving. 2008. *The Political Ideology of Hamas: A Grassroots Perspective.* London: I.B. Tauris.

Kanafani, Nu'man and Sahar Taghdisi-Rad. 2012. 'The Palestinian Economy: Macroeconomic and Trade Policymaking under Occupation'. http://unctad.org/en/PublicationsLibrary/gdsapp2011d1_en.pdf.

Kant, Immanuel. 1795. *Perpetual Peace: A Philosophical Essay.* Translated by Mary Campbell Smith. London: George Allen & Unwin. http://oll.libertyfund.org/index.php?option=com_staticxt&staticfile=show.php%.

Karim, Nasr Abdul, Salim Tamari and Khalid Farraj. 2010. 'The Palestinian Economy and Future Prospects: Interview with Mohammad Mustafa, Head of the Palestine Investment Fund'. *Journal of Palestine Studies* 39(3): 40–51. doi:10.1525/jps.2010.XXXIX.3.40.

Keating, Michael, Anne Le More, Robert Lowe and Royal Institute of International Affairs. 2005. *Aid, Diplomacy and Facts on the Ground: The Case of Palestine.* London: Chatham House.

Kelly, T. 2008. 'The Attractions of Accountancy'. *Ethnography* 9(3): 351–76.

Kershner, Isabel. 2010. 'Palestinian President Suspends Aide in Sex Scandal'. *New York Times,* 15 February. www.nytimes.com/2010/02/15/world/middleeast/15mideast.html.

——2014. 'New Palestinian Town in West Bank Awaits Israel's Approval for Water'. *New York Times,* 26 August. www.nytimes.com/2014/08/27/world/middleeast/rawabi-west-bank-palestinians-israel.html.

Khalidi, Raja. 2012. 'After the Arab Spring in Palestine: Contesting the Neoliberal Narrative of Palestinian National Liberation'. *Jadaliyya,* 23 March. www.jadaliyya.com/pages/index/4789/after-the-arab-spring-in-palestine_contesting-the-.

Khalidi, Raja and Sobhi Samour. 2011. 'Neoliberalism as Liberation: The Statehood Program and the Remaking of the Palestinian National Movement'. *Journal of Palestine Studies* 40(2): 6–25.

Khalidi, Raja and Sahar Taghdisi-Rad. 2009. 'The Economic Dimensions of Prolonged Occupation: Continuity and Change in Israeli Policy Towards the Palestinian Economy'. United Nations Conference on Trade and Development'. www.unctad.org/en/Docs/gds20092_en.pdf.

Khalidi, Rashid. 2006. *The Iron Cage: The Story of the Palestinian Struggle for Statehood.* London: Oneworld Publications.

——2009. *Sowing Crisis: The Cold War and American Dominance in the Middle East.* Boston, MA: Beacon Press.

Khalili, Laleh. 2007. *Heroes and Martyrs of Palestine: The Politics of National Commemoration.* Cambridge University Press.

——2010. 'The Location of Palestine in Global Counterinsurgencies'. *International Journal of Middle East Studies* 42(3): 413–33. doi:10.1017/S0020743810000425.

Khalil, Naela. 2013. 'Is Fatah's Armed Wing Making Comeback?'. *Al-Monitor,* 25 September. www.al-monitor.com/pulse/originals/2013/09/hebron-israeli-soldiers-killed-fatah-intifada.html.

Khan, Mushtaq Husain. 2004. 'Evaluating the Emerging Palestinian State: "Good Governance" versus "Transformational Potential"' in Mushtaq Husain Khan, Inge Amundsen and George Giacaman (eds), *State Formation in Palestine: Viability and Governance During a Social Transformation.* New York: Routledge, pp. 13–64.

Bibliography

——2005. '"Security First" and its Implications for a Viable Palestinian State' in M. Keating, A Le and R Lowe (eds), *Aid, Diplomacy and Facts on the Ground: The Case of Palestine*. London: Royal Institute of International Affairs, Chatham House, pp. 59–73.

——2010. 'Post-Oslo State-Building Strategies and Their Limitations: Transcript of the Yusif A. Sayigh Development Lecture 2010'. http://eprints.soas.ac.uk/2421/1/Prof_Mushtaq_Final_Transcript_Sayigh_Lecture.pdf.

Khatib, Ghassan. 2008. 'Nothing New in Netanyahu's Approach'. *Bitter Lemons*, 24 November. www.bitterlemons.org/previous/bl241108ed42.html#pal1.

——2009. *Palestinian Politics and the Middle East Peace Process: Consensus and Competition in the Palestinian Negotiating Team*. Abingdon: Routledge.

Khoury, Jack. 2013. 'Fatah Militants March in West Bank, Palestinian Sources Say – Middle East'. *Haaretz.com*, 10 January. www.haaretz.com/news/middle-east/fatah-militants-march-in-west-bank-palestinian-sources-say.premium-1.493297.

Khoury, Philip Shukry and Joseph Kostiner. 1990. *Tribes and State Formation in the Middle East*. Berkeley: University of California Press.

Kimmerling, Baruch. 2003. *Politicide: Ariel Sharon's War Against the Palestinians*. New York: Verso.

Klein, Naomi. 2008. *The Shock Doctrine: The Rise of Disaster Capitalism*. New York: Penguin.

Koenig, I. 1976. 'Top Secret: Memorandum-Proposal–Handling the Arabs of Israel'. *Journal of Palestine Studies* 6(1): 190–200.

LaFranchi, Howard. 2007. 'Global Donors Exceed Palestinian Expectations at Paris Conference'. *Christian Science Monitor*, 19 December. www.csmonitor.com/2007/1219/p06s01-woeu.html.

Landler, Mark. 2011. 'Obama Seeks Reset in Arab World'. *New York Times*, 11 May. www.nytimes.com/2011/05/12/us/politics/12prexy.html.

Laor, Yitzhak. 2002. 'Diary'. *London Review of Books*, 3 October.

Laqueur, Walter and Barry Rubin. 2008. *The Israel-Arab Reader*, revised edn. New York: Penguin.

Larudee, Mehrene. 2012. '*Who Shared the Fruits of Growth in the Palestinian Economy, 2006–2010*'. MAS – The Palestine Economic Policy Research Institute. http://bit.ly/1d1K2QL.

Leech, Philip. 2014a. 'After "Security First": An Analysis of Security Transition and "Statebuilding" in the West Bank 2007–11'. *New Middle Eastern Studies* 4. www.brismes.ac.uk/nmes/archives/1337.

——2014b. 'Who Owns "the Spring" in Palestine? Rethinking Popular Consent and Resistance in the Context of the "Palestinian State" and the "Arab Spring"'. *Democratization*, 1–19. doi:10.1080/13510347.2014.899584.

——2014c. 'Recognising Palestine: Six Critiques of the PLO's Internationalisation Strategy'. *Middle East Monitor*, 13 October. www.middleeastmonitor.com/articles/europe/14642-recognising-palestine-six-critiques-of-the-plos-internationalisation-strategy.

Leech, Philip and Jamie Gaskarth. 2015. 'British Foreign Policy and the Arab Spring'. *Diplomacy & Statecraft* 26(1): 139–60. doi:10.1080/09592296.2015.999631.

Leech, Philip and Anan Quzmar. 2012. 'Palestine: The Precarious Present'. *Open Democracy*, 19 July. www.opendemocracy.net/phil-leech-and-anan-quzmar/palestine-precarious-present.

Leibovitz, Liel and Stephanie Butnick. 2014. 'BDS Will Target SodaStream Even after the Company Shutters West Bank Factory. Why?' *Tablet Magazine*, 11 November. http://tabletmag.com/scroll/186957/sodastream-to-remain-target-of-bds-boycott.

Lewis, Paul and Harriet Sherwood. 2014. 'US Condemns Shelling of UN School in Gaza But Restocks Israeli Ammunition'. *The Guardian*, 31 July. www.theguardian.com/world/2014/jul/30/us-firm-condemnation-shelling-un-school-gaza.

Lia, Brynjar. 2006a. *Building Arafat's Police: The Politics of International Police Assistance in the Palestinian Territories after the Oslo Agreement*. New York: Ithaca Press.

——2006b. *A Police Force without a State: A History of the Palestinian Security Forces in the West Bank and Gaza*. New York: Ithaca Press.

Lis, Johnathan. 2011. 'Israel Passes Law Banning Calls for Boycott'. www.haaretz.com/news/diplomacy-defense/israel-passes-law-banning-calls-for-boycott-1.372711.

Luft, Gal. 1998. 'The Palestinian Security Services: Between Police and Army'. www.washingtoninstitute.org/policy-analysis/view/the-palestinian-security-services-between-police-and-army1.

Lynch, Marc. 2011. 'America and Egypt After the Uprisings'. *Survival* 53(2): 31–42. doi:10.1080/00396338.2011.571008.

Maan News. 2010a. 'Fayyad Concedes PA Tortured Hamas Detainees'. www.maannews.net/eng/ViewDetails.aspx?ID=251967.

——2010b. 'PA Hands out Blacklisted Settlement Goods List'. www.maannews.com/Content.aspx?ID=285299.

——2010c. 'Fayyad Denies UAE Cut Aid to PA'. www.maannews.com/Content.aspx?ID=309638.

——2012. 'Source: New Batch of Officials to Be Charged with Corruption'. www.maannews.com/Content.aspx?ID=502598.

Mackinlay, John and Alison Al-Baddawy. 2008. 'Rethinking Counterinsurgency'. www.rand.org/pubs/monographs/MG595z5.html.

Mackinnon, Mark. 2007. 'Growing Muslim Movement Offers Alternative to Hamas'. *Globe and Mail*, 22 August.

MADAR. 2013. 'The Underlying Objectives behind the Demand for Recognition of Israel "a Nation-State of the Jewish People"'. *MADAR: The Palestinian Forum for Israeli Studies*, November. http://bit.ly/1HmBqRA.

Madhoun, Husam. 2006. 'The Palestinian Security Services: Past and Present'. *MIFTAH*, 30 May. www.miftah.org/display.cfm?DocId=10400&CategoryId=21.

Mahle, Melissa Boyle. 2005. 'A Political-Security Analysis of the Failed Oslo Process'. *Middle East Policy* 12(1): 79–96. doi:10.1111/j.1061-1924.2005.00188.x.

Makhool, Basim. 2003. 'Small Enterprises in North Palestine: Reality and Needs'. www.bisan.org/web_files/publications_file/SSE.pdf.

Mansbach, Daniela. 2009. 'Normalizing Violence: From Military Checkpoints to "Terminals" in the Occupied Territories'. *Journal of Power* 2(2): 255–73. doi:10.1080/17540290903072591.

MAS. 2011. *Round Table (5): Financial Crisis of the Palestinian National Authority*. MAS: Palestine Economic Policy Research Institute.

Massad, Joseph. 2001. *Colonial Effects*. New York: Columbia University Press.

——2014. 'Peace is War: Negotiations, Israeli Settler Colonialism, and the Palestinians'. *The Austin School*, 26 February. www.youtube.com/watch?v=CVh9GL0mJzo&feature=youtube_gdata_player.

194 Bibliography

McGreal, Chris. 2003. 'Israel May Kill Arafat, Deputy PM Says'. *The Guardian*, 15 September. www.theguardian.com/world/2003/sep/15/israel.

Mearsheimer, John and Stephen Walt. 2012. 'Mr Obama Must Take a Stand against Israel over Iran'. *Financial Times*, 4 March. www.ft.com/cms/s/38c9382a-65f8-11e1-979e-00144feabdc0,Authorised=false.html?_i_location=http%3A%2F%2Fwww.ft.com%2Fcms%2Fs%2F0%2F38c9382a-65f8-11e1-979e-00144feabdc0.html&_i_referer=http%3A%2F%2Fwww.thinkir.co.uk%2Fmearsheimer-walt-and-the-missing-palestinians%2F#axzz1oj0L9FtZ.

Milne, Seumas and Ewen MacAskill. 2015. 'CIA Attempted to Contact Hamas Despite Official US Ban, Spy Cables Reveal'. *The Guardian*, 23 February. www.theguardian.com/us-news/2015/feb/23/spy-cables-leak-cia-contact-hamas-us-ban.

Milton-Edwards, Beverley. 2013. 'Hamas and the Arab Spring: Strategic Shifts?' *Middle East Policy Council*. www.mepc.org/journal/middle-east-policy-archives/hamas-and-arab-spring-strategic-shifts.

Milton-Edwards, Beverley and Stephen Farrell. 2010. *Hamas: The Islamic Resistance Movement*. Cambridge: Polity Press.

Mitnick, Joshua. 2007. 'Restive Nablus Challenges Fatah's Abbas'. *Christian Science Monitor*, 5 November. www.csmonitor.com/2007/1105/p04s01-wome.html.

Moors, A. 1994. 'Women and Dower Property in Twentieth-Century Palestine: The Case of Jabal Nablus'. *Islamic Law and Society* 1(3): 301–31.

Morley, Jefferson. 2005. 'Israeli Withdrawal From Gaza Explained'. *Washington Post*, 10 August. www.washingtonpost.com/wp-dyn/content/article/2005/08/10/AR2005081000713.html.

Morris, Benny. 2001. *Righteous Victims: A History of the Zionist-Arab Conflict, 1881–1999*. New York: Random House.

Mustafa, Tahani. 2015. 'Damming the Palestinian Spring: Security Sector Reform and Entrenched Repression'. *Journal of Intervention and Statebuilding* 9(2): 1–19. doi:10.1080/17502977.2015.1020738.

Mustafa, Umm. 2008. 'Why I Left Hizb Ut-Tahrir'. *New Statesman*, 28 February. www.newstatesman.com/politics/2008/02/party-hizb-tahrir-members.

Nakhleh, Khalil. 2011. *Globalized Palestine: The National Sell-out of a Homeland*. Trenton, NJ: Red Sea Press.

Nasr, Mohammed. 2004. 'Monopolies and the PNA' in Mushtaq Husain Khan, Inge Amundsen and George Giacaman (eds), *State Formation in Palestine: Viability and Governance During a Social Transformation*. New York: Routledge, pp. 168–92.

New York Times. 2015. 'Mr. Netanyahu's Unconvincing Speech to Congress', 3 March. www.nytimes.com/2015/03/04/opinion/netanyahu-israel-unconvincing-iran-speech-to-congress.html.

Nieuwhof, Adri. 2008. 'Palestinian Workers Exploited at West Bank Settlement Factories'. *The Electronic Intifada*, 5 October. http://electronicintifada.net/content/palestinian-workers-exploited-west-bank-settlement-factories/7745.

Niksic, Orhan, Nur Nasser Eddin and Massimiliano Cali. 2014. *Area C and the Future of the Palestinian Economy*. Washington DC: World Bank Publications.

Nitzan, J. and S. Bichler. 2000. 'Inflation and Accumulation: The Case of Israel'. *Science & Society*, 274–309.

——2002. *The Global Political Economy of Israel*. London: Pluto Press.

Nugent, Jeffrey and Abla Abdel-Latif. 2010. 'A Quiz on the Net Benefits of Trade Creation and Trade Diversion in the QIZs of Jordan and Egypt'. *Economic Research Forum Working Papers* 514. http://erf.org.eg/wp-content/uploads/2014/08/514.pdf.

Office of the United Nations High Commissioner for Human Rights. 2010. 'Report of the Special Rapporteur on Extrajudicial, Summary or Arbitrary Executions, Philip Alston, Addendum: Study on Targeted Killings'. United Nations General Assembly: Human Rights Council. www.ohchr.org/english/bodies/hrcouncil/docs/14session/A.HRC.14.24.Add6.pdf.

Ophir, A., M. Givoni and S. Hanafi. 2009. *The Power of Inclusive Exclusion: Anatomy of Israeli Rule in the Occupied Palestinian Territories*. New York: Zone Books.

Padico. 2014. 'United Nations Global Compact Communications on Progress Report'. www.unglobalcompact.org/system/attachments/cop_2014/108881/original/UNGC_Final_2014_1.pdf?1411053725.

Palestinian Authority (PA). 2007. 'Palestine Reform and Development Plan (PRDP)'. www.mop-gov.ps/web_files/issues_file/PRDP-en.pdf.

——2010. 'Homestretch to Freedom'. www.mopad.pna.ps/en/?option=com_content&view=article&id=6&Itemid=142&hideNav=true.

Palestinian Central Bureau of Statistics (PCBS). 2008. '2007 Census'. www.pcbs.gov.ps/Portals/_PCBS/Downloads/book1487.pdf.

——2011. 'Child Statistics Series'. www.pcbs.gov.ps/Downloads/book1740.pdf.

——2015. 'Labour Force Survey Q4/2014'. www.pcbs.gov.ps/portals/_pcbs/PressRelease/Press_En_LFS-Q4-2014-e.pdf.

Palumbo, Michael. 1990. *Imperial Israel: The History of the Occupation of the West Bank & Gaza*. London: Bloomsbury Publishing.

——1999. 'De-development Revisited: Palestinian Economy and Society since Oslo'. *Journal of Palestine Studies* 28(3): 64–82.

——2002. 'Ending the Palestinian Economy'. *Middle East Policy* 9(4): 122–65. doi:10.1111/1475-4967.00087.

——2004. 'The Palestinian-Israeli Conflict and Palestinian Socioeconomic Decline: A Place Denied'. *International Journal of Politics, Culture, and Society* 17(3): 365–403.

——2006. *Failing Peace: Gaza and the Palestinian-Israeli Conflict*. London: Pluto Press.

——2011. *Hamas and Civil Society in Gaza: Engaging the Islamist Social Sector*. Princeton University Press.

Pappe, Ilan. 2007. *The Ethnic Cleansing of Palestine*. London: Oneworld Publications.

Paris, Roland. 2004. *At War's End: Building Peace after Civil Conflict*. Cambridge University Press.

Pelham, Nicolas. 2012. 'Gaza's Tunnel Phenomenon: The Unintended Dynamics of Israel's Siege'. *Journal of Palestine Studies* 41(4). http://palestine-studies.org/jps/fulltext/42605.

Peres, Shimon and Arye Naor. 1993. *The New Middle East*. New York: Henry Holt & Co.

Perry, Mark. 2011. 'Dayton's Mission: A Reader's Guide'. *Al Jazeera*, 29 January. www.aljazeera.com/palestinepapers/2011/01/2011125145732219555.html.

Petti, Alessandro. 2010. *Archipelagos and Enclaves*. Center for Arab Unity Studies. https://dl.dropboxusercontent.com/u/38469511/Archipelagos%20and%20Enclaves.pdf.

Philps, Alan. 2000. 'A Day of Rage, Revenge and Bloodshed'. *Daily Telegraph*, 12 October. www.telegraph.co.uk/news/worldnews/middleeast/israel/1370229/A-day-of-rage-revenge-and-bloodshed.html.

Pina, Aaron. 2006. 'Palestinian Elections'. CRS Report for Congress. www.fas.org/sgp/crs/mideast/RL33269.pdf.

Pineschi and Anis F. Kassim. 1988. *The Palestine Yearbook of International Law 1987–1988*. Leiden: Martinus Nijhoff.

Portland Trust. 2012. 'Palestinian Economic Bulletin'. www.portlandtrust.org/sites/default/files/peb/issue67_apr_2012.pdf.

Putz, Ulrike. 2010. 'The Palestinian Workers Who Build Israel's Settlements'. *Spiegel Online*, 10 November. www.spiegel.de/international/world/double-pay-for-betrayal-the-palestinian-workers-who-build-israel-s-settlements-a-722424.html.

The Quartet. 2007. 'Statement by the Middle East Quartet'. https://unispal.un.org/DPA/DPR/unispal.nsf/53936ddf3dd093a1852575530073f2e6/4610112c40316738852573b50047322f?OpenDocument.

Qumsiyeh, Mazin B. 2010. *Popular Resistance in Palestine: A History of Hope and Empowerment*. London: Pluto Press.

Ram, Uri. 1999. 'The State of the Nation: Contemporary Challenges to Zionism in Israel'. *Constellations* 6(3): 325–38. doi:10.1111/1467-8675.00149.

Ravid, Barak and Jack Khoury. 2014. 'PA Security Questions Salam Fayyad's Aid NGO over Campaign to Help Gazans – Diplomacy and Defense'. *Haaretz.com*, 28 August. www.haaretz.com/news/diplomacy-defense/.premium-1.612458.

Razin, Assaf and Efraim Sadka. 1993. *The Economy of Modern Israel: Malaise and Promise*. University of Chicago Press.

Retzky, A. 1995. 'Peace in the Middle East: What Does it Really Mean for Israeli Business?' *Columbia Journal of World Business* 30(3): 26–32.

Reuters and *Al Arabiya*. 2013. 'Al-Aqsa Brigades Fire Rockets into Israel as Tensions Rise', 26 February. http://english.alarabiya.net/articles/2013/02/26/268375.html.

Robson, Victoria. 2008. 'Padico'. *Middle East Economic Digest*, 18 January. www.meed.com/sectors/finance/padico-meed-assessment/3091832.article.

Rosato, Sebastian. 2003. 'The Flawed Logic of Democratic Peace Theory'. *American Political Science Review* 97(4): 585–602. doi:10.1017/S0003055403000893.

Rose, David. 2008. 'The Gaza Bombshell'. *Vanity Fair*, 1 April. www.vanityfair.com/politics/features/2008/04/gaza200804.

Roy, Sara. 1996. 'Economic Deterioration in the Gaza Strip'. Middle East Report 200: 36–9, doi:10.2307/3013267.

Rubinstein, Danny. 2005. 'A Palestinian Government of Experts'. *Haaretz.com*, 28 February. www.haaretz.com/print-edition/opinion/a-palestinian-government-of-experts-1.151548.

Rynhold, Jonathan and Dov Waxman. 2008. 'Ideological Change and Israel's Disengagement from Gaza'. *Political Science Quarterly* 123(1): 11–37.

Sahliyeh, E. 1986. 'The West Bank Pragmatic Elite: The Uncertain Future'. *Journal of Palestine Studies* 15(4): 34–45.

Saif, Ibrahim. 2006. *The Socio-Economic Implications of the Qualified Industrial Zones in Jordan*. Amman: Center for Strategic Studies, University of Jordan.

Samara, Adel. 2000. 'Globalization, the Palestinian Economy, and the "Peace Process"'. *Journal of Palestine Studies* 29(2): 20–34.

Samour, Sobhi and Raja Khalidi. 2014. 'Palestinian Authority's State-Building Programme' in Mandy Turner and Omar Shweiki (eds), *Decolonizing Palestinian Political Economy: De-Development and Beyond*. London: Palgrave Macmillan, pp. 179–99.

Sansour, Vivien and Alaa Tartir. 2014. 'Palestinian Farmers: A Last Stronghold of Resistance'. *Al-Shabaka*. http://al-shabaka.org/briefs/palestinian-farmers-a-last-stronghold-of-resistance/.

Save the Children. 2009. 'Life on the Edge: The Struggle to Survive and the Impact of Forced Displacement in High Risk Areas of the Occupied Palestinian Territory'. www.savethechildren.org.uk/sites/default/files/docs/English_Research_Report_with_Cover_low_res_1.pdf.

Sayigh, Yezid. 2000. *Armed Struggle and the Search for State: The Palestinian National Movement, 1949–1993*. Oxford University Press.
——2007. 'Inducing a Failed State in Palestine'. *Survival* 49(3): 7–39. doi:10.1080/00396330701564786.
——2009. '"Fixing Broken Windows": Security Sector Reform in Palestine, Lebanon, and Yemen'. *Carnegie Endowment for International Peace*, October. http://carnegieendowment.org/2009/10/27/fixing-broken-windows-security-sector-reform-in-palestine-lebanon-and-yemen/1w9o.
——2011a. 'Policing the People, Building the State: Authoritarian Transformation in the West Bank and Gaza'. http://carnegieendowment.org/2011/02/28/policing-people-building-state-authoritarian-transformation-in-west-bank-and-gaza/jke.
——2011b. '"We Serve the People": Hamas Policing in Gaza'. Brandeis University. www.brandeis.com/crown/publications/cp/CP5.pdf.
Schiff, Zeev. 1989. 'Security for Peace: Israel's Minimal Security Requirements in Negotiations with the Palestinians'. www.washingtoninstitute.org/policy-analysis/view/security-for-peace-israels-minimal-security-requirements-in-negotiations-wi.
Schneer, Jonathan. 2011. *The Balfour Declaration: The Origins of the Arab-Israeli Conflict*. London: A&C Black.
Sciolino, Elaine. 2000. 'Violence Thwarts C.I.A. Director's Unusual Diplomatic Role in Middle Eastern Peacemaking'. *New York Times*, 13 November. www.nytimes.com/2000/11/13/world/violence-thwarts-cia-director-s-unusual-diplomatic-role-middle-eastern.html.
Shaban, Omar. 2013. 'No Prospects for Palestinian Currency'. *Al-Monitor*. www.al-monitor.com/pulse/originals/2013/03/palestinian-currency-dreams.html.
Shachar, Nathan. 2009. 'The Good Cops of Nablus'. *Prospect*, 18 November. www.prospectmagazine.co.uk/2009/11/the-good-cops-of-nablus/.
Shalhat, Antoine. 2015. *Benjamin Netanyahu: The Doctrine of 'No Solution'. MADAR: The Palestinian Forum for Israeli Studies*. http://bit.ly/1DepxWa.
Sharon, Ariel. 2003. 'Prime Minister's Speech at the Herzliya Conference'. *Haaretz. com*, 18 December. www.haaretz.com/news/prime-minister-s-speech-at-the-herzliya-conference-1.109089.
Sharon, Gilad. 2011. *Sharon: The Life of a Leader*. New York: HarperCollins.
Sharp, Heather. 2009. 'Dilemma of Palestinian Settlement Builders'. *BBC*, 26 August 2. http://news.bbc.co.uk/1/hi/8220680.stm.
Sheehan, Neil. 1988. *A Bright Shining Lie: John Paul Vann and America in Vietnam*. New York: Vintage Books.
Shlaim, Avi. 2010. *Israel and Palestine: Reappraisals, Revisions, Refutations*. New York: Verso.
Sikimic, Simona. 2014. 'Profile: Mohammed Dahlan, Gaza's Comeback Kid'. *Middle East Eye*, 7 April. www.middleeasteye.net/news/profile-mohammed-dahlan-gazas-comeback-kid-1305037516.
Silver, Charlotte. 2012. 'Leaked Documents Show PA Outsourced Palestinian Land and Rights to Turkish Firm'. *The Electronic Intifada*, 19 September. http://electronicintifada.net/content/leaked-documents-show-pa-outsourced-palestinian-land-and-rights-turkish-firm/11680.
Smith, Ray. 2011. 'Interview: Raja Khalidi on the Neoliberal Consensus in Palestine'. *The Electronic Intifada*, 25 April. http://electronicintifada.net/content/interview-raja-khalidi-neoliberal-consensus-palestine/9870.

Bibliography

Supreme Court of Israel. 2011. 'The Public Committee against Torture in Israel and Palestinian Society for the Protection of Human Rights and the Environment vs. The Government of Israel, The Prime Minister of Israel, The Minister of Defense, The Israel Defense Forces, The Chief of the General Staff of the Israel Defense Forces and Shurat HaDin – Israel Law Center and 24 Others'. www.law.upenn.edu/institutes/cerl/conferences/targetedkilling/papers/IsraeliTargetedKillingCase.pdf.

Swisher, Clayton. 2012. 'Al Jazeera Investigates – What Killed Arafat?' www.youtube.com/watch?v=KBT7o0piZ8E&feature=youtube_gdata_player.

——2015. 'Spy Cables: Abbas and Israel Ally against 2009 UN Probe'. *Al Jazeera*, 23 February. www.aljazeera.com/blogs/middleeast/2015/02/spy-cables-abbas-israel-ally-2009-probe-goldstone-palestine-report-gaza-guardian-150222142146258.html.

Tabar, Linda and Sari Hanafi. 2004. 'Donor Assistance, Rent-Seeking and Elite Formation' in Mushtaq Husain Khan, Inge Amundsen and George Giacaman (eds), *State Formation in Palestine: Viability and Governance During a Social Transformation*. New York: Routledge, pp. 215–39.

——2005. *The Emergence of a Palestinian Globalized Elite*. Ramallah, Palestine: Institute of Jerusalem Studies & Muwatin, The Palestinian Institute for the Study of Democracy.

Tawil-Souri, Helga. 2012. 'Digital Occupation: Gaza's High-Tech Enclosure'. *Journal of Palestine Studies* 41(2): 27–43. doi:10.1525/jps.2012.XLI.2.27.

Thrall, Nathan. 2010. 'Our Man in Palestine'. *The New York Review of Books*, October 14. www.nybooks.com/articles/archives/2010/oct/14/our-man-palestine/.

——2014. 'Hamas's Chances'. *London Review of Books*, August 21.

Tilly, Charles (ed.). 1975. *The Formation of National States in Western Europe*. Princeton University Press.

——(ed.). 1985. 'War Making and State Making as Organized Crime' in Peter B. Evans, Dietrich Rueschemeyer and Theda Skocpol (eds), *Bringing the State Back in*. Cambridge University Press, pp. 169–91.

Transparency International. 2013a. 'Case Study/West Bank: Opening the Door to Security Integrity'. http://s173807.gridserver.com/what-we-do/news-events/blog/129-case-study-west-bank-opening-door-security-integrity.html.

——2013b. 'Palestinian National Authority'. Transparency International Government Defence Anti-Corruption Index. http://government.defenceindex.org.

Turner, Mandy. 2015. 'Peacebuilding as Counterinsurgency in the Occupied Palestinian Territory'. *Review of International Studies* 41(1): 73–98.

Turner, Mandy and Florian P. Kühn. 2015. *The Politics of International Intervention: The Tyranny of Peace*. Abingdon: Routledge.

United Nations. 1990. *Yearbook of the United Nations, 1985*. Leiden: Martinus Nijhoff Publishers.

United Nations Conference on Trade and Development (UNCTAD). 2009. *Aftercare Strategy for Investors in the Occupied Palestinian Territory*. UNCTAD/GDS/APP/2009/1. New York and Geneva: United Nations Conference on Trade and Development (UNCTAD). http://82.213.48.101:4000/Publishing%20Documents/After%20Care%20Strategy%20for%20investors%20in%20the%20Occupied%20Territory.pdf.

——2010. 'Report on UNCTAD Assistance to the Palestinian People: Developments in the Economy of the Occupied Palestinian Territory'.

——2011. 'Report on UNCTAD Assistance to the Palestinian People: Developments in the Economy of the Occupied Palestinian Territory'. https://unispal.un.org/DPA/DPR/unispal.nsf/1ce874ab1832a53e852570bb006dfaf6/63503f7b0aeddfb4852578f5006780a6?OpenDocument.

——2012. 'Services Sector Holds Key to Developing Countries' Growth'. http://unctad.org/en/pages/newsdetails.aspx?OriginalVersionID=68.

United Nations Development Programme (UNDP). 2013. 'The Palestinian Industrial Estate and UNDP Sign an Exchange of Letters Funded by the Government of Japan'. www.arabstates.undp.org/content/rbas/en/home/presscenter/pressreleases/2013/02/07/the-palestinian-industrial-estate-and-free-zone-authority-and-the-united-nations-development-programme-sign-an-exchange-of-letters-funded-by-the-government-of-japan.html.

United Nations Relief Works Agency (UNRWA). 2008. 'Balata Refugee Camp Profile'. www.ochaopt.org/documents/opt_campprof_unrwa_balata_nov_2008.pdf.

——2011. 'UNRWA West Bank Livelihood Programme: 2011 Emergency Appeal'. www.unrwa.org/userfiles/2011051512917.pdf.

——2015. 'Where We Work'. www.unrwa.org/where-we-work/west-bank/camp-profiles.

Urquhart, Conal. 2004. 'Arafat "Ruining His People" Says Protege'. *The Guardian*, 2 August. www.theguardian.com/world/2004/aug/02/israel.

US Consulate Jerusalem. 2006. 'Salam Fayyad on Hamas'. *WikiLeaks Cables*. https://wikileaks.org/plusd/cables/06JERUSALEM801_a.html.

Urquhart, Conal. 2007. 'PM Fayyad and CODEL Ackerman: Security Checkpoints and Salaries'. *WikiLeaks Cables*. https://wikileaks.org/plusd/cables/07JERUSALEM1831_a.html.

——2008a. 'PM Fayyad and Security Chiefs Argue for Increased Coordination, Security Presence'. *WikiLeaks Cables*. www.wikileaks.org/plusd/cables/10JERUSALEM43_a.html.

——2008b. 'Fayyad-Dayton: Jenin Coordination, Hamas and the MOI'. *WikiLeaks Cables*. https://wikileaks.org/plusd/cables/08JERUSALEM1384_a.html.

——2009. 'Fayyad on Detainees, Nablus, and Internal Politics'. *WikiLeaks Cables*. https://cablegatesearch.wikileaks.org/cable.php?id=09JERUSALEM1516.

US Department of State. 2007. 'An Action Plan for the Palestinian Presidency'. http://media.mcclatchydc.com/static/pdf/actionplan.pdf.

US Embassy Tel Aviv. 2004a. 'Economic Implications of Gaza Pull-out'. *WikiLeaks Cables*. https://cablegatesearch.wikileaks.org/cable.php?id=04TELAVIV1453.

——2004b. 'Military Implications of a Gaza Pull-out'. *WikiLeaks Cables*. https://cablegatesearch.wikileaks.org/cable.php?id=04TELAVIV1451.

——2004c. 'Political/Institutional Implications of a Gaza Pull-out'. *WikiLeaks Cables*. https://cablegatesearch.wikileaks.org/cable.php?id=04TELAVIV1452.

——2004d. 'UN Envoy Previews Arafat "Ascension" Proposal'. *WikiLeaks Cables*. https://wikileaks.org/plusd/cables/04TELAVIV1707_a.html.

——2004e. 'Israeli Officials Brief Djerejian on Improved Regional Security Situation; Unilateral Disengagement Plans'. *WikiLeaks Cables*. https://wikileaks.org/plusd/cables/04TELAVIV1952_a.html.

——2004f. 'Peres: Gaza Disengagement Incomplete'. *WikiLeaks Cables*. https://cablegatesearch.wikileaks.org/cable.php?id=05TELAVIV6176.

——2004g. 'Sharon and Codel Hagel/Biden: Commitment to Working with New Palestinian Leadership'. *WikiLeaks Cables*. https://wikileaks.org/plusd/cables/04TELAVIV6387_a.html.

Bibliography

———2005a. 'Sharon to Codels: We Need to Build in the Settlement Blocs and Please Leave Us Alone'. *WikiLeaks Cables*. https://cablegatesearch.wikileaks.org/cable.php?id=05TELAVIV2761.

———2005b. 'VPM Olmert Predicts His Own Political Future, and That of the 2006 GOI Budget'. *WikiLeaks Cables*. http://cables.mrkva.eu/cable.php?id=44377.

Uttering, Kate. 2009. 'The Information Campaign and Countering Insurgency: Lessons from Palestine 1945–1948'. www.rusi.org/analysis/commentary/ref:C4AB7E3B86C0B8/.

Verter, Yossi. 2005. 'Netanyahu Quits Government over Disengagement'. *Haaretz.com*, 7 August. www.haaretz.com/news/netanyahu-quits-government-over-disengagement-1.166110.

Wainer, David. 2014. 'SodaStream Closing West Bank Factory after Boycotts'. *Bloomberg.com*, 29 October. www.bloomberg.com/news/articles/2014-10-29/sodastream-to-close-factory-at-center-of-israel-palestinian-spat.

Wallerstein, Immanuel Maurice. 2004. *World-Systems Analysis: An Introduction*. Durham, NC: Duke University Press.

Weiss, Hadas. 2011. 'Immigration and West Bank Settlement Normalization'. *PoLAR: Political and Legal Anthropology Review* 34(1): 112–30. doi:10.1111/j.1555-2934.2011.01142.x.

Weizman, Eyal. 2007. *Hollow Land: Israel's Architecture of Occupation*. New York: Verso.

Whitaker, Brian. 2002. 'UN Report Details West Bank Wreckage'. *The Guardian*, 2 August. www.theguardian.com/world/2002/aug/02/israel.

Who Profits? 2009. 'Privatizing Security – Corporate Involvement in the Checkpoints'. http://whoprofits.org/content/privatizing-security-%E2%80%93-corporate-involvement-checkpoints.

———2013. 'Palestinian Workers in Settlements: Who Profits' Position Paper'. http://whoprofits.org/content/palestinian-workers-settlements.

Wildeman, Jeremy and Alaa Tartir. 2014. 'Unwilling to Change, Determined to Fail: Donor Aid in Occupied Palestine in the Aftermath of the Arab Uprisings'. *Mediterranean Politics* 19(3): 431–49. doi:10.1080/13629395.2014.967014.

Williamson, John. 1990. 'What Washington Means by Policy Reform'. *Latin American Adjustment: How Much Has Happened* 1. http://time.dufe.edu.cn/wencong/washingtonconsensus/whatwashingtonmeans.doc.

———1993. 'Democracy and the "Washington Consensus"'. *World Development* 21(8): 1329–36.

Wilson, Woodrow. 1917. 'Address of the President of the United States to the Senate'. http://wwi.lib.byu.edu/index.php/Address_of_the_President_of_the_United_States_to_the_Senate.

Wines, Michael. 2002. 'Al Qaeda in Lebanon and Gaza, Sharon Says'. *New York Times*, 6 December. www.nytimes.com/2002/12/06/international/middleeast/06MIDE.html.

World Bank. 1993. 'Overview: Developing the Occupied Territories'. http://documents.worldbank.org/curated/en/1993/09/698867/developing-occupied-territories-investment-peace-vol-1-6-overview.

———1994. 'Technical Assistance Program'. http://documents.worldbank.org/curated/en/1994/03/443653/emergency-assistance-occupied-territories-vol-2-2-technical-assistance-program.

———1995. 'Advancing Social Development: A World Bank Contribution to the Social Summit'. www-wds.worldbank.org/external/default/WDSContentServer/WDSP/IB/1995/03/01/000009265_3970716143624/Rendered/PDF/multi_page.pdf.

——2008a. 'Implementing the Palestinian Reform and Development Agenda'. Economic Monitoring Report to the Ad Hoc Liaison Committee. http://siteresources.worldbank.org/INTWESTBANKGAZA/Resources/WorldBankAHLCMay2,08.pdf.

——2008b. 'Progress with the Parallel Actions Towards Palestinian Revival and Growth'. Economic Monitoring Report to the Ad Hoc Liaison Committee. http://siteresources.worldbank.org/INTWESTBANKGAZA/Resources/AHLCSept15,08.pdf.

——2011. 'Building the Palestinian State: Sustaining Growth, Institutions, and Service Delivery'. Economic Monitoring Report to the Ad Hoc Liaison Committee. http://siteresources.worldbank.org/INTWESTBANKGAZA/Resources/AHLCReportApril2011.pdf.

——2012. 'Fiscal Crisis, Economic Prospects: The Imperative for Economic Cohesion in the Palestinian Territories'. Economic Monitoring Report to the Ad Hoc Liaison Committee. http://siteresources.worldbank.org/INTWESTBANKGAZA/Resources/AHLCReportFinal.pdf.

——2015a. 'Electricity Non-payment and Arrears Destabilize the Palestinian Economy'. www.worldbank.org/en/news/press-release/2015/04/08/electricity-non-payment-and-arrears-destabilize-the-palestinian-economy.

——2015b. 'Economic Monitoring Report to the Ad Hoc Liaison Committee'. www.worldbank.org/en/country/westbankandgaza/publication/economic-monitoring-report-to-the-ad-hoc-liaison-committee.

York, John Rossant, Neal Sandler, Amy Borrus and Stanley Reed. 1994. 'The Peace Dividend for Israel and Jordan'. *BusinessWeek: Online Magazine*, 8 August. www.businessweek.com/archives/1994/b338471.arc.htm.

Zanotti, Jim. 2010. 'U.S. Security Assistance to the Palestinian Authority'. Congressional Research Service.

Zayyad, T. 1976. 'The Fate of the Arabs in Israel'. *Journal of Palestine Studies* 6(1): 92–103.

Zilbersheid, U. 2007. 'The Israeli Kibbutz: From Utopia to Dystopia'. *Critique* 35(3): 413–34.

Index

'Arab Spring' 3, 108, 110, 124–5, 165, 174, 178
'asymmetric containment' 46–8, 58, 64, 67, 129; bantustanisation 48; cantonisation 48–9
3G network *see* Internet penetration
Abbas, Mahmoud 3, 11, 21, 62–3, 85, 88, 92–3, 95–6, 101–3, 105–6, 109–11, 115, 118–19, 122–26, 165
Abu Nidal Organisation 41
Abu Sharif, Bassam 42
agriculture 22, 138–9, 153
Al-Aqsa Martyrs Brigade 101–2, 112
Al-Qaida 20, 68
Al-Quds University 160
Al-Rafah Microfinance Bank 152
Algeria 141
Allenby Bridge 137
An-Najah National University 67, 165
anti-corruption *see* corruption
anti-Semitism 48
Aquarian (Palestine Real Estate Investment Company) 55
Arab Bank 54
Arab Uprising (1936) 6
Arafat, Yasser 10, 21, 23, 41–5, 49–50, 55, 62–4, 71, 91–2, 97–98, 119–21
austerity 2, 132, 163–5, 175–7

Balata Refugee Camp 6, 8, 65, 101
Bannerman Associates 70–1
Basic Law (1997) 29, 90–2
Beirut 41, 49–50
Ben-Ami, Shlomo 74
Bethlehem 64, 92, 105, 154
biopolitics 67
Birzeit University 27–8
Blair, Tony 4, 21, 89, 130, 172
border police 73, 75
Borj Cedria 41
Bourguiba, Habib 41

Boutros-Ghali, Boutros 18
boycott 36; international aid 4, 159; Arab Boycott 35, 38–9; boycott divestment and sanctions 159–63; Palestinian Authority's boycott campaign 148–9, 159–62;
bribery 23, 78, 151
Britain *see* United Kingdom (UK)
brutality 89, 98
'bully praetorian republic' 23–6, 49, 150, 152
Bush, George H. W. 35

cablegate 90
Cairo Accord 44
Canada 11, 119
Center for New American Security 117
checkpoints 48, 65–7, 75–7, 101, 136–7, 172
Chevrolet 75
Church of the Nativity 64
CIA 66–7, 121–3
Civil Administration 21, 40, 140
civil society 8, 14, 32, 45, 57, 80, 95, 151, 161–2, 166
class 6, 14–15, 23–4, 26, 32, 36, 38, 50, 53, 56–8, 152, 160
clientelism 149
closure 7, 24, 26–7, 31, 47–8, 52–3, 151
Cold War 18–21, 29–30, 35, 37, 44
colonialism 15–16, 17, 20, 41, 114; post-colonial 15–16
construction 5, 46, 74–5, 136–40, 143, 153
core governance *see* governance
corruption 3–4, 23–24, 50, 52–53, 57, 80, 82, 84, 89, 94, 96–7, 111, 113–14, 120, 131, 144, 149–50, 159–1, 166, 176–77
criminal gangs 69, 100, 104
crony capitalism 50, 54, 58

Index

Damascus 7
Darwish, Mahmoud 44
Dayton, Keith 119, 121–2
Dead Sea 139–40
Declaration of Principles (DOP) 44–9, 54
decolonisation *see* colonialism
democracy 17–18, 20–1, 30, 35, 37, 51, 62, 95, 105, 125, 171–4
Department for International Development (DFID) 4, 11, 75, 80–3, 149, 173
detainees 98, 100
disengagement 3, 64, 69–74, 76–7, 119, 129

economic 'boom' 2010 130, 153, 172, 176
economic development 4, 11, 22, 25, 29, 33, 53, 63, 77, 115, 118, 126, 131, 139, 147, 150, 171
Economic Stabilisation Plan 36–8
education 24, 32, 49, 78, 134, 141
elections 62, 83: Israeli (1996) 48; Palestinian presidential (2005) 62; Palestinian legislative (2006) 4, 62, 69, 78, 93, 95–6, 98, 103, 150, 174
electricity 10, 65, 138, 157–8; prepaid meters 158, 165; Erikat, Saab 85
ethnic cleansing 20, 35, 37
European Economic Community 38; European Union (EU) 27, 62, 93, 96–7, 118–19, 162–3; Commission 162; Police Coordinating Office for Palestinian Police Support (EUPOL COPPS) 119–20
Executive Force 96

Fafo Foundation 44
Fatah 44, 45–46, 49–50, 52, 62, 69, 88, 92, 94–9, 101–2, 104, 113–14, 126; Central Committee 44; Revolutionary Council 41; Old Guard 85, 123, 174
Fayyad, Salam 3, 10–11, 28–9, 63–4, 69, 77, 79–83, 85, 88–90, 94–7, 99–106, 109–12, 115, 118, 120–21, 123, 125–6, 147–50, 153, 161, 164–6, 174, 177–8
fiscal: crisis 2010–11 132, 163, 173–4; leakage 11, 132–4, 144, 157, 164, 175–6
foreign aid 1, 3–4, 11, 22–3, 26–31, 33, 50, 56–7, 62, 74, 76–7, 7–80, 82–3, 89, 94, 97, 102–3, 115–16, 130–2, 122, 126, 135, 139, 143–4, 149, 151–2, 154, 158, 163, 172–77
foreign donors *see* foreign aid
France 17, 108, 154

free markets *see* neoliberalism
Free Trade Agreement 38
Friedman, Thomas 178
Fukuyama, Frances 18, 29
functionalism 3, 29

Gaza pull-out *see* disengagement
Gaza–Jericho Agreement Annex IV Protocol on Economic Relations between the Government of the State of Israel and P.L.O., Representing the Palestinian People *see* Paris: Protocol
Glaser, Daniel 99
globalisation 37–9, 51, 56, 149
good governance 19–23, 29, 53, 78, 80, 83–4, 144, 147–52
Gramsci, Antonio 2, 13–15, 21, 31–2, 180
green line 51, 74, 157
gross domestic product (GDP) 132, 138–40, 148, 153, 155, 176
Gulf 45, 50, 54, 79; Crisis (1991) 35–7, 43, 47, 51

Hamas 2, 4, 8, 23, 28, 30, 45, 48, 51–2, 62–4, 66, 69, 73, 75, 81, 84, 88–91, 93–105, 110–15, 119–25, 150, 164–5, 172, 174
Hamdallah, Rami 165
Hebron 100, 119, 154: Agreement 46; massacre 48
hegemony 15–16, 23, 38, 54, 56
Hirschfeld, Yair 44
Histadrut 36
historic bloc 21, 28, 33–4
Hizb al-Tahrir 98
Homestretch to Freedom 4, 153, 159
human rights 20–1, 75–6, 90, 97–8, 100, 104–5, 112, 120
human rights abuses *see* Human rights
Hussein, Saddam 25, 43, 45

industrial zones 76, 148, 153–5, 165–6; Qualified Industrial Zones (QIZs) 11, 39, 79, 155–6; Palestinian Industrial Estate and Free Zone Authority (PIEFZA) 79
integral state 14–16
Interim Agreement on the West Bank and the Gaza Strip *see* Oslo II (1995)
International Criminal Court (ICC) 108–9, 133
international law 160
International Monetary Fund 17, 19, 176

Index

international non-governmental organisations (INGOs) *see* non-governmental organisations
International Quartet 4, 81, 84, 130, 137
internet penetration 137–8
Intifada: First 21, 35–47, 51; Second 1, 7, 8, 10, 27, 29–31, 49–52, 56, 62–9, 74–77, 84, 88–98, 101, 105, 113, 122, 149–50, 154, 172–4, 179
Iran 141
Iraq 25, 141; War (2003) 20; War (1991) *see* Gulf Crisis (1991)
Ireland 108
Iron Curtain *see* Cold War
Islamism 2, 23, 40–5, 51–2, 57, 95–6, 98, 101, 117, 130
Israel 1–5, 7–9, 11, 13–6, 18, 21–2, 24–7, 29–34, 35–47, 62–85, 88–99, 101–5, 108, 110, 112, 114, 116–18, 120–5, 129, 132–9, 142–3, 147–8, 154–66, 171–3, 175, 177, 179; Ministry of Foreign Affairs 70; occupation of West Bank and Gaza Strip 1–4, 6–7, 9–10, 11, 13, 21, 25, 30–1, 36, 40–3, 48, 50, 52–3, 56–7, 64, 68–9, 72, 74–7, 80, 84–5, 92, 94–5, 97, 108, 114, 118–19, 123, 125–6, 131, 135, 141, 144, 147, 149, 150–1, 153, 155–7
Israel's Preferential Treatment Agreement *see* Free Trade Agreements
Israeli Airport Authority *see* border police
Israeli Military Operations: Cast Lead 100, 172; Protective Edge 172
Israeli settlements 3, 5, 7, 46, 68, 70, 72, 74, 82, 136, 158; Palestinian labour in 24, 133, 142, 147, 156, 161–2; boycott of *see* boycott: Palestinian Authority's boycott campaign
Istanbul 7

Jabal an-Nar *see* Nablus
Jalama 76, 137, 154–5
Japan 17
Jenin 64, 74, 76, 96, 119, 137, 154
Jericho 25, 44, 119, 154
Joint Economic Committee 134
Jordan 42, 51, 54, 134, 137, 154–6: International Police Training Center (JIPTC) 119; Civil War 41; River 2, 39; Valley 79
Judea and Samaria *see* West Bank

Kant, Immanuel 16–7
Kibbutz Crisis 36
Knesset 163

Labor Party 36, 39
labour force 36, 47, 55, 78–9, 130–35, 39, 140–2, 149, 155–6, 161–2, 175
labour market *see* labour force
law and order 19, 30, 77, 109–10, 112, 149
League of Nations 17
legitimacy 14, 15, 17, 24, 47, 57, 68, 84, 95, 98, 105, 108–11, 115, 123, 125–6, 133, 149, 160, 162, 165
liberal peace theory 3
Libya 25, 141
Likud Party 48, 73
Livni, Tzipi 72

Madrid conference 35, 43–4, 58
Majid, Faraj 106
Masri, Subih and Munib 54, 56
Mecca agreement 96
MI6 *see* UK: clandestine forces
mining 138–40
Mofaz, Shaul 165
moqata'a 64
Morsi, Mohammed 125
Mubarak, Hosni 124
Mukhabarat (secret police)
Muslim Brotherhood 123

Nablus 2, 6, 45, 56, 65, 68, 74, 78, 88, 90, 92, 96, 100–2, 104–5, 111–16, 119, 142, 149, 152, 158, 173, 179; Old City 7, 8, 64, 80, 160
Nakba 35
National Guidance Council 40
natural resources 137–8, 175
Nazareth 76, 137
neoliberalism 3, 9, 28–30, 37, 149, 153, 175, 177
Netanya 135
Netanyahu, Benjamin 39, 48, 73–4, 125, 129–130, 135
New York 20, 125
non-governmental organisations (NGOs) 24; NGO-isation 56: globalised elites 51–2, 56–7, 75, 90, 113, 151, 166
North Atlantic Treaty Organisation (NATO) 118
Norway 119
nuclear option 108

Olmert, Ehud 129
opinion polls 111–12, 123, 125
Oslo II (1995) 25, 46–8, 64, 136, 138

Palestine Liberation Organisation (PLO) 21, 39–54, 62, 66, 70, 84–5, 90, 108–9, 114, 116–17, 124, 160
Palestinian Authority 1–4, 9–11, 14–16, 21, 23–6, 28–32, 44, 46–55, 57–8, 62–3, 69, 71, 73–5, 77–84, 88–105, 109, 111–30, 131–4, 136–8, 140, 143–4, 147–66, 171, 174–9: leadership 9, 11, 14, 23–4, 30, 52, 78, 80, 92, 104, 113; budget; Ministry of Finance 79, 134; Ministry of Planning 81; National Security Council 92; legal framework 91–2, 131
Palestinian Islamic Jihad 23, 45, 48
Palestinian Liberation Army 49
Palestinian Monetary Authority (PMA) 25
Palestinian Reform and Development Plan (PRDP) 78, 80–1, 84, 97, 118, 120, 143
Palestinian Securities Exchange 54
Palestinian security forces 2–3, 26, 68, 75, 88–90, 92, 94, 100, 102, 118, 121, 155
Palestinian Spring; popular unrest 132, 156
Palestinian Telecommunications (Paltel) 54
Paris 47, 71, 143–4; conference 4, 30; Protocol 25–6, 28, 31, 46, 79, 131, 133, 135, 159–60, 175
patronage 25, 43, 49, 92, 97
peace dividends 39, 51–2, 56
peacekeeping 20
Peres, Shimon 39, 44, 48, 72, 159
permits 26, 47–8, 68, 140, 162
Philadelphia corridor 73
Pillar of Defence 172
political Islam *see* Islamism
political violence 30, 65, 68, 100
politicide *see* political violence
poverty 21, 27, 99, 143, 156–7
private sector 11, 24, 30, 33, 53–5, 58, 76, 79, 118, 134, 142–3, 147, 150, 153, 164–5, 176–7
private security 75
privatisation 19, 38; of the occupation 75–6, 155

public sector 2–3, 24, 33, 50, 53, 99, 134, 142, 150, 154, 165, 175–7

Qalandia 76
Qaryut 6, 7, 158
Qassem, Abdul Sattar 114
Qray, Ahmed 44
Qualified Industrial Zones *see* industrial zones

Rabin, Yitzak 44, 48
Ramallah 2, 26, 64, 92, 101, 119, 120, 140, 159–60, 166: lynching 94
RAND Corporation 116–17
Rawabi 140
refugees 116–17
remittances 156
rent-seeking 24–5, 28, 53–5, 58, 150–2
road map 71, 89, 92, 122
Rød-Larsen, Terje 44
Rwanda 20

safety and security 78, 111–12
Said, Edward 44
Saudi Arabia 96
Save the Children 156–7
seam zone 74, 82, 157
Second World War 15, 17
Secret Intelligence Service (SIS) *see* UK: clandestine forces
security coordination 123
security sector reform 90, 97, 118–19
Separation Wall 157, 172
September 11 terror attacks (2001) 20
settlements *see* Israeli settlements
Shamir, Yitzhak 44
Sharon, Ariel 64, 68–74
shopping festivals 7
Shouman, Abdel Majid 54
Somalia 20
South Africa 48, 158, 160
spoilers 71, 91
strategic envelope 1, 77, 83–5
surge 2, 88–9, 101, 103–4, 109, 111–16, 119
surveillance 74–6, 156

taxes 22, 25, 36, 132–4; value added (VAT) 133
technocrats 63, 85, 98, 104, 105, 126, 147
Tenet, George 122
terminals 75–7
textiles 7, 78–9, 142, 149

The Palestinian Investment and
  Development Company (Padico)
Third Way 54–5
Tilly, Charles 13–14
torture 67, 84, 98, 100, 103–4, 112, 120
tourism 139–40
trade 22, 25, 33, 38, 53, 78, 132, 134,
  137, 138, 151, 155, 166, 172, 175
Turkey 38, 149, 154
two-state solution 2, 42, 45–6, 80, 82–3,
  129, 166, 172–3

unemployment 26–7, 54, 140–2, 156–7
Union of Soviet Socialist Republics
  (USSR) 43
United Kingdom (UK) 17, 108:
  Government 3, 80–4, 89, 103,
  118, 174; Department for
  International Development (DIFD)
  4, 11, 30, 75, 80–3, 149, 173;
  Mandate of Palestine 17, 21, 91, 116;
  clandestine forces 62, 84, 89, 100,
  121–2
United Nations (UN) 17, 63, 109,
  111, 124, 126, 142; Security
  Council 2; General Assembly 3,
  5, 108, 125, 172; Relief Works
  Agency (UNRWA) 18; Development
  Programme (UNDP); Conference on
  Trade and Development (UNCTAD)
  130, 133–4, 153; High Commissioner
  for Human Rights (UNCHR) 66;
  Global Compact Communications
  on Progress 55
United States 2–4, 17–18, 20–1, 30, 35–8,
  42–5, 50–1, 55, 62–4, 67–8, 70–3, 80,
  89–93, 96–100, 102–4, 110, 114, 116–
  19, 121–5, 129–30, 155, 174: Security
  Coordinator (USSC) 119, 121–3;
  USAID 76, 137, 152; Department of
  State 55, 125
unity government 62–3, 69, 96–7, 103,
  122, 165

Village Leagues 40
violence 7, 20, 27, 30, 33, 36, 48, 56,
  64–9, 74, 77, 89, 95–100, 103, 178–80;
  spatial 65–6, 68; systemic 67, 99;
  kinetic 66–7; political 30, 65, 68, 100

wages 26, 140, 142, 147, 152, 156
War of Position 2, 32–3
War on Terror 2, 30, 68, 94, 121
Washington Institute 121
water 38, 47, 81, 138–9, 157–8
Who Profits? 75, 162
Wikileaks 71, 90
Wilson, Woodrow 17–19
Wilsonianism *see* Wilson, Woodrow
World Bank 78, 137, 139–40, 144, 154, 164
Wye River Memorandum 46

Yanoun (Upper and Lower) 6–8, 158
Yemen 25, 141
Yugoslavia 20

Zakat committees 99
Zionism 35, 37–8